Swed

from Poverty to Affluence

The assistance of the Swedish Institute,

of Stockholm, in the publication of this volume

is gratefully acknowledged

The contribution of the McKnight Foundation to

the general program of the University of Minnesota Press,

of which the publication of this book is a part,

is also gratefully acknowledged

Sweden's Development from Poverty to Affluence 1750-1970

edited by STEVEN KOBLIK

translated by
Joanne Johnson in association with the
University of Minnesota Press
and Steven Koblik

University of Minnesota Press, Minneapolis

Acknowledgments

I would like to thank the many people and institutions that have had a part in the construction of this volume; Ingrid Arvidsson, Sverker Oredsson, Franklin Scott, and the Swedish Institute have all given special help without in any way being responsible for the volume's final form. The work was initiated during the year 1971–1972 when I was a member of the Historical Institute in Lund, Sweden. My colleagues in Lund, especially Professor Birgitta Oden, provided me with the opportunity to extend my own understanding of modern Sweden and to complete this manuscript. The volume was first written and published in Swedish although it was intended primarily as an English-language work on Sweden. Translation and editing of the text has proven extremely difficult and time consuming. Often names and terms were used in the Swedish text which, while familiar to a Swedish reader, demanded considerable explanation or elimination from the English version. I have received support in this trying task of editing from the University of Minnesota Press.

Steven Koblik

Claremont, California
June 1975

Contents

Sweden's Development
from Poverty to Affluence

Introduction

by Steven Koblik

Sweden: The Middle Way, written by Marquis Childs and published in 1936, stimulated an interest in contemporary Sweden that has continued until the present day. Despite its small size and relative unimportance as a European state, Sweden has been examined and reexamined by a host of foreigners who are anxious to prove that Sweden is either a paradise or a hell on earth. No other similarly sized European country has received anywhere near the same kind of attention. Articles in newspapers and popular magazines appear regularly. Sweden, at least in the United States, has become synonymous with the idea of the "welfare state" or "cradle to grave" security, and proponents and opponents of these ideas often use Sweden as an example to show the benefits or the dangers that accrue with the establishment of welfare programs. President Eisenhower in 1960, for instance, could not resist the temptation to note that welfarism in Sweden had led to increased suicide, socialism, alcoholism, and promiscuity. Even though this interest has now spanned nearly forty years, what do we know of Sweden? How accurate are the accounts of contemporary Sweden that we so often see in our media? How did

Sweden reach its present level of development? These are the questions often asked of social scientists specializing in twentieth-century Sweden. To respond intelligently to these questions is not always as easy as it might first appear.

Most scholars of Sweden are painfully aware of how rudimentary is our knowledge of modern Sweden. My purpose in this volume is to provide the English-speaking reader with a series of essays by leading Swedish scholars who can give us dependable and up-to-date information about the growth of modern Sweden. Additionally, this work should acquaint the reader with Swedish historiography and historians. *Sweden's Development from Poverty to Affluence* is an introduction to the study of modern Swedish history; it will not answer definitively the questions posed in the preceding paragraph. But the essays should suggest how scholars are approaching some of the issues related to those questions.

My own work has left me highly skeptical about the accuracy of the type of study represented by Childs, David Jenkins (*Sweden and the Price of Progress*), and Roland Huntford (*The New Totalitarians*). These popular accounts of contemporary Sweden often tell more about the author than they do about Sweden. Childs, for example, misunderstood the role of cooperatives in Swedish society, while Huntford assumed that the political system and values of Great Britain should serve as the model for any democratic state. Jenkins's study is simply too impressionistic. Still there is value in these accounts and the critical reader may make use of them. One of the most challenging aspects of Huntford's book is his theory of Swedish historical development. His view that Sweden has been able to reestablish a new form of corporatist society in a postindustrial state because of its relatively late and rapid industrialization contains seeds of ideas that were developed by Swedish political scientists and need to be examined more carefully by historians.

Historians of Sweden both native and foreign have not yet produced any broad consensus view of modern Sweden. The best general studies of Sweden in English, Ingvar Andersson's *A History of Sweden* and Stewart Oakley's *A Short History of Sweden,* emphasize the earlier periods of the country's development and do not confront the major issues of the recent past. Even the best of the Swedish general histories of the modern era, volume 2 of *Svensk historia,* by Sten Carlsson, is too descriptive to be as helpful as we would wish. There is such a paucity of analytic works on modern Sweden primarily because of the way in which Swedes approach historical research. Foreign scholars are dependent upon the work of native historians and therefore mirror in most regards the strengths and weaknesses of historical scholarship in Sweden.

How do Swedes approach history as a field of study? The study of history is a time-honored tradition and historical literature is extensive and intensive. Since the mid-nineteenth century, Swedish historical writing has been heavily influenced by the Germanic tradition. The purpose of the historian is to be as empirical as possible, to make historical research approximate the accuracy of the hard sciences, and to remove the subjective influences of the historian himself. The result has been that the best works on Swedish history tend to be exhaustive, monographic studies of the early modern or medieval periods. The monographic tradition lends itself well to empiricism because the scholar is able to focus precisely on carefully defined problems and to bring his critical methods fully to bear on the documentary evidence. The earlier periods have received the greatest attention because of the documents available on them. Indeed so prolific have been the studies of these periods that numerous stimulating works of synthesis have been produced. The modern period, however, has just begun to be researched; historical studies on the late nineteenth and the twentieth centuries were rare before 1960. No important syntheses of the modern period have yet been written by historians.

The best thematic studies of the modern period have been done by economic historians. The most important of these is the six-volume study by Eli Heckscher, *Sveriges ekonomiska historia.*

Although Heckscher's methods and findings have been attacked at virtually every point, his influence on our understanding of modern Sweden has been greater than that of any other scholar. A similar contribution has been made by his colleague Arthur Montgomery with such works as *Den Industriella Revolutionen i Sverige.*

What we would like to see now is more books similar to the studies of Heckscher and Montgomery but based on modern theoretical foundations and recently released documentary material. This will not be an easy task. Those historians who try to meet such a challenge will need much time to assimilate the newer methods and theories of social science and to use them in organizing what is an overwhelming amount of primary materials. Further there is still considerable skepticism about the value of syntheses, and about the legitimacy of social science theories, among historians locked firmly in the empirical tradition. In the meanwhile the need still exists for those who wish an overview of Sweden's modern history to find sources to increase their understanding. It is my hope that *Sweden's Development from Poverty to Affluence* will contribute to fulfilling that need.

The thirteen essays in this volume are by well-known Swedish scholars, most of whom are historians, but among the authors are two political scientists, an economic historian, and a sociologist. It was impossible in the compass of this book to cover all aspects of Swedish development. We have tried to focus upon critical problems within that process. The advantage with such a problem-oriented approach is that it most closely resembles the way in which historical research occurs in Sweden.

The essays therefore will offer the reader the opportunity to study not only the specific problems but also the latest methods in historical research used by Swedish historians. In some cases the essays attempt to study problems that have not been examined previously. In order to help the reader understand and appreciate each author's research methods and interpretations, I have added a brief introduction to each essay. The introductions do not summarize the contents of the essays but try to establish their significance, to relate them to each other, and to fill in, where necessary, factual background.

Each author has been free to define his subject in his own way. This has meant that there is wide diversity in approach and methods. There is also a broad range of topics. Some essays deal with specific and narrowly defined issues, while others attempt to view a large historical period from a thematic perspective. This variety is one of the strengths of the book if the reader will note the introductory remarks and compare the articles. All historical methods have advantages and disadvantages in the study of the historical process. A comparison of the different methods and approaches used in the following essays should be illuminating.

As for source references, I felt it important that the authors keep footnotes to a minimum, using them chiefly to clarify particular points within the context of the essay. In this fashion, the essays are largely independent of other materials and holistic in their conceptualization. However, for those who wish to examine in more detail either the issues discussed in this volume or other problems related to the development of modern Sweden, sources may be found in the bibliography. I hope the reader will use the materials cited there for a closer examination of problems that are of interest to him.

With all historical studies there is the question of where to begin chronologically and when to end. The primary concern in this volume is the process that has created contemporary Sweden. History is a continuing succession of unique events, situations that neither "begin" nor "end." Every attempt to establish periods of history is therefore artificial, yet this is a task that cannot be ignored. I have chosen the middle of the eighteenth century as the starting point here, a traditional choice in the writing of Swedish history. Important political, social, and intellectual developments at this time would eventually produce a Sweden quite different from the country that had been a Great Power in the preceding period.

"The Age of Freedom" is the name that the era from 1718 to 1772 has received in Swedish history. Its reference points are the two periods of royal absolutism that precede and follow it. By the middle of the age, the ideas of the Enlightenment had begun to make important inroads into Swedish intellectual life and the political discussions of the day; the first essay here is a study of this phenomenon. The founding of the Royal Academy of Science and the contributions of Swedish scientists, most notably Karl von Linné (Linnaeus), demonstrate that Sweden participated significantly in the contemporary European growth of scientific inquiry. Of equal importance were the new philosophical trends in Sweden in the early 1740s that encouraged the consolidation of peasant landholdings. The changes produced as a result of consolidation and the enclosure movement are among the most critical changes of all Swedish history. But the process was slow. At the beginning of the nineteenth century the great majority of Swedes lived in villages in much the same manner as those in previous generations.

In economic and social terms the eighteenth century was more a transitional than a revolutionary period. Sweden was, in light of contemporary Western European standards, a relatively poor but stable country. Heckscher believed that the average calorie intake per capita in eighteenth-century Sweden was lower than it had been in the previous century. Newer research has, however, suggested that Heckscher overestimated the general living standards of the earlier period. Malthus used his observations of southern Sweden, among other places, to formulate his famous law that population grows exponentially while agrarian production increases arithmetically. Malthus concluded that during good times significant sections of the population would exist at minimum levels and that in hard times they would starve. Recent historical research has noted that the periods of rapid population growth during the eighteenth century coincide with the periods of the best weather. The impression one gets from these studies is that a significant part of the Swedish people lived hard and exposed lives.

Another sign that the development of Sweden proceeded more slowly than that of Western Europe generally was the weakness of the middle class. The political upheavals initiated in France and Great Britain by middle-class groups in the late eighteenth and early nineteenth centuries had no counterparts in Sweden until well into the middle of the nineteenth century. In summary it appears that the eighteenth century in Sweden was a period of accommodation and slow change. The Great Power era was over and the country was forced to find a realistic place in European society. While it is true that Sweden continued to hold some of the territories gained during the earlier periods, there was a gradual diminution of its holdings on the southern Baltic. These areas were lost with a minimum of economic and political difficulty, although the immediate ramifications were important and not without their consequences for later development. Some of the essays discuss the most critical of these issues. The cosmopolitanism of the seventeenth century that had dominated the country between 1600 and 1720 ebbed, and a more introverted period began. Industrial growth stagnated, partly as a direct result of governmental policy. The country's significance for European trade, particularly in copper and iron, decreased even though Sweden's own production levels were not lowered. Agricultural activities continued to engage an overwhelming portion of the Swedish people. It has been estimated that 75 to 80 percent of the population was involved in agricultural pursuits during the late eighteenth century. One hundred years later, the corresponding figure was still 72 percent. These statistics indicate the slow rate at which industrial development occurred in Sweden. But from another perspective the figures are highly misleading. During the hundred-year period 1770–1870 there occurred in Sweden a veritable agrarian revolution.

During this period extraordinary changes took place in the age-old pattern of living in villages and in the methods of holding and tilling the land. The three forces most influential in this process were government-sponsored programs of enclosure, an extensive exploitation of newly reclaimed agricultural lands, and a steady, spectacular rise in the population of the country. A fourth factor might be included: the introduction of new crops, most critically the potato. In Great Britain, enclosure led to the creation of large holdings owned primarily by the aristocracy and gentry with a resultant migration from rural areas into the new industrial centers. By contrast, the enclosure movement in Sweden led to development of a class of independent farmers who held relatively small-sized pieces of land. The traditional way of village life altered markedly. The village community, especially in the richer provinces such as Skåne, ceased to be the focal point for activity in the area. Families moved out to their own land-holdings, and the successful among these farmers became an important influence on the continued growth of the country. On the other hand, there were a growing number of landless rural workers who could not, or did not, take advantage of the reform programs. Since no parallel growth occurred in the industrial sector as had taken place in England, these landless or poor farmers had no alternative but to remain in the countryside and serve as a rural proletariat. The increase in these rural groups, whose existence was so exposed, was remarkable, as the accompanying tabulation suggests. The first column, "Bondeklassen," is the independent farmer group; the next three groups should be considered part of the rural poor despite the differences that exist

Year	Bondeklassen	Tjänar-klassen	Backstugu-och Inhyses-klassen	Torpar-klassen
1775	 1,052,725	266,577	98,948	183,302
1800	 1,102,120	277,184	197,116	261,127
1870	 1,395,543	369,459	482,261	436,486

between them. In 1775 the total population was 2,020,847; in 1800, 2,347,303; and in 1870, 4,168,525.

The agrarian revolution in Sweden is of fundamental importance for Sweden's modern development. Throughout Swedish history the countryside has taken an unusually important role in comparison with other European states. The peasantry was never enserfed as were similar groups elsewhere in Europe but participated, however passively, in the struggle for political power during the entire period 1600–1800. In the nineteenth and twentieth centuries farmer representatives had critical roles in the political process. Perhaps even more remarkable is the part that the Agrarian party has played during the time Sweden has been guided by the Social Democrats.

The Agrarian party is currently called the Center party; it is the largest opposition party and has formed coalition governments with the Social Democrats during the periods 1933–1945 and 1951–1957. Although the party's composition has changed significantly in the past forty years, its ties with the countryside remain strong. Indeed one is tempted to comment that the recent success of the Center party is due partly to the romanticism about rural life that continues to dominate the country. Swedes probably have the highest per capita number of second homes in the world; these homes are often located in rural settings and permit the Swedes to keep their roots in the countryside.

Of course there are other historical themes besides the activities of the peasantry that have been of great importance for modern Sweden. A few of the most critical might be mentioned:

1. *The existence of a powerful state church.* Although the initial conversion to Lutheranism from Catholicism occurred more for political than for religious reasons, the Lutheran tradition soon firmly established itself among the Swedish people. Over time the church provided both a solid basis for religious and ethical attitudes and a foundation of stability enabling existing holders of power to maintain their position. By the nineteenth

century the church hierarchy had rigidified to the extent that it
had difficulty in responding to new forms of religious concern.
Since church and state had become so closely intertwined (church
officials operated as parish registrars), religious revolt had immediate political ramifications.

2. *Respect for the law.* Law has ruled Sweden even during times
of royal absolutism. Violent political upheavals are very rare.
Respect for the law is so ingrained that Swedes themselves rarely
appreciate its importance in the construction of a modern society.

3. *The homogeneity of the Swedish people.* From the end of
the Great Power period until after World War II Sweden experienced no significant immigration. A sense of family, community,
and shared experiences exists in Sweden that would be difficult
to reproduce in more heterogeneous countries. The spirit of community, which clearly does not operate at all times, produces both
a degree of trust on the part of the governed and a sense of
responsibility in those who govern that is fundamental to the
"middle way" Sweden seeks.

4. *The importance of government.* Organized government has
existed for a very long time in Sweden. Also, the tradition of
responsive government has been strong. As a result government
has been seen as a proper medium by which to solve problems. The
need for, or desirability of, private initiative decreases when government demonstrates effectiveness and a sense of responsibility.

5. *The effectiveness, honesty, and influence of the bureaucracy.*
The modern bureaucracy or civil service began its development
during the Great Power period. It was staffed primarily by members of the aristocracy or talented laymen and its influence served
as a brake on royal power. Even after 1866 when its formal political power waned, it continued to draw upon the traditions established earlier. As a result part of the cream of every Swedish generation is attracted into bureaucratic service where prestige and
considerable influence are guaranteed.

6. *The weakness of the middle class.* The absence of a strong

classical liberal tradition has had many ramifications. Governmental institutions—particularly administrative bureaucracy—and the concept of government "interference" were not attacked as early or as forcefully as they were elsewhere in much of Western Europe. The combination of a weak classical tradition and a vibrant social libertarian movement has meant that middle-class parties were late in developing in Sweden and yet in the recent period have made important contributions to the growth of social democracy.

7. *The tendency within Swedish intellectual life toward rationality and practicality.* Sweden has been called a land of engineers; indeed, the country has produced a large number of practical inventions. This pragmatism has also been applied to politics.

Most of these themes will be discussed in the context of one or more of the following essays. Should the reader wish to examine more carefully their importance in the earlier periods the proper place to begin would be volume 1 of *Svensk historia* by Jerker Rosén.

Introduction to Chapter 1

One of the great watersheds of Swedish history was the loss by
Sweden during the Great Northern War (1700–1721) of Great
Power status, which occurred simultaneously with the absolutist
reign of Karl XII (1697–1718). Sweden's institutions continued
to be shaped by its experiences in the Great Power period, 1618–
1720, but internationally it ceased to play an important active
role in European affairs even though it fought two wars with
Russia (1741 and 1789) and one with Prussia (1757–1762) and
participated in the Napoleonic wars, by which it lost Finland but
gained Norway in a monarchal union. Indeed Sweden became,
particularly between 1720 and 1772, an area for Great Power
intervention. The Age of Freedom in Sweden witnessed a degree
of external intervention in domestic affairs unequaled in Sweden's modern historical experience. This fact led nineteenth-
century Swedish historians, under the influence of a growing
nationalism, to view the period in very negative terms and to
applaud the restoration of self-reliance under the guidance of
Gustav III in 1772. For generations of Swedes, the term Age of
Freedom was synonymous with foreign domination and interfer-

ence in Swedish domestic life. Relatively ignored by this historical perspective were the important political and social advancements achieved once royal absolutism had been overthrown and the burden of Great Power status removed.

In eighteenth-century Europe the status quo was challenged in many fields. Traditional institutions and philosophies were attacked in the names of reason, science, progress, and man. Great scientific breakthroughs, commonly associated with Sir Isaac Newton's work, occurred in the earlier part of the period, while the latter part of the age was dominated by political philosophers' attacks on established political institutions and personages. This philosophical movement became the intellectual base for "the age of the democratic revolution" that shook the Atlantic community after 1760.

It was the American historian R. R. Palmer who suggested in his two-volume work *The Age of the Democratic Revolution* that all the states of Western Europe and their North Atlantic dependencies went through a common intellectual and political experience during the last forty years of the eighteenth century—an experience that was essentially directed toward the overthrow of the old social and political order and toward the establishment of a new community based upon a modern, "democratic" idea of justice. In short, Palmer saw the foundation of the modern European (and North American) state as a product of this age. He placed not only the obviously revolutionary developments in the thirteen colonies and in France within this context but also the relatively nonviolent experiences of such countries as Sweden. Palmer's work since its publication in 1959 has become a focal reference for research on the late eighteenth century in the countries of the North Atlantic community. His theories have fared surprisingly well.

Nineteenth-century Swedish historians, in emphasizing the negative aspects of the Age of Freedom, had not perceived that Sweden too was involved in the progressive development of a modern political system and a freer society. However, out of historians' reexamination of the Age of Freedom in the past fifty years has come a clearer, more positive view of the political development of the era. Professor Sten Carlsson of Uppsala University, who has been very active in these new probings, will, in the following essay, examine the political forces at work during the latter part of the Age of Freedom and test Palmer's thesis against the Swedish experience.

1

Sweden in the 1760s

by Sten Carlsson

In the first part of his masterly work *The Age of the Democratic Revolution*, R. R. Palmer says that "a revolutionary era" began in Western civilization around 1760. It manifested itself in various ways: confidence in the justice or reasonableness of existing authority was undermined, old loyalties and responsibilities were no longer accepted, respect for superiors was felt as a "form of humiliation," "existing sources of prestige seem[ed] undeserved, hitherto accepted forms of wealth and income seem[ed] ill-gained," and the distance between the governors and the governed grew. The ties between social classes were also transformed into "jealousy and frustration."

Palmer touches upon the general state of affairs in Sweden during the Age of Freedom (1718–1772) as well as upon the bitter battles between the country's two political parties, the Hats and the Caps, in the 1760s; he also makes note of developments of Gustav III's reign (1771–1792). But an examination of Palmer's general interpretation of social changes in Europe and North America during the decades before the French Revolution shows that Sweden fits into his grand design even better than his own investigations reveal. What makes Sweden especially interesting from an international perspective is its combination of old-fashioned agrarian and patriarchal forms of production on the one hand and unusually well-developed instruments for broad social activities along with strivings for self-government on the other.

In the 1760s, Sweden (including Finland) had a population of about two and a half million, of which barely a half million belonged to the Finnish part of the kingdom. Swedish Pomerania and Wismar, Sweden's German territories, had a unique position and were not represented in the Swedish Riksdag; they will not be taken into consideration here. More than 90 percent of the population lived in the countryside, and more than 75 percent was occupied in the agricultural sector, which included stock raising, fishing, and forestry. Sweden was still a society of estates, but the structure of the estates was considerably different from the continental model.

The nobility was relatively few in numbers—less than half of 1 percent of the total population—and it was not as strictly distinguished from the higher commoner groups of society as was true in many other countries. It retained exclusive right to the highest offices, however, and played a leading role in the bureaucracy and the military forces. Land favored with special tax reductions*—a third of the land in Sweden, less than a tenth in Finland—was still held primarily by noblemen. The manors, which encompassed the most valuable part of this land, were reserved for the nobility in principle, while other tax-exempt farmsteads could be acquired by commoners, although not by peasants. Within the four-estate Riksdag, the nobility played a leading role and held far more than one fourth of the political power. The clerical estate, which contained barely 1 percent of the people,

---

* *Frälsejord* was land held by either nobles or commoners that was exempt from taxes by virtue of service provided by the owner to the crown. In this essay, such land will be called tax-exempt land.

was still a very important spiritual and political force, but its position was somewhat weakened by the strong expansion of lay education: in time, the university came to be less and less dominated by theologians. Academic education for judges and civil officials expanded during the Age of Freedom, and the natural sciences enjoyed a veritable golden age under the guidance of Linnaeus and others. The burgher estate contained about 2 percent of the people and controlled retail trade and handicraft production through the use of mercantilist legislation. In social status and influence, the big merchants in Stockholm and Göteborg were almost on a level with the high nobility. A group of so-called commoner gentry—government officials, officers, teachers, owners of industrial operations (about 2 percent of the population)—emerged alongside the three higher estates. This group was not represented in the Riksdag, but its importance in social and economic life was growing. The peasant estate included about half the total population. The peasants were completely free personally and, as one of the four estates of the Riksdag, held greater political power than the peasants of any other European country, although not as much as the three higher estates. In the Riksdag only those peasants were represented who owned their own land and paid taxes or who leased their land from the crown, while the peasants who worked tax-exempt property were excluded from political influence. More than 40 percent of the population was entirely unpropertied. These people were primarily agricultural proletarians—crofters, cottagers, farm workers paid in kind, farmhands, servant girls, etc.—but also workers in the merchant industries, industrial hands, unskilled laborers of all kinds, lower civil and military officers, and so on. Although the number of people in many of these categories grew very quickly, there was never any question of giving them political power. They were free personally, but regulations giving masters great power over their workers limited their actual freedom of movement.

With the death of Karl XII in 1718, the absolutist royal power collapsed. His sister Ulrika Eleanora (1718–1720), her husband Fredrik I of Hesse-Cassel (1720–1751), and his successor Adolf Fredrik of Holstein-Gottorp (1751–1771) were incapable of holding their own against the estates. An attempted royalist coup in 1756 was smothered and its consequences for the royal house were humiliating. The Riksdag held almost all the political power. Two political parties, the Hats and the Caps, had emerged in the Riksdag, and after 1738 the Swedish parliamentary system was better developed than the contemporary British system. The Older Caps—to some extent a counterpart to the Whigs in Great Britain—dominated from 1719 to 1738, while the Hats—who were similar to the Tories—controlled the government from 1738 to 1765. During the 1760s, the Younger Caps, who represented a more radical political line than their predecessors in the 1730s, appeared in opposition to the Hats.

The Hats represented an active, dynamic element in Swedish social life when they came to power in the 1740s. They demanded a more powerful and purposeful policy than the Caps had aspired to. The social base of the Hats was narrow, however: it was actually composed largely of officeholders and entrepreneurs, although the party also had won a foothold in the peasant estate. As the four-estate Riksdag was constructed, however, the political situation could be dominated by a minority group that had sufficient support from the noble government officials and from the bourgeois entrepreneurs and local officials, especially if the group won control of the powerful Secret Committee—the central governing body of the Riksdag composed of fifty noblemen, twenty-five clergymen, and twenty-five burghers under the chairmanship of the speaker of the House of Nobles. The Secret Committee was particularly concerned with public finances and foreign policy. The peasants, to their great indignation, were excluded from this central body; their lack of language skills was the usual argument for not allowing them entry.

The dominant philosophy of the Hats was arch-mercantilistic:

above all they supported the iron industry and other export enterprises with duties, regulations, and direct aid. Their special favorites were the textile manufacturers, whose businesses were relatively unimportant in size. The Hats were also centralistically inclined, both economically and administratively. They wanted to concentrate control of foreign trade in the hands of specific business interests and to protect the Bothnian trade constraint, which they inherited and which prohibited the cities on the Gulf of Bothnia north of Gävle and Åbo from conducting their own foreign trade; this legislation especially favored Stockholm's merchants. The Hats also sought to retain legislation against merchandising in the countryside. They became more and more bureaucratic with time. Their interest in administration could be progressive—for example, in their demand for increased theoretical education for civil servants—but it could also be restrictive. In the Government Service Report of 1756, careful instructions were given on how to announce vacancies and on the principles for promotion, in which special weight was given to seniority. At the same time, the juridically educated mayors and aldermen (civil administrators) of the towns tried to usurp power from the ordinary burghers, i.e., the merchants and craftsmen. The regulations for voting and eligibility for posts in the administration of towns were changed to favor the incumbent public officials, and the freedom of assembly of the burghers was limited. The Hats' interest in civil rights was generally cool; among other things, they maintained a rather strict political and ecclesiastical censorship.

The Hats tended to support aristocratic interests. They did not approve of the attacks on noble privileges by the commoner estates and did not like the moderate demands for equality raised in the 1760s. However, they did not erect any barriers to the slow process of equalization within the civil administration that had begun in the 1730s and that meant public officials born in the commoner estates could advance quite far without ennoblement; promotion to the highest posts did entail ennoblement. By the

1760s, the government had become uneasy about this latter development: in 1762, the House of Nobles was closed to the introduction of new families until its membership declined to less than eight hundred families, which could not be expected to happen in the near future. This decision, which aroused great bitterness among the commoners, meant that no person born in a commoner estate could be promoted to any of the highest civil and military posts—not even if the king gave him a noble letter of escutcheon. The Hats were also not of a mind to comply with the peasants' demands for equality. A Hat decision in 1763 stopped the royal peasants from buying the homesteads that they worked and thereby advancing from tenant farmers to peasant proprietors, an opportunity that formerly had been much appreciated and frequently used. The Hats, with the help of the royal huntsmen, also tried to limit the peasants' hunting and fishing rights.

The basic characteristics of the Hats' foreign policy were friendliness to the French and enmity to the Russians. French subsidies and bribes played a large role in Hat policy, while the Caps accepted money from Russia and Great Britain. The Hat government led the country into war twice, against Russia in 1741–1743 and against Prussia in 1757–1762, during the Seven Years War. Both wars were fiascoes for Sweden, primarily because the Hats, despite promising beginnings and an active foreign policy, had failed to make the Swedish military forces effective. After the catastrophic reverses against Russia in the 1740s, the Hats succeeded in retaining power by skillfully exploiting the Caps' engagement on the Russian side. For many Swedes, Russia continued to loom as the hereditary enemy, and it was easy to brand anyone with sympathies in that direction as a traitor. The war with Prussia was conducted in Pomerania, where both Sweden and Prussia had possessions, and it too resulted in reverses, although not as disastrous as those in the 1740s. This war had greater effects on party politics than the war with Russia; it lacked popular support in

Sweden and it caused a violent inflation, evoking widespread dissatisfaction. This unhappiness fanned the hopes of the Caps.

The Caps were mercantilists but not in the same conspicuous way as the Hats. Their program gave more priority to demands for thriftiness and economic freedom than the Hats' did, and they criticized the commercial policy that benefited a limited group of entrepreneurs while the country's many craftsmen and other small businessmen were ignored. The Caps also favored decentralization: they wanted to abolish or relax the Bothnian trade constraint and expand the opportunities for peasants to engage in trade with their own products. The Caps were also antibureaucratic: they wanted to save money through the abolition of certain positions, especially in the military sector, and they took the side of the burghers against local officials. The Caps also advocated greater freedom of assembly and freedom of the press. Without being democrats in the modern sense, they supported a certain equality, for example in promotions of civil servants; however, there were conflicts of interest between noble and commoner Caps in this regard. The peasants' demands for equality were greeted with more sympathy from the Caps than from the Hats.

The Caps did not like the Hats' connections with France; they were primarily anglophiles and also sought support from Russia, Prussia, and Denmark-Norway, and they accepted bribes from foreign legations. Great Britain often inspired the Caps' demands for freedom, but they did not want to collaborate as intimately with Great Britain as the Hats did with France. Above all, they wished to carry on a policy of peace, and the severe military setbacks under the leadership of the Hats worked in their favor. Developments among the Great Powers, with defeats for France in Europe as well as in India and North America, also benefited the Caps. The British government had reason to believe that a victory for the Caps would help Great Britain commercially as well as diplomatically; the protectionist policy of the Hats had been very unpopular in London.

The Caps' strength showed itself at the election of Riksdag members in 1764 when they were victorious in all the commoner estates. The nobility, which was represented by the heads of the various families or authorized deputies, held no election, but when the estate met in 1765, it was apparent that the tide had turned there too. In the contest for speaker, the powerful Hat leader Axel Fersen the elder was defeated by a fairly wide margin by the Caps' candidate T. G. Rudbeck. All the commoner estates elected Caps as speakers. Under the parliamentary system of the time, control of the government (Privy Council) was transferred to the Caps. Carl Gustaf Löwenhielm, a factory owner from Värmland, became president of the chancellery (prime minister); previously a Hat, he had become more and more critical of Hat policies that favored the big export firms at the expense of the factory owners. To some extent it was symptomatic of the period that Löwenhielm came from the countryside, not from the capital, and that he belonged to a newly ennobled family. He had been a commoner until he became a nobleman at the age of twenty-four through his father's ennoblement. Löwenhielm's foremost co-worker in the new Privy Council, Esbjörn Reuterholm, a representative for the landowning nobility in Finland, also represented the countryside.

The prime ideologue among the victorious Caps, however, was not among these aristocrats, but was a newly ennobled businessman with a purely bourgeois background, Anders Nordencrantz. He came from Norrland and had been a merchant in Sundsvall for many years, even representing that city in the burgher estate of the Riksdag. Later he had been involved in consular activities and the iron industry, and for fifteen years he had been a member of the Board of Trade. He became a nobleman in 1743. He thus had unusually varied experience when he threw himself seriously into the political debate in the mid-1750s. Although he had originally been closest to the Hat party, in time he became strongly opposed to that party and in the 1760s he emerged as a kind of oracle for the Caps. In his extremely long-winded writings, almost unreadable today, he primarily attacked the two groups that supported the Hat regime: the noble government officials and the bourgeois mercantilists. In his arguments he especially protested against the strong position of power held by government officials in the four-estate Riksdag and their opposition to increased public control. He wanted a completely new body of representatives, based on property but independent of the estates, with government officials not eligible for election. He proposed that judgeships and certain other public offices be filled by popular election and for limited terms. He had lived in England during his younger days, and many of his ideas were influenced by ongoing English debate. Something often overlooked by both his contemporaries and posterity is that many of his expostulations against officialdom concerned conditions that had arisen during the 1750s and that were not typical for the Age of Freedom as a whole.

Nordencrantz was strongly influenced in his economic thinking by his own experiences in operating a factory. He had sustained heavy losses and thought that one of the large merchant houses in Stockholm had made unreasonable profits at his expense. He did not regard the inflation following the Pomeranian War as a consequence of the increase in the supply of money in circulation but blamed the exporters, who he felt had undermined the value of money through criminal manipulations. He developed ideologically from a mercantilist to a "prephysiocrat" under the influence of such French and British thinkers as Rousseau, Voltaire, Montesquieu, Mirabeau the elder, and Hume. In accordance with physiocratic ideals, he placed greater emphasis on the agricultural sector than the mercantilists usually did. At the same time, he attacked aristocratic luxury and corruption and the whole prevailing system of economic and social privilege. Nordencrantz embodies the background and philosophy of the Younger Caps in an extraordinary way: his Norrland origins, his opposition to the exporters, his antibureaucratism, and his ties to Great Britain are especially illustrative.

The transition from Hat to Cap politics entailed no great problems for the clerical estate. The Hats had never had a sure hold on this estate, although many clergymen, especially bishops and other prelates, had united with the Hat party. An important factor in the party orientation of the clergymen was the Hats' tendency to tolerate increasingly pious religious groups—cherished not the least by many aristocratic groups—which stood in opposition to Lutheran orthodoxy and which were exemplified by the pietists and Herrnhutians. Despite the Caps' sympathy for freedom in principle, on religious matters they were less tolerant and more orthodox in practice. The Caps took command of the clerical estate during the 1760–1762 Riksdag, and in 1765 their majority was very clear. At the same time, dominance of the estate shifted from the bishops to the parish clergymen, who wanted to make the holding of a parish position the basis for belonging to the estate. In 1766 those prelates (mostly bishops) who had accepted nobility for themselves or their children were formally excluded from the clerical estate of the Riksdag.

There were Caps even in the episcopacy. Bishop Jacob Serenius of Strängnäs was especially talented and influential. Like Nordencrantz, he had spent part of his life in London, where he was the pastor of the Swedish congregation. He had been greatly impressed by English church organization and learning. As an anglophile and utilitarian, he had vehemently attacked the Hats' war policy both in 1741–1743 and in 1757–1762. He had also urged that the four estates support agriculture instead of granting favors to the manufacturers, and, like many other Caps, he worked for improvements in the school system.

In 1765, Serenius, Löwenhielm, and Nordencrantz were all about sixty-five years old—rather elderly men by the standards of the time. A younger generation was coming to power, led by

Anders Chydenius. A thirty-six-year-old chaplain from Österbotten, he was elected into the clerical estate, representing a relatively poor social group that could rarely make its voice heard in political debate. Chydenius himself was not poor, however. He belonged to a clerical family that was both rich and culturally prominent, with ties to merchant families in Åbo and Stockholm. When he spoke out for mitigation of the restrictions making servants dependent on their masters, he was not acting in his own interest. As he pointed out later (1778), he had twelve or thirteen bonded servants each year and thus should have "sung the same tune" as many other masters. In his opinion, the servants' oppression and lack of freedom were the most important causes for the emigration of so many of them; like many of his contemporaries, he had an exaggerated idea of the extent of such emigration. In this matter, Chydenius let his interests give way to his principles. In his attacks on the Bothnian trade constraint, his principles and interests were in harmony. With greater consistency than many who shared his opinions, he made his demand for expanded freedom of trade a unifying element in a general criticism of the entire mercantilist regulatory system. He thereby foreshadowed economic liberalism. He was also liberal in his demands for freedom of the press. Like Nordencrantz, he strongly censured the exporters and mercilessly demanded accountings from all who could be regarded as responsible for the miserable condition of the state's finances. Before long, he even attacked the Caps' financial policy and thereby aroused such displeasure among the members of his party that his own estate expelled him from the Riksdag for the meeting then in session and the following one.

Within the burgher estate, the Hat-minded merchants, supported by numerous members of the civil administration and small-town burghers, had long held control. In the 1764 election, however, the wind changed: sixty-four of the members elected to the estate could be classified as Caps and thirty-four as Hats, while eight were more or less undecided. The Hats' defeat in Stockholm was especially marked. Only one of the electing groups there— characteristically, the entrepreneurs—supported the party. The Hats' most reliable support was now in Göteborg and other cities on the west coast; the Caps' most secure footholds were in Norrland and Österbotten, where discontent with the Bothnian trade constraint was an important factor. A good half of the Hats in the burgher estate were local officials and the rest were wholesalers, businessmen, government officials, or manufacturers; none were craftsmen. A third of the Caps were government officials; about half were wholesalers or businessmen; none were manufacturers. All nine of the craftsmen in the estate were Caps. The Caps' victory meant a regional and social shift, but it should be remembered that even they had good connections among relatively well situated bourgeois groups and in the civil administration bureaucracy. It was the obvious interests of exporters and government officials that suffered from the party shift. Many of the Caps combined government officeholding with bourgeois activities, as was the case with Mayor Anders Ekman of Åmål, for example, who carried on trade in Göteborg and Värmland from his small hometown in western Sweden. He was not particularly wealthy but he had an ample library, which included the writings of Nordencrantz.

The internal situation in the burgher estate was greatly affected by the 1765 party shift. It was decided in 1766 that persons who had, or who had previously had, the "character" of government officials (i.e., a real office or an honorary title, such as sheriff, royal comptroller, or judge) could no longer be members of the estate. This disqualification, which may be compared to the closing of the House of Nobles and the exclusion of noble bishops from the clerical estate, did not affect the civil administration officials, although a few of the most radical Caps wanted to bar them too. Factory owners and entrepreneurs living in the countryside who were not town residents with the rights of burghers were also excluded. At the same time, provisions for the election of magistrates in Stockholm were reformed in an antibureaucratic direction. One regulation that was abolished was a rule, introduced in 1756, whereby local officials were given great influence on magistrate elections in the kingdom; in the future, these elections were to be a purely burgher matter. The same tendency was evident in a decision to annul a regulation reducing the freedom of assembly of the burghers that had been introduced in 1752.

Pure party politics meant less in the peasant estate than in the three higher estates. The peasant members of the Riksdag worked primarily to achieve full equality among the estates, to ameliorate tax burdens on peasant land, to strengthen the tax-paying peasants' right of ownership, and to fulfill the local desires their various principals instructed them to present. Party grouping occurred even within the peasant estate, however, especially among the more influential members; for example, the speaker of the estate from 1738 to 1762, Olof Håkansson from Lösen in Blekinge, was a pillar among the Hats at least from the beginning of the 1750s. Many peasants were drawn to the Cap party, however, because of its position on foreign-policy questions, its greater inclination for economy, its ideas of equality, and its sympathies for increased freedom of trade. During the 1760–1762 Riksdag, it was difficult for Håkansson to keep his support, and he was defeated in the election for speaker in 1765 by Joseph Hansson from Mossebo in Västergötland.

Hansson, like Håkansson, was a long-time member of the Riksdag and had been close to Håkansson, but during the 1760–1762 session their paths began to diverge. As the representative for a district where rural trade in the form of house-to-house peddling had long held a strong and, in some respects, privileged position, Hansson had reason to sympathize with the Caps' economic program, to ally with those who wanted to abolish the Bothnian trade constraint. He also disapproved of the Hats' war policies, although his generally moderate disposition kept him from uniting with the Hats' most vengeful opponents. As an orthodox Lutheran, he was disturbed by the Hats' tolerance for the Herrnhutians. In questions of financial policy, he gladly listened to Nordencrantz. Although Hansson was a spokesman for purely peasant interests and at times expressed distrust of those countrymen who were socially close to the gentry, he was no typical peasant himself. Through mill and sawmill activities, management of property, public services, and probably also, in his younger days, peddling, he built up a position of wealth that was perhaps unparalleled in the peasant estate. He was a prominent example of the west Swedish peasants who thrust themselves into the property market of the nobility during the Age of Freedom and acquired manors and other tax-exempt property in various ways— usually through mortgages—even though they were not supposed to hold this property.

In the rest of Europe during the mid-eighteenth century there were no peasant politicians of the stature of Olof Håkansson and Joseph Hansson. The Riksdag of 1765–1766 was of great importance for the social aspirations of the peasants. Although they did not succeed in gaining entry to the Secret Committee, they again received the right to purchase the taxable lands they worked. A formal order to the royal huntsmen not to meddle in the hunting and fishing rights of the tax-paying peasants was another triumph for them. The peasant estate also forced through an act freeing peasant navigation within the kingdom, so that the men of the countryside could trade their own products by sea in various places, which often meant they traveled past the towns in their home provinces and went directly to Stockholm. Chydenius and members of the Riksdag from Stockholm worked for this measure, while representatives from towns in northern Sweden were opposed. A warning was also given to the authorities who placed barriers in the way of the peasants making trips by land to trade their own wares.

These reforms changed the social position of the commoner estates in various ways. The most important results of the 1765–1766 Riksdag were more general, however, and came about through cooperation among the various estates. A major and successful attack on the Bothnian trade constraint was undertaken under the leadership of Chydenius and others. Their arguments were not accepted in Stockholm but won response in many areas in central and southern Sweden as well as in Norrland and Österbotten. The fear that Finland's trade would go to the east if the trade constraint was not discarded contributed to their success. All four estates therefore agreed in 1765 to give six cities in Norrland and Österbotten the right to sail to foreign ports, although they were not given the right to receive foreign vessels. Other coastal cities on the Gulf of Bothnia could use the six privileged cities' right of staple and thus did not have to go through Stockholm or Åbo; they also were to be permitted a certain freedom of movement on the Baltic. At the same time, internal navigation between cities, including those on Lake Mälar and Lake Hjälmar in central Sweden, was freed of restraints. This decision had great importance for the development of Österbotten, at least, and was a break with the arch-mercantilist and centralist policy of the Hats.

The position the Riksdag took on freedom of the press was equally important. Here the commoner Caps, led by Chydenius, split from their political friends in the House of Nobles, some of whom were opposed to the demand for freedom of the press. In 1766, a historic act on freedom of the press appeared after a decision by the three commoner estates: censorship was abolished, except in theological areas. While the four estates, the royal house, and government offices, as well as religion, were protected from abuse, freedom of the press in principle was unrestricted. The freedom of the press act was incorporated into the constitution, which meant that it could be abolished or changed only after action at two meetings of the estates and with the agreement of all four estates. Elsewhere, only in Great Britain and the Netherlands was there freedom of the press at all in the modern sense, and, in being made part of the constitution, the Swedish freedom of the press act can be considered unique. The result of the act was open discussion in press and pamphlets without precedent in Sweden.

Otherwise the 1765–1766 Riksdag was marked by the Caps' characteristic thriftiness, which, among other things, affected the military, especially the fortresses and the archipelago fleet, and the factories, which were forced to reduce, and in some cases halt, their activities. An act forbade all use of coffee, chocolate, alcoholic punch, and various wines, and orders were issued against luxury in clothes, furniture, porcelain, and coffins. The consumption taxes on tobacco were removed, however, and the right of home distilling—considered to be one of the country folk's inalienable rights—was extended to people below the peasant estate, such as crofters, garrisoned soldiers, members of the cavalry, and ordinary seamen. Strict financial audits of businesses were set in motion; as a result a number of leading Hat businessmen were sentenced to pay damages or serve prison terms for failure to meet legal requirements. Inflation was stopped with far-reaching deflationary measures. The Government Service Report of 1756 was replaced by a new ordinance that was less bureaucratic to some extent and that discarded seniority as a general principle; it also limited the king's right to disregard the appointment recommendations made by the civil authorities. In foreign policy, the alliance with France was liquidated and a new, but rather restricted, pact with Great Britain was made instead. The Caps concentrated more on limiting Sweden's foreign policy and defense activities than on achieving closer cooperation with Great Britain, Russia, Prussia, or Denmark-Norway.

Thus the Caps' takeover of power brought increased freedom, openness, and vigor to political discussion. Socially, a shift in influence took place from government officials and big merchants to country gentry, parish clergymen, retailers, craftsmen, and peasants. This constellation was hardly "democratic" in the twentieth-century sense, but by the standards of the time it had an unprecedented breadth. Various parallels can be discerned in

Great Britain, Ireland, North America, and Geneva, and in countries with absolute rulers, such as Denmark-Norway, France, Prussia, and Austria. There were tendencies throughout the Western
world toward new political and social groupings of the type
Palmer has described; what made Sweden's position interesting
was that the reforms were linked to the old traditions of popular
rule within the bourgeoisie and peasantry.

The change in political leadership also had a regional aspect.
The historical tendency toward centralization (with Stockholm
the focal point) had become all the more obvious over the years
of Hat dominance and corresponded to the general trend of the
Age of Enlightenment; it was broken now in favor of bases in the
countryside, not the least in its most peripheral parts. Nordencrantz from Norrland and Chydenius from Österbotten were representative of this decentralization.

Despite the fact that the Caps were allied with strong, international social, economic, and ideological forces, their regime was
short-lived. The Cap government was forced to call together the
four estates at the end of 1768, and in the following elections, the
Hats won. They retained power until the spring of 1772, when
the Caps relieved them once again, but only temporarily. In
August of the same year, the new king, Gustav III, carried out a
coup d'état that overturned the four estates' domination and laid
the foundation for a new constitution based, in principle, on a
division of powers but with a strong emphasis on personal royal
power. Gustav effectively pointed to the instability that characterized national life during the political party shifts from 1765 to
1772.

The reasons why the Caps ruled so briefly were many, their
financial policy being the most immediate. The deflation they set
in motion in 1765 worked too precipitously and led to catastrophic changes in the currency situation. It had especially disastrous consequences in Bergslagen, an important mining area in
west central Sweden where the Caps had had many supporters.

The change in commercial policy was also very abrupt. The failure of the Caps to win any British or Russian subsidies to replace the French support lost in 1765 was a serious blow to state finances. In general, the Caps' foreign policy was unsuccessful: the interests of Russia, Great Britain, Prussia, and Denmark-Norway were far too divergent to enable them to act together in support of the new regime. The Russians were increasingly occupied with their Polish and Turkish affairs, the British were generally skeptical of Russia as well as Sweden, Frederick II of Prussia was primarily concerned with conditions in northern Germany and was contemptuous of the whole Swedish political system with its four-estate rule, and the Danes were fairly unclear in their party sympathies. The Caps were shaken internally by the conflict between noble and commoner groups. Characteristically, they did not succeed in achieving a real change in the bureaucratic promotion system. The actual relations between noble and commoner were not changed much during the Caps' time, and the House of Nobles remained closed. Another Cap weakness was their lack of respect for the principles of tolerance they themselves preached. They were guilty, for example, of clear encroachments on the rights of certain members of the Riksdag whom they regarded as undesirable and who in several cases were ejected from their respective estates; and they set in motion regular persecutions of politicians who criticized their policies. As was mentioned, Chydenius himself was a victim of this intolerance. Behind some of the Caps' actions can be discerned a vague ideological notion that in principle the majority is always right and the minority must comply silently.

The practical results of the Cap exercise of power for four years were nonetheless considerable. The limitations in the Bothnian trade constraint remained. Even the coercive legislation surviving the reforms of 1765 was slowly abolished. Although under his strengthened powers Gustav III repealed the freedom of the press act of 1766, he did not do away entirely with freedom of the press;

even today the ideas of 1766 are the basis for Swedish legislation in this area. The reforms of the clerical estate were abolished by the Hat regime, but the Caps' changes in the composition of the burgher estate, in the election of local officials, and in the burghers' freedom of assembly remained. The peasants' right to purchase taxable land they had leased was limited by the Hats and stopped by Gustav III, but he renewed it in 1789. Peasant navigation endured. Many of the Caps' antibureaucratic and egalitarian efforts were carried further by Gustav III, especially after he broke with the nobility in 1789.

Gustav III never admitted, however, that he could be regarded in any way as an heir to the Caps. Still less would he admit that his coup d'état weakened or cut off many fruitful tendencies in Swedish social development. The royalistic historiography of the Gustavian age was very critical of the Age of Freedom in general and of the Caps in particular. This negative attitude largely survived the fall of the Gustavian regime in 1809, although the "men of 1809" connected themselves to the Age of Freedom and to the Caps on several points. One exception to the generally anti-Cap stance of the historians of the nineteenth century was Anders Fryxell, who, with his generally moralizing and utilitarian point of view, can be considered a late-born Cap. He was a nephew of the prominent Cap politician Mayor Ekman—a fact perhaps not without influence on his writing. During the twentieth century, Fredrik Lagerroth above all others has stressed the modern aspects of the Caps' policies; at times his accounts of them have had a slightly panegyric tone. In the present essay, Younger Caps have been seen as suffering from fatal weaknesses—shortsightedness, clumsiness, intolerance—but many of their ideas and efforts have given impressive testimony to the innate possibilities of Swedish popular rule. At the same time, the Caps stand as representatives of international currents that would come to have decisive importance for the social life of the modern Western world.

Introduction to Chapter 2

Even if the developments of the latter part of the Age of Freedom suggest that Sweden experienced relatively early the growing pains of a modern political system, there can be little doubt that many influential sectors of Swedish society tired by the early 1770s of the ever more bitter conflicts that arose between the various groups within the Riksdag and that the same period witnessed increasing social as well as political struggles. These problems were aggravated by economic difficulties in 1771–1772. Under the circumstances, the opportunity presented itself for a restoration of a more monarchal, traditional form of government under the guidance of young King Gustav III. Allying himself with the conservative bureaucratic and aristocratic elements of Swedish society, he staged a successful bloodless coup d'état on August 19, 1772. The coup was followed shortly by the installation of a new constitution that, while ambiguous and contradictory, was in general terms a return to the constitutional forms of the Great Power period. The control of the state lay, by and large, in the hands of the king and the aristocracy with the real powers of the Riksdag sharply curtailed. The power of the king increased throughout his reign; and in a second coup against the aristocracy in February 1789, he established a new form of royal absolutism, recorded in the Act of Association and Security.

The reign of Gustav III, 1771–1792, has attracted great historical interest, not least because of the fascinating personality of the king, who so completely captivated his age. However, the long-range historical impact of his reign does not appear very great. True, there were important cultural achievements, many of them stimulated by the king himself. Swedes continued to make impressive contributions to the ongoing scientific experimentation, the enclosure movement was supported more widely, older forms of class differentiation became less marked after the 1789 coup, and Sweden fought an inconclusive war with Russia. But the royal absolutism that he established was a throwback to another age and a no longer extant social order. It is difficult to avoid the conclusion that even if Gustav had survived the shot at the Opera, he would have been plagued by the same kind of problems that his son, Gustav IV, proved so incapable of handling. The social changes and political tensions of the late eighteenth century made it extremely difficult to govern in a traditional and conservative fashion. It was during the reign of Gustav IV, 1792–1809, that momentous changes were to take place in Sweden's political life.

The background against which the drama of the years between 1805 and 1809 unfolds was the upheaval caused by the French Revolution and the threat of Napoleon Bonaparte to the European status quo. Until 1805, Sweden remained aloof from the actual struggles on the continent, but as early as the last years of Gustav III's reign Swedish policy had been hostile to the forces of the French Revolution. This hostility increased dramatically after 1804 as Gustav IV developed a paranoiac hatred of Napoleon. Sweden's entrance into the Napoleonic wars in 1805 was more a product of the curious personality of the king than a rational evaluation of how to protect Sweden's interests. Sweden's position in the wars was complicated enormously by the agreements between Napoleon and Alexander at Tilsit in 1807. If Sweden wished to remain at peace with Russia, in short to retain Finland, it would have to abandon its anti-Napoleonic alliance. This step the king could not take and in a series of Swedish defeats in 1807–1808, Russia gained control over all of Finland and threatened the Swedish heartland proper. These events encouraged a group of Swedish officials to stage a coup d'état on March 13, 1809, to overthrow Gustav IV, who was forced into exile, and to initiate the drawing up of a new constitution.

The writing of the 1809 constitution has traditionally been seen by Swedish historians as an important event in the history of Sweden. This belief has been reinforced by a long-standing historiographical tradition of studying constitutional questions. The following article by Professor Nils Stjernquist of Lund University examines the origins of the new constitution and the circumstances surrounding the writing of it. The reader should keep in mind Professor Carlsson's preceding examination of the last years of the Age of Freedom. The connection between many of the ideas he discusses and those of the men of 1809 is clearly apparent.

2

The Creation of the 1809 Constitution

by Nils Stjernquist

The Swedish constitution of 1809 is the second oldest constitution in the world; only the United States constitution is older. A lively debate about its creation and character has been conducted in scholarly literature. Essentially, three questions have been raised: Who wrote the constitution and what took place at its creation? Was the constitution a radical or conservative product for its time? Last—the question arousing the most heated discussion—to what extent did Swedish or foreign examples serve as models for the constitution; in other words, was it national in character or not?

The view held by the general public in Sweden and taught in the public schools is the following: The constitution was worked out in a very short time within the Riksdag's constitutional committee and the chief credit belongs to the committee's secretary, Hans Järta. In many ways it is a compromise between radical and conservative views. A middle road was sought between the Riks-

NOTE: This essay was originally written in 1959 as a contribution to *Minnesskriften till regeringsformens 150-årsjubileum*. It was published at the same time in *Statsvetenskaplig tidskrift* and six years later in the collection *Kring 1809, om regeringsformens tillkomst* . . . edited by Stefan Björklund. It is published here in revised and shortened form.

dag rule of the Age of Freedom and the absolutism of the Gustavian age. It builds on Montesquieu's philosophy of a division of powers, although the building blocks were gathered to a great extent from Sweden's own experiences.

The actual course of events at the creation of the 1809 constitution will be traced in this essay. Such an analysis primarily provides the background material necessary to answer the first question cited above; but since the three questions are interrelated, it also sheds light upon the other two, although neither of them can be explored fully.

At the beginning of 1809, Sweden was at war with almost all the surrounding world—with Napoleon, with Russia, and with Denmark-Norway. Pomerania was occupied, Russian troops had conquered Finland and were on the verge of advancing in Norrland and against Åland, clearly threatening Stockholm. The country's finances were in miserable condition, the conduct of the war was scarcely better, and the king, Gustav IV, to put it mildly, was not equal to his task. Ferment was growing among the military and civil officials. At the beginning of March, the Western Army, stationed at the Norwegian border under the command of Lieutenant Colonel Georg Adlersparre, turned its back on the enemy and marched toward Stockholm, with the intention of revolting. Adlersparre, however, was anticipated by a group of civil and military officials in the capital led by Adjutant General C. J. Adlercreutz, renowned from the Finnish War, and this group arrested the king on March 13 and took over the government.

After the coup the problems of peace and royal succession were the most burning issues, but the constitutional question soon emerged in the foreground. It was clear to the new ruling group that the Gustavian constitution, i.e., the constitution of 1772 and the 1789 Act of Association and Security, with all that they entailed of absolutism and lack of freedom, should be replaced by a new constitution with a genuine division of powers, and it was equally clear that the new constitution must be written as quickly as possible because of the crisis in foreign affairs: Russia would negotiate for peace only with a legal government. Two possibilities existed. Either the old constitution could be used as a point of departure or an entirely new document could be drafted. The choice depended on the answers to a number of questions. How many and how great were the changes the old constitution could accommodate? How much value was placed on having a stylistically and logically satisfactory constitution? How highly regarded were the ties to old forms, formulas, and formulations? And how much time was available? The objection that historically in constitution writing neither of these alternatives appears in pure form is certainly reasonable; there are always paragraphs that must be completely reworded, and even in an entirely rewritten constitution, formulations from its predecessor easily slip in. But the point of departure is ˚fundamental in selecting the techniques for preparing a constitution, and the alternatives should be kept in mind as we seek to understand the creation of the 1809 constitution.

What materials are available for reconstructing the course of events at the creation of the 1809 constitution? Most importantly, the preliminary drafts of the constitution and memorandums on them exist. Along with the actual preliminary documents we have the debates in the plenums of the four estates and the discussion in the press and pamphlets. Much factual information can also be gathered from contemporary letters and diaries written by the main actors or by persons close to them. The most significant are some diary notations by Hans Gabriel Wachtmeister, son of the lord high chancellor at the time, C. A. Trolle-Wachtmeister. Finally, we have reports and interpretations of the events that were written much later.

Descriptions of the creation of the 1809 constitution have tended to accept uncritically the surviving materials. The actual preliminary work on the constitution is obviously an appropriate basis of analysis, but it should be noted that the source material is incomplete—considerable amounts have been lost or were never

committed to paper. Statements from the main actors are preserved only to a limited extent; there is also the risk that they are
tendentious or simply wrong, and the same may be the case with
the diary notations. Finally, the reports and judgments made long
after 1809 are marked by the particular context in which they
appeared. As a result, a legend has arisen around the creation of
the 1809 constitution that needs close investigation.

As usual after a revolution, the battle for political power and
leadership was confused during the early stages. At least two
groups appeared. One consisted of men from the top echelon of
the central administration, such as Lord High Chancellor Trolle-
Wachtmeister, President of the Exchequer (for our purposes
"Finance Minister") C. E. Lagerheim, and Undersecretaries Carl
Lagerbring and Mathias Rosenblad. The governor in Karlskrona,
an experienced Riksdag tactician, Anders af Håkanson, who was
asked to come to Stockholm immediately after the revolution, also
belonged to this group. These men had generally been critical of
Gustav IV and had often shown passive resistance to him. Now
it was primarily this group that took power.

There were, secondly, a number of persons who had appeared
more openly in opposition. Among them were L. A. Mannerheim
and Hans Järta (both known as opposition men from previous
Riksdags); the principal assistant secretary, Gudmund Göran
Adlerbeth, better known as a poet; and the secretary of the House
of Nobles, A. G. Silverstolpe. They had various ties with those
mentioned above, but also disagreements. Georg Adlersparre,
who took quarters with his troops in Stockholm, occupied a special position. It may be added that Gustav IV's uncle, Duke Karl,
who stepped in as regent, was hardly more than a pawn in the
struggle for power.

As far as can be judged, the men behind the revolution of 1809
did not have any definite constitutional plans. Hans Wachtmeister related in his diary on March 30, 1809, that at the suggestion
of his father (the lord high chancellor) a committee had been

appointed under the elder Wachtmeister's chairmanship to work out recommendations for constitutional changes that would be made in the Riksdag, called to meet on May 1. The secretary of the Court of Appeals, F. Gyllenborg, along with Håkanson, Adlerbeth, Adlersparre, Järta, Justice G. Poppius, and others were members of the committee. It was expected that the committee would seek the views of a number of other people. The committee was clearly to have a broad base with representatives from the government, from the more active opposition, and from the nobility, the clerical estate, and the burgher estate.

In his diary for April 20, however, Wachtmeister said that the proposed constitutional committee existed only on paper. Supposedly, Adlerbeth, Poppius, and Järta did not want to cooperate in working out plans and submitting them to Håkanson, to whom editing of the constitution had been assigned. Adlerbeth had already given several "points" to the lord high chancellor but he asked to have them returned after Håkanson had seen them, and with this he ceased to be involved. Järta and Poppius stopped working because "they thought that it was only a matter of working for someone else who would reap the glory alone." "Such a lack of cooperation was to be expected," Wachtmeister added, ". . . since everyone wants to be the sole legislator on such occasions and not submit his recommendations to any modifications." On the other hand, Gyllenborg contributed a large part of the notations and additions made at this stage. Adlersparre, who no doubt also had a share in the proposal that Håkanson was occupied with, said that he completely approved it "as resting on those principles he in consultation with Håkanson thought should serve as the foundation."

Wachtmeister's diary notations are colored by his sympathies and antipathies. They cannot give us a complete picture of what occurred within the constitutional committee, but it is clear there was opposition and tension between the higher public officials and a number of the others. It may be added that, according to another tradition, reported by Järta, Håkanson "took possession of the duty" of working out the constitutional proposal.

There is a document in the National Archives that is usually called Anders af Håkanson's first draft of the constitution. It is wholly in his handwriting. The document was a working copy and reflected the situation at an early stage. It can thus hardly be doubted that Håkanson took an active part in the committee's work and was the "editor"; it is harder to say where the ideas actually came from. A "Memorandum with Regard to the Question of a New Constitution 1809" that Poppius submitted to the lord high chancellor also is extant. The memorandum contains a number of notations and suggestions proceeding from the 1772 constitution. It is generally agreed that this memorandum was taken into consideration, but it is difficult to determine to what extent it inspired ideas that were incorporated in the proposed constitution. It contains many comments that can be characterized as public property. Suggestions naturally came from other quarters as well, surely also from Håkanson himself.

In his diary on April 15 Wachtmeister reported that Håkanson had given a recommendation to the lord high chancellor to be conveyed to the other members of the constitutional committee. Wachtmeister noted that acceptance with a few changes appeared certain. Five days later, Wachtmeister related that the proposal for the constitution was examined by a committee summoned by the lord high chancellor. Among others, Håkanson, Adlercreutz, and Adlersparre were present. According to the diary, the committee met at least four more times before May 4.

The government's proposal—generally known as "the Håkanson proposal"—for a new constitution was thereby ready. Numerous handwritten copies of the proposal exist. Most of the copies belonged to members of the 1809 Riksdag constitutional committee, the second constitutional committee of that year, of which more later. The government's proposal is more fully worked out than Håkanson's first draft. It has two main parts: the first is entitled "On the King, His Rule and Power and Those Offices That Most Closely Assist Him in This"; the second, "On the Estates of the Kingdom, the Riksdag, and the Riksdag's Duties." The executive power was ascribed to the king; at his side was to be a cabinet, composed of five ministers of state (heads of departments) and seven other ministers (without portfolio). The king would have two votes in the highest court. The proposal did not return to the tradition of strict administrative regulation apparent in earlier constitutions; that is, the freer hand given to the king by the 1789 Association and Security Act was essentially retained. Legislative power was divided between the king and the Riksdag. The power of taxation and control of the state budget were in principle given to the Riksdag. Even the first draft of the Håkanson proposal contains the statement that the Swedish people's ancient right to tax themselves was to be exercised by the estates of the kingdom in public Riksdag. It is here for the first time that we meet this declaration, which came to be a symbol in the battle for parliamentarianism and democracy. The procedures set up for handling financial matters, however, provided an opportunity for the executive to make its views known and to exercise leadership. Budget estimates were to be prepared by the Secret Committee, where the king was chairman; decisions were to be made by the plenums of the estates, with the important exception that if the estates were evenly divided, two against two, the will of the Secret Committee would be determining. Recommendations for the distribution of appropriations were to be made by the Ways and Means Committee, but if the estates could not agree, the decision would be made at a joint meeting of all the estates in the throne room in the presence of the king. Finally, the draft constitution stated that if the budget was not drawn up and appropriations agreed upon at the end of the Riksdag, the king could "attend to this with the cabinet" until the next Riksdag.

These were the major points of the government's recommendation for a new constitution. In procedure and in content, as compared with earlier constitutional provisions, it was mostly a "new product."

Apparently the constitutional committee intended that the Riksdag would first recognize Duke Karl as king by virtue of his hereditary right and, thereafter, would take a position on the constitutional recommendation; in doing so the Riksdag would have only the right either to accept or to reject the recommendation as a whole. If the Riksdag rejected it, the constitutional provisions valid during Gustav IV's reign (the 1772 constitution and 1789 Association and Security Act) would continue in force; that is, absolute rule would remain. It was a risky procedure, but the committee took what precautions it could. For example, Håkanson was appointed secretary of the peasant estate (despite the fact that the peasant estate had been guaranteed that this position would be occupied by a commoner). This position would presumably make it possible for him to direct the estate's decision.

The committee had to publicize the constitutional recommendation, muster public opinion, and, especially, make sure members of the Riksdag were positively disposed to the recommendation's content. According to Wachtmeister, at the committee's last meeting on May 4, even the knight marshal and the speakers of the three commoner estates had been present; each had brought two additional representatives of his estate. Before the meeting, the diary stated, the lord high chancellor passed out "to the wise men of the estates" as many copies of the government's constitutional recommendations as there had been time to make, so that anyone who wished could present comments, which then were studied by the duke and the constitutional committee. It may be assumed, however, that reports on the recommendation's contents had leaked out far earlier and had been rather generally distributed.

However, the discussion in the estates did not follow the line the constitutional committee had hoped. There was widespread criticism against the procedure the government intended to use as well as against the content of the recommendation. Against the government's plan of "king first—constitution later" the counter-demand "constitution first—king later" was voiced, and the duke's hereditary right to the throne was challenged. According to the May 21 entry in Wachtmeister's diary, Järta was actively support-ing this latter position. Wachtmeister noted in another context on May 13 that disturbing ideas were festering; it was being said that all fundamental laws had been abolished and that revolution prevailed.

Attempts were made privately to persuade the duke to accept a compromise. A discussion took place at the castle on May 7. In attendance were Lord High Chancellor Trolle-Wachtmeister, Court Chancellor Lagerbjelke, all the speakers as well as other representatives of the four estates (including some representatives of the House of Nobles who were in opposition to the government proposal and Håkanson in his capacity as secretary of the peasant estate). A protocol from this deliberation exists.

According to the protocol, Lagerbjelke began by commenting on the "hopeless" foreign-policy situation and sharply underlined the necessity of establishing a legal government so peace negotia-tions with Russia could begin. In this connection, Lagerbjelke said that the duke was concerned about rumors in circulation that a new constitutional recommendation had been presented unex-pectedly to the estates of the kingdom in hopes that their approval would follow without deliberation. Lagerbjelke denied this. Immediately thereafter the duke entered and confirmed the court chancellor's words. The statements he then made on the issues of succession to the throne and the constitution were some-what vague, but denote a more conciliatory attitude than he had earlier expressed. The duke proposed that he first be acknowl-edged king by action of the Riksdag so that his hereditary right to the throne would be established. He would then leave it to the estates to reach agreement on a new constitution although there should be prior agreement by king and estates on certain basic principles. Finally, the constitution worked out by the estates would be delivered to him for his examination and sanction.

The negotiations continued during the evening of May 7. A meeting was then held at the knight marshal's residence, and messages went between there and the castle, with, according to the protocol, agreement finally reached along the lines of the duke's proposal. But, because the situation was so tense, it is questionable whether the protocol accurately represented the agreement as understood by all parties.

In any case the new proposal failed to win general support. The nobles and the burghers did not want the duke to become king before the constitution was accepted or to have the right to sanction it. After the protocol was read at the nobles' meeting on May 8, the knight marshal asked if the estate wanted to concur in the procedure outlined. Not a single voice was heard in favor. Instead, Baron Jacob Cederström, followed by Baron Knut Kurck, moved adoption of the principle "constitution first—king later," to which many agreed. A tactless remark by the knight marshal ignited a hot debate and the meeting disintegrated in confusion. The burghers likewise refused to endorse the protocol. As a contemporary observer wrote, "Now the devil is loose."

A man who was present at the castle on May 8 wrote in a letter to his wife, "The duke looks very old and frail." The duke had earlier insisted he had already made as many concessions as he could. Now, in the face of the outcome in the House of Nobles and in the burgher estate, he is said to have been inclined to retreat still further. In any case on the evening of May 8, the duke made a calming statement through the knight marshal that he would yield to the will of the estates. At a meeting in the throne room on May 10, when Gustav IV was "officially" deposed, the duke exhorted the estates to "consult and agree among themselves" on a new constitution and to "delimit the method of deliberation" that soonest and most appropriately would lead to the intended goal. He promised to remain as regent until the estates had delivered the results of their work to him. He would then give a definite decision on whether he felt able to continue to cooperate. Thus, the government's plan of "king first—constitution later" had been upset. The Riksdag would first establish a constitution and then elect a king (presumably, the duke).

Criticism from the estates had been directed not only at the government's proposed method of procedure, but also at the content of its recommendation for a new constitution. The provisions on taxation and budget estimates especially came under fire. In a letter of May 4, Colonel Baltzar von Platen, best remembered as the builder of the Göta Canal, pointed out that the control of money was not sufficiently under the supervision of the Riksdag. The same desire to guard the Riksdag's power of finances was also supported in some of the political pamphlets that appeared at this time. A well-known example is A. G. Silverstolpe's publication *What Does the General Opinion Seem to Want in a Now Possible Improvement of the Swedish Constitution?* Silverstolpe urged that "the estates, alone the country's levier of taxes," should "have the right to determine all the purposes of taxation in times of peace and appropriate sums for each special need, and only at the occurrence of war grant in lump sum what they [deemed] necessary for its execution." The Riksdag should always have the power to oversee any expenditures arranged solely by the king. It may be added that contemporaries thought that Järta was behind the Silverstolpe brochure.

The debate took its special character from the prevailing personal antagonisms. The duke maintained in a letter to his confidant Lars von Engeström, later minister of foreign affairs, that he could find no reason for criticism of the government recommendation other "than regrettably the usual jealousy that authors feel between themselves." A number, among them Wachtmeister (diary entry of May 5), thought the recommendation contained two or three carelessly phrased paragraphs that could be used by opponents to incite the people. The old governing group came in for severe criticism along with its recommendations for a new constitution. The attacks were concentrated on Håkanson, who, to be sure, was justly regarded as the strongest of the "old ones." The word spread among the opposition that the government proposal was a disguised attempt to return to absolutism. In his diary on April 22, Wachtmeister described the men who formulated and supported the government recommendation as "the monarchy's old knights, who well see themselves forced to hail the spirit of the times in the recommended constitution in order to make the work appealing and get the revolution approved in the Riksdag, but who also in their project prepared numerous hiding places in which the administration could lie in ambush."

The criticisms overwhelmed the old ruling group and it lost its grip on the government. Trolle-Wachtmeister, Lagerbring, and Lagerheim withdrew from the arena and Håkanson was forced in the middle of May to leave his post as secretary of the peasant estate and return home to Karlskrona. Adlersparre remained, but his prestige and influence had greatly declined. Others of the "old ones" who stayed had to accommodate themselves to new leaders, who later came to be called "the men of 1809." Primary among them were L. A. Mannerheim, Hans Järta, A. G. Silverstolpe, Baltzar von Platen, Gudmund Göran Adlerbeth, and Järta's confidants Adolf Göran Mörner and J. G. Gahn. As the men of 1809 gradually became more powerful, they drew support from several new groups on the left—radicals and republicans and, as Wachtmeister called them, all other "undaunted democratizing screamers." Compromise and moderation were watchwords of the new leading group, although they were faced with insistent demands from the groups on the left.

On May 12 and 13 the Riksdag elected its own constitutional committee. Baron Mannerheim, Baron Baltzar von Platen, Adlerbeth, Silverstolpe, Anders Fredrik Skjöldebrand, and Office of

Mines Counselor Salomon von Stockenström were chosen to represent the nobles; Bishop Carl von Rosenstein of Linköping, Bishop C. G. Nordin of Härnösand, and Uppsala Professor (later Bishop of Västerås) Sven Caspersson Wijkman, the clerical estate; Deputy Judge J. G. Gahn, Justice I. Blom, and the industrial estate squire Daniel Eberstein, the burgher estate; and Mats Persson from Utsund in Dalarna, Anders Jansson Hyckert from Ytterboda in Uppland, and Jon Jonsson from Skörje in Blekinge, the peasant estate. The fact that Adlersparre was passed over was regarded as an astounding rebuff. Mannerheim was chairman of the committee by right of rank and age. Järta was appointed secretary. J. D. Valerius, secretary to the chief justice, was made vice-secretary.

The election was generally regarded as a triumph for the men of 1809, because they placed a number of their leaders on the committee, especially from among the nobles. Of the members from the clerical estate, Rosenstein and Wijkman were counted as favorably disposed to the men of 1809. Nordin, however, belonged in the camp of the opposition. He had been an aide and adviser to Gustav III and now aligned himself with Håkanson. Of the members on the committee from the burgher estate, Gahn and probably Blom and Eberstein were allied with Järta.

It was generally expected that the constitutional committee would limit itself to reviewing the government's recommendation and revising it to take account of the criticisms that had been made. Two documents were important in the committee's deliberations: a statement on the constitutional question by Mannerheim which drew on provisions of the 1772 constitution, and a memorandum by Järta putting forth questions the committee should take a position on. Another useful paper was "Reflections in View of the Present Political Situation," which A. G. Mörner wrote in April 1809. As additional working material, the committee had many recommendations from the plenums of the estates and statements from other quarters, such as a document by Principal Assistant Secretary Eric Bergstedt criticizing the government's constitutional recommendation.

The constitutional committee began immediately. The first meeting apparently took place on May 14. Its work was carried on intensively, according to statements made in the estates' plenums. Järta, in his report on the creation of the constitution written twenty-three years later, told of the committee's deliberating daily for ten to twelve hours. And he added, "The secretary had only the remaining part of the day to use for editing the agreed paragraphs, which usually were verified the following day."

Both contemporaries and posterity have taken special notice of Järta's role in the committee. There survives not only the working memorandum already mentioned, but a preliminary draft of the constitution written in his hand. Some days after the constitution was accepted on June 6, 1809, Mannerheim is supposed to have said privately that "we were thirty on the constitutional committee—the members numbered fifteen, but Hans Järta as secretary was equivalent to another fifteen." While his diligence has not been doubted, the nature and extent of Järta's influence have been debated in more recent times. He has often been cited as the author of the constitution; sometimes, with a certain disdain, he has been referred to as merely the committee's secretary. In addition to Järta there were others on the committee who held the same views he did. It would be of interest to know what roles were played in the committee's work by those whose activities were less well known to later generations—men like Nordin, Rosenstein, Wijkman, Blom, and Eberstein. None of them were unimportant.

Whoever was primarily responsible, work within the committee progressed rapidly. In a letter written sometime between May 15 and 20 Platen reported the outlines of the recommendation to be made. Members of the committee were so essentially in agreement that there was no need to resort to voting on issues: in his diary on May 21, Wachtmeister noted that the constitutional committee

was almost finished and that still no vote had occurred. Bishop
Nordin reported in a letter on May 22 that the committee "with
good unity" had gone through "all of the components of the con-
stitution" and the recommendation was "under production."
Nordin added, "No vote has been taken among us, no sour word.
Mannerheim chaired politely and worthily."

Private discussions on the contents of the recommendation now
began in the estates. Engeström and Lagerbjelke, and possibly
Adlersparre, were informed of the terms of recommendation. The
duke also read it and reportedly made no objections.

After the Pentecost holiday on May 21 and 22, the committee
continued to deliberate questions of detail and even some suggestions for extensive reforms. Differences of opinion at this time
became stronger and votes were necessary. Points of conflict can
be clearly seen in the memorandum finally presented to the
estates on June 2 that embodied not only the committee's recommendation for a new constitution but reservations as well. In
handling these points of conflict, the committee leadership sought
to avoid making an issue of proposals that would arouse strongly
differing opinions within the estates and thereby jeopardize or
delay adoption of a constitution. This tactic was obvious with
regard to the sensitive matter of changes in the system of representation in the Riksdag. The memorandum merely stated that
it was basically fair that commoner landowners and those engaged
in running industrial estates should be represented, but because
the committee had not had time to investigate changes in representation—it could not be done hurriedly—no specific suggestions
were made.

Hedging was also apparent in the treatment of two special
proposals that had spokesmen within the committee. One—supported by Platen—concerned the initiation of general national
conscription; the other—advocated by Silverstolpe—dealt with the
introduction of a permanent Drafts Legislation and Economic
Administration Committee in the Riksdag. Neither won sufficient

response to be made part of the recommendation for a constitution, but both proposals were mentioned in the memorandum.

With one exception, the reservations appended to the committee's recommendation were not of a nature to jeopardize the recommendation's acceptance. The exception concerned privileges, which were characteristic of the old society of estates. The most important were economic, for example, freedom from taxes. A slow demise of estate privileges had begun before 1809, but the peasants still felt discriminated against. Within the constitutional committee, the representatives for the three higher estates agreed that the recommendation for the constitution should guarantee that the privileges then existing could not be amended or abolished without the consent of all the estates. The peasants' representatives on the committee demanded that all landholders should be equally taxed and share in the burden of defense, and that privileges, therefore, should not be named and guaranteed in the constitution.

The memorandum delivered to the estates on June 2 reputedly was constructed in one night by Järta. Written with power and elegance, the memorandum belongs to the classic documents in Swedish history. It includes the well-known, though somewhat ambiguous, statement that the committee "tried to form an executive power, active within established limits, with unity in decisions and full power in the means of executing them; a legislative power, wisely slow in action but firm and strong in opposition [to the executive]; a judicial power, independent under the laws but not autocratic over them." The memorandum further said that the committee had "tried to direct these powers to a mutual guarding, to mutual restraint, without blending them together, without giving the restraining power any of the restrained power's capacity for action." The state constitution should "rest on these primary principles of mutual balance of the powers of state." The memorandum also stated that the committee did not recommend "large changes in the old basic forms of our state constitution." It "believed that such forms [should] not lightly be replaced, least of all in the first hours of a rewon freedom, during a time of unavoidable division in ways of thinking." As an introduction, the memorandum emphasized that, because of "the perils of the fatherland," the committee had worked rapidly and that imperfections would surely "be discovered in [its] so hurriedly completed task." It therefore recommended that new methods of making changes in the constitution should be developed—an important innovation on Sweden's part.

The committee's recommendation for a new constitution has many similarities to the government's proposal, but it differs on a few decisive points. One is the organization of the executive. The committee declined the government recommendation of departmental reform, supporting instead the existing division of His Royal Majesty's Council into four offices, each with a secretary of state acting as departmental head and reporter in the council. The cabinet would consist of the minister of justice, the foreign minister, the court chancellor, and six ministers with purely advisory functions. Another decisive point where the committee recommendation differs from the government's is the locus of the financial power—certainly this was understandable considering the vehement criticism directed at this portion of the government's proposal. Budget estimates and other governmental fiscal measures would be prepared by the Riksdag's Appropriations Committee, rather than, as the government had recommended, by the Secret Committee with the king as chairman. If the estates divided evenly on a financial issue, the Secret Committee's will would not automatically prevail, but the decision would be made by the vote of an augmented Appropriations Committee. The augmented committee would also settle disputes concerning the distribution of allocations (the government recommendation had entrusted decisions of this type to a joint meeting of the estates in the throne room in the presence of the king). In the government recommendation the king had been given the power to prepare budget estimates and determine allocations if the estates had not decided on these matters at the end of any given Riksdag. The committee replaced this proposal with a provision that old budget estimates would stay in effect in the event that decisions were not reached by the Riksdag. In the area of governmental power, the committee produced very detailed provisions, which included such innovations as establishment of the office of ombudsman for the judiciary and the civil administration. In addition, the constitutional committee had made in the government's recommendation a number of changes in details and specifications, these often characterized by a desire to further restrict the executive, and it had elaborated on sentences and phrases in many places. Still, much of the intent of the government's draft had been retained in the newer draft.

With regard to style, it has often been said that the constitutional committee's (Järta's) product is decidedly superior to the government's (Håkanson's). Such judgments may be based on Järta's widely acknowledged ability to write elegantly; but if by "superior style" one means legal writing that is easy to interpret and apply, then this evaluation is open to question. The constitutional committee produced paragraphs that later created much difficulty for those with the task of interpreting and applying them. This is the case, for example, with regard to rules concerning the real estate of the crown, which are so complicated and poorly thought-out that they cannot be followed in practice; similarly, another provision outlines such complex restrictions on debate in the Riksdag that many a speaker has rebelled.

Whatever Järta's (or the second constitutional committee's) contributions to the new constitution, it is Håkanson who deserves first place in authorship. His was the "new product" from the point of view of innovative legal writing; the constitutional committee's, through Järta, was a revision.

Private discussions on the committee recommendation began before the memorandum was presented. Information concerning the provisions of the recommendation leaked out gradually, and by the end of May the gist of the document was well known. Members of the constitutional committee cooperated in providing information. Criticism was not slow in coming. In his diary on May 21, Wachtmeister noted that the recommendation "is according to the thought of all wise people splendid, but that does not prevent its rejection without mercy by the House of Nobles' undaunted democratizing screamers, although they have not yet read anything of it but only know of it through private conversation. They and their fellows go so far as to suppose that the members of the committee were partly bought, partly influenced, by the court party. It was an unexpected accusation for men who recently were considered chiefs of the democratic party and in particular this reproach is a new one for Hans Järta." In the days to follow, Wachtmeister related in his diary how "the malicious and exalted" used all their powers to put each paragraph of the recommendation in an unflattering light. Now, in turn, the committee recommendation was called disguised absolutism. The men of 1809 found themselves criticized in precisely the same terms they had used against the government's proposal.

The initial response among members of the House of Nobles boded ill for the recommendation. However, various circumstances arose that stemmed the tide of opposition and brought the nobles to favor the immediate adoption of the constitution as drafted. News was widely circulated about recent successes of the Russian troops. The peasants' demands for the equalization of privileges and for removal of the guarantee of privilege from the constitution aroused fear of what might result if the recommendation were rejected and a new document drawn up. And it was rumored that Adlersparre might intervene with force of arms if the constitutional committee's recommendation was not accepted. The formal discussion by the nobles began on Saturday, June 3, and continued through Monday, the 5th. The opposition was subdued. The high point of the debate was Adlerbeth's elucidation of the division of powers in the recommended constitution that is clearer and more detailed than the more famous description in the constitutional committee's memorandum. "According to the bases on which the theory of the state rests and the testimony of history," Adlerbeth said, "it seems to be pretty well decided that security is best preserved when the legislative power belongs to the nation and its regent jointly, when the power of the execution of the law [is given] to certain corps which should not suffer imposition by either the nation and its representatives or by the government, when the executive power is held undivided by the regent and the power of taxation is held undivided by the people." But "these powers should be so linked together, and exercised so carefully, that none of them can make encroachments on the others, disturb the balance, and drag too much power to the one side or the other; for then, little by little, either the monarchy degenerates to despotism or the people's freedom to lawless mobocracy, license, and anarchy. To find such a balance is the sure but not easily realizable means of giving the state constitution durability."

The nobles accepted the constitutional committee's recommendation by acclamation; they decided at the same time that the observations made in the estates' plenums should be remitted to the constitutional committee for comment and then be acted upon at the next Riksdag. The clerical estate approved the recommendation in the same way. The burgher estate suggested some changes in detail but was not opposed to the adoption of the recommendation if the other estates did not concur with its views.

The outcome in the peasant estate was different. As already indicated, the peasants' representatives on the constitutional committee had strongly objected to the naming and guaranteeing of privileges in the constitution and maintained that all land should share equally in taxation and defense burdens. The peasant estate was unyielding on this point. In order to satisfy the demands of the peasants, the nobles, mostly on Mannerheim's suggestion, had decided on June 2 to abnegate their sole property right to the tax-exempt manors. The nobles further agreed to pay poll tax and allocations for all types of tax-exempt land until the next Riksdag on the condition that the other estates made the same concession with regard to tax-privileged lands belonging to them. The clerical and burgher estates consented immediately. Thus, the nobles had given up their last privileges concerning the right to hold tax-exempt land; anyone could now become the owner of any type of tax-exempt land.

To put further pressure on the peasants, the speaker and four deputies for each estate were called to a meeting in the presence of the duke on the evening of June 3. The topic was once again the threatening foreign situation that necessitated immediate adoption of the constitution and hence resolution of the question of privileges. According to contemporary testimony, the meeting degenerated into open dispute between the peasants and the others.

The majority of the peasant estate was not satisfied with the concessions made by the other estates or impressed by the argument that considerations of foreign policy should take precedence over the peasants' domestic concerns. The most outspoken members of the peasant estate demanded "tax equalization first—constitution later." However, the peasant estate's final decision on June 5 was not so radical: It "accepted and approved the constitutional committee's recommendation for the kingdom's constitution with some few annotations." Since it was "pressed by difficult burdens and made destitute by the war," needing "help and relief," the estate "felt that the last paragraph of the proposal concerning the establishment of privileges should be completely withdrawn." The privileges should be examined during the Riksdag session and "finally be applied according to circumstances." The peasant estate decided unanimously on the next day that it would not sign the constitution "until the requested adjustments in the privileges of the other estates" had been "announced."

All four estates, however, united in the decision to offer Duke Karl the crown. On the evening of June 5, they gathered at the House of Nobles and marched with the knight marshal to the castle, where the duke received them in the gallery. The knight marshal reported the estates' conclusion in a protocol: "His Royal Highness was pleased to express his gratitude and favor to the estates of the kingdom in the most gracious words and with the most extreme emotion." At a meeting of the duke and the four estates in the throne room the next morning, the knight marshal and the speakers related the decisions on the constitutional recommendation of the respective estates, after which the duke agreed to govern the kingdom according to the constitution established by the estates and to ascend the throne under the name Karl XIII.

The constitution is dated on the same day, June 6. In the preamble to it the new king officially accepted the document and stated that the mutual rights and duties of the king and the citizens "had been so clearly delimited that they, along with preservation of the royal power's sanctity and capacity for action, [guarded] the Swedish people's constitutional freedom." In their part of the preamble, the estates proclaimed that, through the changes in the balance of power, they, in their capacity as "the Swedish people's delegates, entered into the right to improve the fatherland's situation in the future through the establishment of a changed state constitution." They had therefore abolished the constitution of 1772, the Association and Security Act of 1789, and other constitutional provisions still in force, and, as the kingdom's primary governing body, enacted a new constitution. The idea of popular sovereignty could not have clearer expression.

Also on June 6 a number of higher positions were filled, including appointments to cabinet offices created by the constitution. Adlerbeth and Platen, among others, entered the cabinet; Järta became secretary of state for trade and finance. At the same time, Blom and Poppius became supreme court justices. Somewhat later during the Riksdag session Mannerheim was elected ombudsman for the judiciary and the civil adminstration. These appointments officially acknowledged the position of power that the men of 1809 had acquired.

Although the original constitutional document is dated June 6, it was not signed by all parties until several days later. Undoubtedly the knight marshal, the archbishop, and the speaker of the burgher estate signed it immediately. But the signature of the speaker of the peasant estate was not forthcoming at once, since the peasant members had forbidden him to sign it before the privileges question had been satisfactorily settled. Numerous ways to break the deadlock were discussed. Should the new constitution be considered approved with support of only three estates? This recourse would be identical to the still highly criticized action that had forced through the Association and Security Act in 1789. Or should it be assumed that the "acceptance" by the peasant estate was sufficient in spite of the fact that it refused to let its speaker sign the constitution? In the end, the situation was handled rather crudely instead of subtly. During the peasant estate's deliberations on the morning of June 27, the temporary court chancellor, Gustaf af Wetterstedt, suddenly appeared and read a royal letter requesting the estate "to present itself immediately at the royal palace in the large gallery." After the peasants had assembled at the stated place, the new king entered, followed by the council of state, and made a speech harshly chastising them. He concluded by saying that he would leave the room so the peasants could express themselves "freely and without constraint" and then vote with secret ballots.

However, according to the protocol of the meeting, there was no discussion or secret voting, and, according to other contemporary reports, Karl XIII remained in the gallery. After the king stopped speaking, Wetterstedt read the following proposition: "Is the peasant estate ready to sign the constitution if His Royal Highness now promises the peasant estate to use his high offices with all the action and power that laws and mutual fairness allow in the questions raised of equalization of privileges and duties, in which the other estates have already declared themselves willing to meet the peasant estate, and moreover assures the peasant estate of full and open right to raise anew and have decided at the next Riksdag all questions concerning the same subject that shall not have been finally and completely decided at the present national meeting?" The protocol continued: "The peasant estate answered this proposition with a unanimous yes, and a general statement that no vote was required. This voluntary consent was combined with visible emotion and the liveliest expression of the estate's faith in and affection for His Majesty. During this unforgettable and solemn time for the king's heart, the speaker Lars Olsson came forward, exhorted thereto by the peasant estate's unanimous voice, and signed the constitution of June 6, 1809, on behalf of the estate and in its presence." According to a report in a contemporary letter, Mats Persson then made "an unexpectedly beautiful" speech to the king requesting him to mediate between the peasants and the other estates.

Obviously, the verbose protocol leaves a false impression of the real situation. The illegality of the pressure exerted by the king on the peasant estate becomes obvious when seen in connection with paragraph 55 of the constitution, which prohibits the estates from deciding on any subject "in the presence of the king."

At the end of November 1809 the constitutional committee presented a report on the estates' reservations to the constitution, but resolution of the problems was not completed until 1815. As a complement to the constitution, three further fundamental laws were accepted at the 1809–1810 Riksdag: the succession act of December 18, 1809; the Riksdag act of February 10, 1810; and the freedom of the press act of March 9, 1810.

The political careers of the men of 1809 were short and hardly brilliant. After they came to power their changed perspective led them to abandon any radical views they had held. They lacked sufficient administrative experience to preside over government affairs and had to seek advice from the old officials, who thus found themselves once again in a position of some power; toward the end of the constitutional Riksdag even Håkanson was invited to return to Stockholm, although he declined. During the Riksdag of 1809–1810, it was the legislative branch that dominated the government. The constitutional Riksdag took many fresh initiatives and discussed great reform plans, such as a new representation system and a radical revision of the allocations system. Its dominance was short-lived.

In 1810 Prince Bernadotte of Pontecorvo became Karl XIII's heir to the throne (taking the name Karl Johan) and thereafter the king largely left matters of state in his hands. Karl Johan was accustomed to exercising command on the battlefields of Europe and thought lieutenants should be nothing but lieutenants. An independent and vigorous Riksdag did not fit into the administrative system that Karl Johan little by little introduced. When the estates next gathered in 1812, the Riksdag was effectively controlled by Karl Johan and those who supported him. Lagerbring, who was knight marshal, Håkanson, and Lagerheim, three of those who in May 1809 had been more or less excluded from authority by the men of 1809, served to a considerable extent as directors of the Riksdag. The men of 1809 were dismayed at the turn of events. Instead of working to improve the recently accepted reforms, the Riksdag leaders evinced a desire to reconstruct completely the machinery of government. The constitution itself came under renewed attack.

Contemporaries of the 1809 constitution did not regard it highly although to some extent they excused its faults—as did the constitutional committee—because of the international situation, which allowed the framers little time for reflection. Gradually, even the men of 1809 became highly critical. The foundations of the constitution were surely right, Silverstolpe maintained in a letter to Karl Johan in 1811. "But," he added, "undoubtedly it suffers in details from real and obvious imperfections." Although Wachtmeister had described the proposed constitution at first as "splendid according to every wise man's mind," at a later time—it is uncertain just when—he crossed out this judgment in his diary and noted in the margin, "mainly modeled on the rejected proposal by the [first] constitutional committee and, according to all moderates, as good as a fast and patch work can be." Karl Johan planned to introduce at the 1812 Riksdag a new constitution, better suited to serve his desires and interests, and recommendations for it were worked out. But the plan was abandoned and the constitution of 1809 remained in force.

After the Napoleonic era, conservative elements reasserted themselves in Europe. Conservatives looked sympathetically on all that was old. The 1809 constitution came to belong with the "old" things that should be preserved. From the point of view of the country's rulers, it became tolerable, even valuable, in that interpretation and application of it could be brought into harmony with the spirit of the time. In the debates over the distribution of power that followed until the emergence of the modern parliamentary system in Sweden, the 1809 constitution remained an important bulwark for proponents of the status quo.

The defense of the constitution received its special stamp from Järta, who in the 1820s and 1830s strongly opposed those who asserted more broad-minded interpretations of the constitution than did those in power at the time or who urged constitutional changes. On various occasions including his 1832 report on the creation of the constitution Järta gave his interpretations of the events in 1809—invariably with a conservative cast; in these accounts he never failed to mention his own accomplishments. His statements were long considered gospel. When the Håkanson draft was rediscovered, in the 1870s, it caused shock waves among political historians and gave rise to much discussion on the circumstances of the constitution's creation in general and Järta's role in particular. The relatively radical milieu in which the 1809 constitution was written was finally placed in balance against the conservative interpretation of Järta.

In conclusion, an approach to answering the three questions posed at the outset might be this: The constitution was written in a short time under pressing circumstances, both within and outside the committee. Järta's role as an active and influential secretary cannot be doubted, but it is difficult to weigh that role in the committee work against the contribution of the other members. Above all, it is important to acknowledge that Anders af Håkanson, the principal person behind the government's first proposal for a new constitution, played a larger role than Järta.

Insofar as the new constitution was a revolutionary reaction against Gustavian absolutism it can be said to be of radical origin. On the other hand, it is clearly marked by compromises, like most other political settlements.

It is hardly possible to determine whether the constitution is primarily a product of native or foreign influences. At this point in Swedish history the national and the general European debates on the best form of government were so interwoven that it is hard to clarify what originated from which country. The men of 1809 were surely acquainted with constitutional conditions in other countries, but it is questionable if they had time to devote themselves to reasoned theoretical discussions and speculations under the circumstances in which they worked.

Introduction to Chapter 3

How does a nation that has once been an important force in international affairs respond to a decline in its influence and to the fact that it has become a small European state? This question is a fascinating one for European history because nearly all European states have experienced at one time or another a period in their history when they could rightfully claim status as a Great Power, only to lose this position and be forced to adjust to their own international insignificance. Certainly behind today's agonies of building a united Europe lie the frustrated hopes of many a German, Frenchman, Englishman, or other national who wished to see his country remain important in world affairs. The transition from Great Power to lesser status is usually difficult and replete with many unfortunate mistakes. It has often been asked how Sweden adjusted to the loss of its Great Power status after 1720. No simple answer can be given.

Internationally Sweden has never retreated to the position of a small state. (The problem of defining "small state" is in itself almost impossible, but I mean in this context a state that conceives of itself as nearly negligible in world affairs and therefore develops a foreign policy that is very limited in aims and activity.) Throughout the eighteenth and nineteenth centuries, Sweden continued to exhibit interest in becoming once more a European power, particularly in northern Europe. Within this context the union between Sweden and Norway, which is analyzed from its origin to its collapse in Jörgen Weibull's essay that follows, takes on special interest. Even after the peaceful, although trying, end of the union, Sweden maintained an active foreign policy. Prime Minister Hjalmar Hammarskjöld dreamed of being a mediator who would end World War I or at least of being the spokesman for the nonbelligerents in Europe. Sweden made important contributions to the League of Nations as it has to the United Nations. These activities have been justified in terms of both the value of collective security and the special role of Sweden in world affairs. Under the leadership of Prime Minister Olaf Palme, the Swedish government in the recent period expressed the belief that it is Sweden's role to speak out clearly and without prejudice on nearly all matters of importance in international affairs. This self-appointed position as the world's conscience may simply have its roots in the increased interest and justifiable concern Swedes have shown for the activities of the Great Powers since World War II. On the other hand, it may also fill a psychological need Swedes have historically had to be something other than a small state.

3

The Union with Norway

by Jörgen Weibull

Nationalism during the nineteenth century led to the unification of Italy and the creation of the German Empire. A number of smaller states that had previously been either disunited or loosely connected but that had the same language and strong cultural ties were collected into national units. At the same time the dissolution of confederated states built on combinations of peoples of various nationalities was also taking place, as in the Balkans, where the old Ottoman Empire fell apart and was replaced by a number of independent states, and in the Austro-Hungarian Dual Monarchy, which eventually disappeared at the end of World War I. In Scandinavia both the aspiration for confederation and tendencies toward dissolution were asserted in the nineteenth century.

At first glance, the union between Norway and Sweden, which occurred in 1814, should have had every possibility of leading to a complete fusion of the two countries. The differences in language were small; between central Swedish dialects and the language spoken in Norway at this time there was less difference in many cases than between, for example, the dialects of Dalarna and Skåne. Geographically the two countries also appeared to belong together. Economically there were no barriers to integration, and at many points the economic life of each country complemented the other. For example, southern and western Sweden's surplus of grain and food should have easily found a market in Norway, while the Norwegian merchant fleet could handle the shipping that Sweden could not manage. In other areas cooperation should have promoted development, through a more effective use of common resources or simply through the larger market created by the union for the growing industry in both Sweden and Norway.

Despite this apparent harmony of interests, the Swedish-Norwegian union never led to any real unity, politically, culturally, or economically. The dissolution of the union in 1905 was not unexpected, even if the brusque procedures of the Norwegians came as a surprise to many in Sweden. Repeated, continuously sharper and sharper controversies characterized the relationship between the two countries during the union, on several occasions leading to open crises. Behind all the controversies there was the same fundamental question: What should Norway's position within the union be? The disputes always arose from Sweden's attempt to assert her supremacy within the union and Norway's demand for a position equal to Sweden's. The documents produced at the time of the union's origin in 1814 became the focal points for intensive analysis and the bases upon which debate over Norway's position in the union raged. Of particular importance were the Treaty of Kiel, by which Denmark's king ceded Norway to the king of Sweden; the Convention of Moss, in which Norway's newly elected king pledged to return the executive power entrusted to him and to leave Norway, while the king of Sweden promised to accept the new Norwegian constitution; and, finally, the changes in the new Norwegian constitution necessitated by the union. Even though all of these important documents bearing on the union were preserved in the original, it was impossible over the years of the union for Swedish and Norwegian leaders or scholars to reach broad agreement on their interpretation. On the contrary, the same acts—the Treaty of Kiel, the Convention of Moss, and Norway's constitution of November 4, 1814—were cited as evidence both for Sweden's supremacy and for Norway's equal status within the union. Intensive analysis and logical deduction in both countries led to irreconcilable conclusions. How was this possible?

The explanation must be sought on a political level. In large measure the analyses and deductions were contributions to the political debate on the union, despite the avowed commitment of their authors to "scientific" methods. All were concerned with the current legal problems of the union. The interpretations were therefore predetermined. Interest during the life of the union was concentrated on legal-constitutional questions concerning the validity and interpretation of the acts fundamental to the union. Very recently, on the other hand, the purely historical aspects of the union—the background of the events at its origin and the circumstances surrounding the writing of the basic documents—have been the primary objects of more penetrating analysis. Only after the acts themselves and various contemporary positions have been interpreted against the background of the political situation in which they appeared can the developments in the history of the union be discussed and clarified.

After the defeat by Russia, the loss of Finland, and the coup d'état in Sweden in 1809, conflicting views on the direction Sweden's foreign policy should take divided the nation's leaders into two camps. In one group were certain government officials and military men who had engineered the coup d'état and who wished and expected the inner revolution to be followed by a change of Sweden's foreign policy: Sweden should seek support for her policies from France in order to retrieve Finland. Among the representatives of this policy were Foreign Minister Lars von Engeström and Chancellor of the Realm Gustaf af Wetterstedt.

The other group wanted to direct Sweden's attention to Norway instead of Finland. These Swedes hoped to exploit the displeasure then widespread in Norway against Denmark's pro-French policy, which through the Continental System and blockade had brought poverty and famine to Norway. Norway's economy was closely tied to Great Britain's. If Sweden—in contrast to Denmark—took an English-oriented position in the war between the Great Powers, the Norwegians might be persuaded to liberate themselves from Denmark and voluntarily unite with Sweden. This plan built upon the long Norwegian isolation from Denmark, brought on by the war, that had made necessary the establishment of a separate administration and aroused strong demands for self-government in Norway. The prime spokesman for this policy was one of the leaders of the coup d'état in 1809, Georg Adlersparre.

The election of the French marshal Jean Baptiste Bernadotte in August 1810 as the successor to the throne in Sweden was forced upon the government and the Riksdag primarily by Gustaf af Wetterstedt and Lars von Engeström. Behind their choice lay the hope of an association with France and Napoleon. But shortly after his arrival, Bernadotte, now Karl Johan, embarked on a policy other than the one his Swedish supporters had expected. Instead of a reconquest of Finland, he entered into plans for acquiring Norway. To this end he began negotiations with England and in the spring of 1812 he joined the Russian-English coalition against Napoleon. The basis for the so-called policy of 1812, which was confirmed in treaties with Russia in 1812 and with England in 1813, was that Sweden would voluntarily renounce all plans for a reconquest of Finland and instead receive Norway.

In May 1813, Karl Johan landed in Germany in order to participate in the campaign against Napoleon at the head of the Swedish army. He played a leading role as the commander of the Northern Army, which was composed of large Prussian and Russian forces in addition to the Swedish army. After the battle of

Leipzig, Karl Johan turned the Northern Army against Denmark in November 1813. The war was short, and on December 15 a truce was concluded. On January 14, 1814, the peace treaty between Denmark and Sweden was signed in Kiel. According to this treaty the Danish king ceded Norway in return for Swedish Pomerania.

In the Treaty of Kiel each provision on the cession of Norway to Sweden had its counterpart in the provisions on the cession of Pomerania to Denmark. In the first Swedish draft of the treaty, these articles were identical in form. This was not the case, however, in the final text of the treaty. On one decisive point, the provision intended to regulate Norway's future position, a change had been made. In the first draft prepared by the Swedes, it had been decreed that "ces Baillage, embrassant la totalité du Royaume de Norvège . . . appartiendront désormais en toute propriété et souveraineté au Royaume de Suède, et lui restent incorporés" ("this bailliage, encompassing the whole Kingdom of Norway . . . will belong hereafter in all property and sovereignty to the Kingdom of Sweden, and remain incorporated in it"). In the draft, however, the words "au Royaume de Suède, et lui restent incorporés" are crossed out and replaced with the words "à S. M. le Roi de Suède, et formeront un Royaume, réuni à celui de Suède" ("to His Majesty the King of Sweden and will form a realm united with that of Sweden"). The provision appeared in this revised form in the Kiel peace treaty. The change in the draft had been made by the Swedish peace negotiator, Gustaf af Wetterstedt, before the actual peace negotiations had begun. It had not been the result of any demand from the Danish side. In establishing Norway's rank as a royal kingdom, united with Sweden under one king, Wetterstedt, completely in agreement with Karl Johan's stated views, was countermanding the Swedish government officials who had formulated the first draft, not conciliating the Danish negotiator.

This change in the fourth article of the Treaty of Kiel came to play an important role in the union debate during the later part of the nineteenth century. The wording of the article was used as an argument both for Sweden's supremacy within the union and for Norway's equality with Sweden. The interpretation of its legal content became the dominant issue; the question of why this change in the article had been made was not given the same attention.

Norway had been won in Kiel, thanks to the Great Powers' guarantees, through an attack directed against Denmark. The propaganda activity Adlersparre had energetically conducted in Norway in his attempt to induce the Norwegians to work voluntarily for their country's union with Sweden was without importance. The approach that Adlersparre had recommended actually failed. Adlersparre himself admitted in November and December 1813 that the atmosphere in Norway, despite all efforts, had become increasingly hostile to Sweden. However, a strange situation developed because of the change in the peace treaty's fourth article: Norway acquired the same position in relation to Sweden as it would have had if the Norwegians themselves had assisted in their country's union with Sweden. The readjustment of the fourth article was no accident. The change was dictated not only by the hope of winning the Norwegians over to the union and inducing them to accept cession of their country without a struggle, but also by the desire to fulfill promises that Karl Johan had given the Norwegian people through agents and proclamations. It meant the completion of a main line—the Adlersparre line—in Karl Johan's Norwegian policy.

The union was in existence only on paper after the Treaty of Kiel. Karl Johan and the Swedish army were engaged in the final battle against Napoleon, and the possibility of supporting by force what had been enacted in Kiel did not exist in the winter and spring of 1814. The long isolation of Norway due to the blockade had encouraged the development there of an independent bureaucracy and a considerable degree of self-government.

At the same time ideas about popular sovereignty had achieved strong influence. After the Danish king had ceded the country at Kiel, many Norwegians believed sovereignty had reverted to the people, giving them the right to decide their own fate. In order to try out this theory in practice, the national assembly, the Storting, was gathered at Eidsvoll and the constitution of May 17 was created. On the same day Prince Christian Fredrik of Denmark was chosen as Norway's king.

Sweden refused to acknowledge Norway's independence and demanded the execution of the Treaty of Kiel. After Karl Johan returned from the continent in June 1814, he sent the Swedish army against Norway. After two weeks of battle, before any decisive military decision, a truce was concluded, the Convention of Moss. Christian Fredrik promised to relinquish executive power and to leave Norway. Karl Johan promised, on behalf of the Swedish king, to accept the Eidsvoll constitution. After long negotiations with the Storting, the necessary changes in Norway's constitution to accommodate the union with Sweden were made. Only when this was done did the Storting "elect and acknowledge" Sweden's King Karl XIII as king of Norway. The union was thereby a fact.

The words "elect and acknowledge" in the Storting's decision of November 4, 1814, typify the art of formulation that characterizes the creation of the Swedish-Norwegian union. With the word "elect" the Storting wanted to make clear that it had voluntarily elected Karl XIII as Norway's king only after the constitution was ratified. Through the word "acknowledge" the Swedish side wanted to make clear that the Norwegian Storting had thereby accepted the Swedish king's right to Norway's crown.

The changes and additions made in Norway's constitution at the negotiations in October and November, along with some further amplifications, were collected in the Act of Union, to be binding on both countries. After the Riksdag in Sweden and the

Storting in Norway had jointly accepted it, the Act of Union was issued on August 6, 1815.

The compromises that resulted in the Swedish-Norwegian union were negotiated only through formulations that allowed both sides to interpret them in their own way. Some of the basic provisions of the documents and agreements that formed the legal foundation for the union were so ambiguously formulated that they were interpreted in different ways from the beginning.

The attitudes toward the union were also different in Sweden and in Norway from the outset. In Sweden the association with Norway was regarded as a compensation for loss of Finland. High hope existed that the union would successfully bring together the two peoples. In Norway the union was regarded as a defeat. It frustrated the demands for national independence that had grown strong during recent years and had been manifested in the appearance of the constitution and in the royal election of May 17. The union, it was felt, had been forced upon Norway by the Great Powers and by military might. Every attempt to extend the union was regarded in Norway as a threat to the country's national independence. These attitudes remained essentially the same during the entire union period. Sweden made various efforts to strengthen the union, and its goal was a merging of the two kingdoms into one. In Norway every proposal was repulsed that signified a curtailment of the country's internal self-government. The joint king was the link in the union. Each strengthening of the royal power, therefore, was a strengthening of the union ties. The scope of the king's authority in Norway became the chief issue of conflict within the union during the 1820s.

The Eidsvoll constitution of 1814 was far more democratic than any other contemporary constitution in Europe and gave the people through their representatives more authority than in any other country except the United States. It is true that the king had the executive power and appointed his ministers, but agreement of the popular representatives—i.e., of the Storting—was required in order to legislate and to impose taxes. The Storting could also initiate new laws, which, if the king refused them his sanction, went into force after the Storting had approved them three times with intervening elections. The king thus had only a suspensive veto. When the union's King Karl XIV Johan (1818–1844) demanded an absolute veto in 1821 after the Storting, among other things, abolished the nobility against his will, the Storting refused to give in, even though the king tried to frighten the representatives with military demonstrations. In the face of the unanimous opposition, Karl XIV Johan was forced to give up, and the Storting's position of power became Norway's permanent defense against the union king's—that is, in reality, the Swedish king's—attempts to merge the two countries. In the 1820s, Norway began celebrating May 17—the day the constitution was adopted at Eidsvoll in 1814—as its national day. When the king tried to forbid the celebration, violent demonstrations erupted, which culminated in the *Torvslaget* (Battle of the Square) in 1829. During the 1830s, the king also gave in on this point.

The next epoch in the union's history, from the mid-1830s to 1860, was characterized by attempts to replace the ambiguous documents of 1814–1815 with a treaty of union that would establish clearly the two countries' mutual position and the functions of their common organs. After long negotiations a committee was formed in 1839—the so-called first union committee—composed of four Norwegian and four Swedish members. The result of its work did not become available until the fall of 1844, after the death of Karl XIV Johan. In its recommendation for a new treaty of union, the relations of the two countries were carefully regulated in not fewer than 150 paragraphs. The main points were that the union should entail (1) a common royal house; (2) commonality in questions of foreign relations; (3) independence in internal affairs; and (4) complete equality between the kingdoms within the union. The duties and rights of both kingdoms were carefully fixed. Under the recommendation, for example, a joint foreign minister might be either a Swede or a Norwegian. He would head a joint department of foreign affairs and be responsible to a union congress consisting of twelve Norwegian and twelve Swedish members. This body would have the deciding voice if the Storting and the Riksdag differed on union questions. Originally the recommendation had spelled out full equality for the countries in matters regarding the king's title, the national coat of arms, and the flag. That is, the king would put Norway before Sweden in his title when conducting Norwegian business and he would use the Norwegian coat of arms; also, the Norwegian flag would be placed equal to the Swedish through the introduction of, among other things, a special Norwegian naval flag instead of the union flag, which had been used up to then and which marked Sweden's supremacy.

At his accession to the throne, Oskar I had decided to put into immediate effect these reforms in use of the king's title, the national coat of arms, and the flag, reforms which had been vigorously espoused by the Norwegians. Thereafter interest in the adoption of a new treaty of union declined among the Norwegians. Only in February 1847—after more than two years—was the Norwegian government ready to make a statement on the treaty. In its report it formally supported the recommendation, but this was on condition of such large changes that it really entailed a rejection. For one thing, the Norwegians opposed the establishment of a common union congress. Also, Norway wanted permission to conclude its own treaties with foreign powers and to establish a separate consular service. A new treaty with these provisions would have weakened, not strengthened, union ties and would have been unacceptable to the Swedish government. In order not to intensify the conflicts between the countries, the Swedish government simply let the recommendation circulate and recirculate among political leaders—for fourteen years. Only on April 9, 1861, was the first union committee's report taken up for consideration in joint—i.e., union—cabinet. In February 1862, the cabinet decided to set aside the recommendation without any action other than that the documents were made public. Since the situation in the 1860s was completely different from that when the first union committee was established and when it drafted its recommendation, the release of the texts was of little interest. The whole matter of a new treaty of union was lost in the shadow of the first serious crisis in the Swedish-Norwegian union—the 1859–1860 battle of the governor.

Since it had been assumed from the beginning that the union king would normally reside in Sweden, the revised Norwegian constitution directed that a governor would represent the king in Norway. This provision, insisted upon by Sweden, was one of the most obvious signs of Norway's subordinate position within the union. Strong demands that the office of governor be abolished had therefore been made time after time in Norwegian quarters. In 1854 the Storting even proposed a formal change in the constitution on this point; however, the king refused to sanction it.

From the point of view of practical politics, the issue at this time had become unimportant. Since 1829 the office had been occupied exclusively by Norwegians and it had been unoccupied during long periods. When it fell empty again in 1855, Oskar I failed to name a new governor. Instead, the following year, Crown Prince Karl—later king under the name of Karl XV—was named vice-king in Norway. This measure was greeted with great satisfaction in Norway.

With youthful energy, Crown Prince Karl set to work on his duties as vice-king and regent in Norway. His goal was to draw the union ties tighter. For this purpose he initiated a committee to investigate a new structure of common defense for the union kingdoms. He also tried to promote trade connections between the two countries through further reduction of or freedom from tolls and other fees. Finally he also took the initiative on planning a railroad between Norway and Sweden.

In most cases Crown Prince Karl met firm opposition in the Storting. Despite this, his service as vice-king in Norway in 1856–1857 was a period of close cooperation within the union. In the background, however, Norwegian demands for equality and independence within the union grew, finding expression in such ways as the appearance of the Venstre party under the leadership of Johan Sverdrup. The first serious conflict came shortly after Karl XV became king.

As crown prince and regent, Karl XV had promised the Norwegians that at his accession he would abolish the office of governor. His purpose was to increase the popularity he had won in Norway and to create the conditions necessary for a more permanent resolution of the union question. Immediately after the death of Oskar I in 1859, the Storting decided to abolish the office of governor itself, counting on the new king's sanction in accordance with his earlier promises. But the Swedish government, led by the powerful minister of finance, J. A. Gripenstedt, opposed the intention of the king to give his sanction to the act in a meeting of the Norwegian cabinet. The office of governor, said Gripenstedt, was a provision of the union and therefore could not be abolished by Norwegian officials alone; action in joint cabinet was required. When the Norwegians refused to accept this interpretation, the Swedish government threatened to resign and won strong support in the Riksdag. The king was forced to refuse to sanction in the Norwegian cabinet the Storting's decision on the abolition of the office of governor. From the Swedish point of view this meant that the government with the support of the Riksdag maintained its position against the king. The dispute over the office of governor can be said to begin the tug-of-war for power between the king and the Riksdag that characterized Sweden's political history during the later part of the nineteenth century.

For Karl XV personally, the outcome of the governorship battle —at the very beginning of his regime—was a bitter defeat. His royal word had shown itself to be an empty promise. On the union's part, the dispute laid bare the deep opposition between Sweden and Norway, which had often been glimpsed previously but now appeared clearly. All attempts during the 1860s to rework the basic provisions of the union ended without result. A recommendation prepared by the second union committee (1865–1867) was rejected in 1871 by the Storting. The only progress was the abolition in 1873 of the office of governor, which had been unoccupied since 1855; Sweden finally agreed that the question could be decided in the Norwegian cabinet.

The political history of Sweden and Norway during the rule of Oskar II, who succeeded Karl XV in 1872 and reigned until 1907, is marked to a large degree by conflicts over the union, which led in 1905 to its dissolution. The first phase of this period is dominated by Oskar II's stubborn fight to maintain royal power in Norway; the second, by the fight over a common or separate Norwegian foreign-affairs administration and the establishment of a special Norwegian consular service.

Shortly after Oskar II became king a demand for parliamentarianism was seriously made in Norway. A law was enacted that allowed cabinet ministers to participate in the Storting's deliberations—and thereby become de facto representatives of the Storting, not of the king. Oskar II refused to give the law his sanction. After the Storting had approved it the three times necessary under the constitution to override the king's opposition, he still refused to issue it on the grounds that it involved a change in the constitution; on such measures the king, according to his understanding, had an absolute, not merely a suspensive, veto. The Norwegian prime minister, who countersigned the Storting's decision, was placed before the Swedish court of impeachment. After this court had taken the Storting's side and in 1884 removed the conservative government in Norway, Oskar II was forced to appoint a Venstre government under the leadership of Johan Sverdrup, which was accepted by a majority of the Storting. Parliamentarianism had thereby won a decisive victory in Norway.

But new problems arose immediately. Even if Norway had won full internal self-government in 1884, the country was represented outwardly by the Swedish-Norwegian king and his envoys in the Swedish foreign ministry. A reorganization of the foreign-affairs administration that would satisfy Norway's demands for full equality with Sweden now became the major problem within the union. In Sweden a reform was carried out in 1885 that gave the Riksdag increased control over foreign policy. This reform, in itself democratic, had fateful consequences for the union with Norway, since now Norway's foreign policy came to an even greater degree than before under purely Swedish authorities.

Sharp voices were raised insisting on a separate Norwegian administration for foreign affairs. In the 1891 election the Venstre party won a decisive election victory on a platform that included a demand for a separate Norwegian foreign minister. Despite this the Venstre government did not take up the question of a separate foreign minister but instead pursued the more limited demand for a separate Norwegian consular service. Even this was rejected by Oskar II, however, after strong pressure from the Swedish side. When the Storting thereafter tried to carry out this reform on its own, the king refused to give the law his sanction. Long negotiations followed; during this period the Venstre party succeeded in retaining its majority—if by a narrow margin—at the Storting election in 1894. The crisis became acute in the spring of 1895, when the king asked that the Riksdag's Secret Committee be called together for deliberations on the question. The threat of military measures became obvious, and the Storting was forced to give in. In November 1895, the third union committee was appointed. The Swedish demand for a general revision of the operative provisions for the union—instead of reforms worked out point by point—had triumphed.

On January 29, 1898, the union committee released its conclusions. It had not been possible to achieve agreement within the committee. There was disagreement not only between Swedes and Norwegians but also between representatives from each country. The committee's work resulted in four different reports, two Swedish and two Norwegian. But the most important division was between the Swedish recommendations on the one side and the Norwegian on the other. Both Swedish recommendations aimed at strengthening the union ties through provisions making clear statements on such issues as a joint foreign minister and full equality, all to be summarized in a new treaty of union that carefully regulated the relationship between the two countries. The two Norwegian recommendations differed more, one from the other, than the Swedish but both recommended only changes in the already existing Act of Union, not any new union organs or joint directives. Also both recommended that each country should have a separate consular service—which in effect would weaken the union. The three Norwegian representatives of the Venstre party went farthest in this direction. They proceeded from the view that the union meant only a joint king and commonality in the event of war, and, therefore, they demanded a separate Norwegian foreign minister, separate diplomatic negotiations by Norway, and a separate Norwegian consular service.

The Venstre government with the support of an absolute majority in the Storting announced advocacy of the recommendation of the three Venstre men in the union committee. The Swedish government at the same time concurred in the recommendation by the Swedish majority on the committee of a joint foreign minister and common diplomacy and consular service, all confirmed in a new Act of Union. In light of this situation further negotiations became meaningless. In joint cabinet on October 21, 1898, it was decided that no further action should be taken on the union committee's reports. The attempt to obtain a general revision of the fundamental provisions for the Swedish-Norwegian union, long recommended and anticipated with great hopes in Swedish quarters, was a complete failure. The only result was that the conflicts within the union were further sharpened.

Shortly thereafter the "flag dispute" took the spotlight. The Storting voted for the third time to abolish the union symbol from the Norwegian merchant flag, overriding the king's veto; he protested, but the Storting's decision was upheld legally. The hostility to the union in Norway was further underlined by the large appropriations earmarked by the Storting for defense and by the appearance of a number of fortresses on the border with Sweden.

In this situation a last attempt was made to reach a settlement on the point where the sides were closest: the question of the right to a separate consular service. After long deliberations, the communiqué of March 24, 1903, was issued. The prime ministers of both countries and the ministers participating in the negotiations declared themselves in agreement on the establishment of a "special consular service for Sweden and for Norway," but at the same time they stressed that they "had been obliged to try to achieve such an arrangement of the consular question that leaves the status quo undisturbed with regard to the position of the minister for foreign affairs and the missions."

The communiqué was immediately interpreted in different ways in Sweden and in Norway. On the Swedish side it was believed that the statement about "leaving the status quo undisturbed" meant a recognition of the Swedish foreign minister's position and thereby bound Norway to a permanent joint administration for foreign affairs. In Norway on the other hand, the same passage was interpreted as an agreement to solve the consular question as a separate issue and to let the "status quo" prevail for the time in the matter of the foreign minister, but the right to present in the future a demand for a separate Norwegian foreign minister remained.

During the continued negotiations on the practical execution of the decision, the different interpretations of the communiqué were mercilessly disclosed. Swedish Prime Minister E. G. Böström tried to find an acceptable and clear formulation on the issue of the status of the foreign minister and the consular service but was immediately attacked by the Norwegians for breaking Sweden's earlier promise. "A contract which is meant in one way by the one side and in another by the other leads not to peace but to battle," wrote one of the leaders of the Swedish Riksdag to Böström several days before the latter signed the communiqué in 1903. Böström ignored the warning. But the letterwriter was proved true. On February 7, 1905, it was stated in joint cabinet that the negotiations on the consular question had definitely broken down. The union conflict thereby became acute.

The Norwegians in this situation took matters into their own hands. In March the government resigned and was replaced by a national coalition government under the leadership of Christian Michelsen, with solution of the consular question as the primary point on its program. On May 23, 1905, the Storting unanimously accepted a recommendation for a law establishing a separate Norwegian consular service. On the 27th this recommendation was presented to Oskar II in Norwegian cabinet in Stockholm. He refused to give it his sanction. Prime Minister Michelsen and the other ministers of the Norwegian government then submitted their resignations, which had been prepared in advance. The king stated: "Since it is clear to me that no other government can now be formed, I do not accept the resignations of the ministers." Several days later, on June 7, the Norwegian government's members let it be known to the king that they had vacated their offices, despite his refusal to allow them to resign. The message was delivered to the Storting at the same time. This body decided unanimously that since the king had declared himself unable to provide the country with a new government, the cabinet as "the Norwegian government" would exercise the authority of the king for the present and at the same time declared the union with

Sweden under one king to be dissolved "as a consequence of the fact that the king has ceased to function as Norwegian king." The Swedish-Norwegian union had thereby de facto ceased to exist. The Norwegians' quick and resolute course of action came as a shock in Sweden. A long crisis and continued negotiations had been expected. When the Norwegians simply declared the king deposed and the union dissolved without giving the king the opportunity to abdicate and Sweden the opportunity to agree on conditions and forms for the dissolution of the union, general bitterness was aroused in Sweden. Norway's method of action was considered to be a humiliation of the old king and a challenge to Sweden. Liberals and conservatives united in refusing to accept Norway's course of action and demanded negotiations on the dissolution of the union. The daily press, the Riksdag, and the public placed themselves almost unanimously behind this demand in the summer of 1905.

The Swedish Riksdag, summoned to an extraordinary meeting immediately after the union break, drew up the conditions for Sweden's acceptance of dissolution of the union. The most important of these politically were, first, that a Storting election or a popular plebiscite be held to determine if the Norwegian people supported dissolution of the union, and, second, that a neutral zone be established along the border with Sweden, which meant that the newly erected Norwegian border fortresses would have to be razed. In order to underline the seriousness with which the Riksdag regarded the situation, it at the same time placed large military appropriations at the government's disposal.

After the Norwegian people at a plebiscite approved the government's and the Storting's policy on union with a crushing majority—368,208 votes to only 184—negotiations on conditions for a dissolution of the union were begun. At a conference in Karlstad, after sometimes dramatic confrontations, accord was reached on the Swedish demands with modifications concerning, especially, some of the border fortresses. Shortly thereafter, the Storting and the Riksdag annulled the Act of Union. De jure as well as de facto, the Swedish-Norwegian union ceased to exist.

Even if the union did not lead to a closer relationship between Sweden and Norway politically and constitutionally, did the union, it might be asked, result in closer economic cooperation and increased contacts on the cultural and social level?

One of the few results of all the Swedish efforts to bring the countries closer together was the law of 1825 regulating interstate relations, which reduced and partially abolished tolls and fees between the two kingdoms. But the law's significance was diminished rather quickly by the introduction of free trade by most of the countries of Europe in the middle of the nineteenth century. When Sweden reintroduced protective tolls in the 1890s, while Norway continued to espouse free trade, the law was revoked without thereby noticeably changing foreign trade for either party. Economically the union hardly brought—despite interstate regulations—any closer cooperation than that which was a result of industrialization and better communications and which surely would have come without the union.

With regard to culture, Norway had been closely tied to Denmark before 1814. The written language was Danish, the school system Danish, the literature Danish; priests, teachers, and government officials had been educated at the University of Copenhagen. Close cultural ties with Sweden did not exist before 1814, and the union brought less change than one could have expected. To be sure, Norway had established its own university in Christiania (later Oslo) shortly before the union with Sweden, but the professors were recruited almost exclusively from Copenhagen, the books used in courses were published in Copenhagen, and the students in large measure continued to travel to Copenhagen in order to benefit from the widened perspective and richer cultural life of a large university. Norwegian priests, teachers, and government officials continued to be educated or to complete their education in Copenhagen throughout the period of the union. The University of Christiania for a long time was almost a branch of the institution in Copenhagen. No close relations with Swedish universities ever came about: Norwegian students at Swedish universities or Swedish students in Christiania remained a rarity. Swedish books were never read in Norway to anything like the extent Danish books were. Closer relations between Sweden and Norway during and after union were evident only in theater, art, and music—and these in large measure thanks to the interest that the king and his court evinced toward them. Sweden, it must be said, failed to use the opportunities the union provided for closer cultural cooperation. The return that cooperation in education and research, for example, could have produced in the long run in the form of increased understanding was apparently not understood.

If we look at population movements, the labor market, and purely social contacts, it can be seen immediately that the Swedish emigration to Norway increased strongly during the union period and that at the beginning of the twentieth century there were not fewer than 50,000 Swedish-born persons in Norway. In the opposite direction, however, the stream was much smaller and the number of those born in Norway then living in Sweden amounted to only 8000. In determining whether the union had any influence on these population movements, we must take account of the fact that the industrial development in the area around the Oslo fjord in Norway for a long time was ahead of that in the nearest bordering area in Sweden, especially during the later part of the nineteenth century. A sign that this and not the union was the primary cause of the population movements is that the population exchange between Sweden and Denmark was of exactly the same character as that between Sweden and Norway. The proportionally large emigration of Swedes to Norway during the later part of the nineteenth century was composed primarily of workers, especially laborers in railroad construction, farmhands, and workers in sawmills and mines. In Norway they were called "work Swedes" or "gray Swedes," the railroad laborers often also "raw Swedes."

Among the higher social classes there were surprisingly few personal contacts. Within the state administration, the educational system, and the business world, contacts among individuals were slight, in certain areas almost nonexistent. Only within three categories is it possible to say that the union led to closer personal association, namely the royal court, the theater, and the timber industry. But the Swedes and Norwegians in these areas who did intermix were all too few to have any importance for the union as such.

The union was created from the geographical unit which the Scandinavian peninsula forms, without regard to existing communications, economic ties, and cultural development. Through skillful formulations Karl Johan and his negotiators tried in 1814 to conceal what was lacking in economic, social, and cultural solidarity. The history of the Swedish-Norwegian union shows, however, that treaties, conventions, and common bodies are not of much use where the real will for cooperation does not exist. The prerequisite for political cooperation and a melting together into a political unit is a knowledge of belonging together that can only be created by common economic interests and from close cultural cooperation.

Introduction to Chapter 4

After the turbulent years, 1805–1815, Sweden's political life
became more tranquil and stable than it had been in the previous
decades. Indeed in Europe as a whole, the immediate post-
Napoleonic period was one of general political reactionism which
slowly dissipated after 1830. In Sweden there was clearly a conservative wind blowing the ship of state during most of the reign
of Karl XIV Johan, 1818–1844. Sweden's new constitution was
interpreted in such a way that the traditionally influential groups
—the bureaucracy and aristocracy—retained a high degree of control over the political process. Yet even if the older elites remained in control of Sweden, the means by which they exercised
their authority had been altered and liberalized through the constitution of 1809. The new political forms were constructed so
that they could, and would, be sensitive to changing social and
economic conditions. The challenges to the existing order which
began to take form in the late 1830s came primarily from groups
whose own importance was a product of the economic and social
changes that were occurring in Sweden at the same time. Indeed
it was the great social and economic changes of nineteenth-cen-

tury Sweden that were to have such critical ramifications on its political forms after the turn of the century.

The process by which European countries shed their older forms of economic activity and means of production both in agriculture and in industry and adopted forms in these fields that we recognize as "modern" is generally called the Industrial Revolution. The term is obviously imprecise and implies a rapid, drastic change which in fact rarely occurred. There were a series of changes in a variety of fields over an extended period of time all of which contributed to this great development. In the case of Great Britain, which was the first country to experience this process, some of the factors generally emphasized are these: specific technological innovations and their adaptation to the economic system, adequate accumulation of capital, modern forms of economic institutions and organizations, population "surplus" in rural areas which could be drawn upon as a working force for the new enterprises, availability of the necessary agrarian resources to feed increasing numbers of nonagrarian elements of the population, cheap transportation systems, an entrepreneurial spirit, and the availability of certain natural resources. The peculiar combination of these factors which produced late-nineteenth-century Britain did not take place in a brief period of time but rather over an extended period. The critical period for this industrialization process is usually regarded as the years between 1775 and 1850. By the latter date, the British economy had taken a form which most historians would label "industrial." This economic upheaval eventually was to occur in the other European countries but under circumstances particular to the time and the geographical area.

The Swedish Industrial Revolution occurred at a rather late date comparatively. It is usually suggested that between 1870 and 1914 Sweden emerged from its primarily agrarian economic system into a modern industrial economy. The following essay by Docent Lennart Jörberg is an analysis of the particular forces that produced industrial Sweden. It is of interest to note not only which factors made significant contributions to the process of industrialization but also what might be called the "time element." Of what significance is the fact that Sweden's transformation to a modern industrial society came so late for a European country? A careful reading of Docent Jörberg's work will suggest certain conclusions as will many of the later articles in this volume which also touch upon this problem.

4

Structural Change
and Economic Growth in
Nineteenth-Century Sweden

by Lennart Jörberg

During the nineteenth century, Sweden, like other European countries, underwent a drastic economic change. Swedish economic expansion had many features common to Europe in general, but also features that differed from what can be considered normal in Europe. England's economic expansion is usually taken as an example of the general pattern in European development. But it is questionable whether that can help to explain the first stage of development on the continent of Europe or in Sweden. The development in England was in many ways unique. Its initial position was vastly different from that of countries on the continent. The economic growth factors which started the industrialization of England were not the same as those that initiated the development on the continent, although England, as the first industrial country, influenced the economic growth in other countries. In Sweden the economic growth rate accelerated during three short periods when production had an irregular development: in the 1850s, in the 1870s, and in the 1890s. The first acceleration greatly influenced agriculture, and the international demand for Swedish grain was a contributing cause of the changes that took place. In the 1870s there occurred the industrial break-through, which was strongly affected by the international boom period, whereas the expansion in the 1890s reflected the bigger demand by the home market. Swedish industry began to be self-generating, although international developments were extremely important in influencing the irregular tendencies in the Swedish economy.

Like all other European countries, Sweden was agrarian, perhaps more so than most others at the beginning of the nineteenth century. Agriculture employed more than 80 percent of its population, whose growth was relatively slow; agricultural production was scarcely sufficient to support the farm families. Sweden depended on imported grain, although to a dwindling extent, up to about 1830. At this time, a change occurred. Agriculture developed to such an extent that it was able to support an increasing population as well as to produce a surplus for export. Swedish agricultural exports during a short period after the middle of the nineteenth century competed with iron exports for second position among exports. Timber exports held the lead.

We here face a situation of considerable interest. In the pre-industrial phase, Swedish agriculture achieved a production capacity so great that it could support a rapidly increasing population (more than 30 percent from 1830 to 1860) and could also yield substantial exports, which during the same period multiplied tenfold. We do not know whether the living standard of the population fell, i.e., whether the exports were at the expense of the home market. References have been made to the lower classes in agriculture being proletarianized, but no proof of such an assertion has been produced. Certain factors, for example the increase in the birthrate and the reduced mortality rate after 1845, may instead indicate that a positive improvement in the national economy took place after this time.

Coincident with the expanding agricultural yields after 1830, signs can be detected of industrial growth. Iron mining, the production of pig iron and of bar iron, expanded at about 3 percent per annum between 1830 and 1860, and the textile industry showed a very rapid upward trend. The production of cotton yarn multiplied more than twentyfold, and the production value of cotton fabric and linen fabric rose by about 20 percent per annum. The number of workers employed in the factories increased, according to industrial statistics, by about 3.5 percent per annum; at the same time the production value rose by about 10 percent per annum, which means that productivity improved substantially.[1]* This may seem to be clear proof that an industrial breakthrough had taken place, but it would be unwise to draw such a conclusion. Very large percentage increases show, in this case, that the initial position was extremely low and that modest absolute changes led to large relative increases. The iron industry, which had for a considerable time been well established, was given a positive jolt. This was intensified by the greatly increased competition from England and from those continental countries beginning to industrialize. At this time the Swedish timber industry also began to develop. Exports multiplied fivefold between 1830 and 1860, and the old water-driven sawmills began to be replaced by steam sawmills whose capacity was larger. This allowed them to change their location from the inland waterfalls to the coast.

The economic expansion of the 1870s can be characterized as an industrial revolution, however, if by revolution is meant a rapid change in Sweden's economic structure. Naturally, the conditions for this rapid change had been created during the previous decades. In an analysis explaining the factors contributing to industrial development, it would be impossible to concentrate on the changes taking place during the brief period of takeoff. But if we analyze only this takeoff, we can disregard some of the conditions that are believed to be fundamental and concentrate on the short-period changes.

* The notes begin on p. 134.

In the 1870s an extremely rapid expansion took place in most industrial branches. Investments reached new heights. They were concentrated in a few sectors strategic from an economic standpoint. From the 1870s up to World War I, Swedish national income rose at the rate of about 3 percent per annum, i.e., it more than doubled during this period. The industrial growth was even stronger. At the outbreak of World War I, the part played by

Table 1. Swedish Economic Growth, 1870–1914

Item	Annual Percentage Growth	Absolute Growth (in Millions of People/Kronor)	
		1870	1914
Population	0.7	4.2	5.7
Town population	2.3	0.5	1.5
National income	2.8	800	3,300
Industrial production	4.4	320	2,200
Gross investments	5.0	50	450
Investments in machinery	4.0	10	90
Exports	3.1	140	790
Imports	3.2	150	800

Source: L. Jörberg, "Growth and Fluctuations of Swedish Industry 1869–1912," *Studies in the Process of Industrialization* (Lund, 1961), p. 27. Percentage growth has been calculated exponentially by the least squares method.

industry in national income was considerably greater than that played by agriculture. (See Table 1.) In subsequent pages some of the factors will be discussed that have probably contributed to this development, and the consequences for further economic growth will be analyzed.

Some Basic Theoretical Factors

Intensive studies made during the past two decades into the problems of economic growth have led to a large number of factors being considered relevant for study when one is seeking an explanation for this growth. For a long time the raw-material sector was concentrated on. It was believed that access to raw materials was decisive in bringing about economic expansion. The availability of capital later played a leading role as an object for investigation, and the degree of investment in relation to national income was considered to be a criterion of a country's ability to initiate and maintain economic expansion. However, some authors have pointed out that scanty savings are not necessarily an insuperable obstacle to the start of industrial growth. Furthermore, it has been shown that savings and investment are, to an equally high degree, a result as well as a cause of economic development. A theory that has recently been debated anew is Joseph Schumpeter's regarding the strategic role played by innovations and entrepreneurs in the development process. Innovations lead to structural changes both for enterprises and for branches of economy, i.e., they can result in changed relations between branches of economy or industries. For underdeveloped countries the lack of entrepreneurs has been thought to be a big obstacle to economic development. Availability of capital and entrepreneurial activity are sometimes considered complementary, but it has also been suggested that the influence of entrepreneurs in the development process is more important than capital.

Albert Hirschman in his book *The Strategy of Economic Development* has stressed that the usually long list of "necessary" conditions for economic development does not justify the conclusion that the difficulties are insurmountable for the underdeveloped countries of today. Instead, he emphasizes that economic development can be brought about by many different means. It is necessary to break "the vicious circle," but the break-in can occur in many places. When the development has started, it leads upwards as more and more conditions for expansion come into being.

The most debated theory of economic growth has been W. W. Rostow's stage-by-stage exposition, in which his "take-off" thesis is the most prominent feature. His aim has been to find a general explanation of how economic growth begins, and he believes his theory to be applicable to all communities; at the same time he considers it to have value in prognosis. However, he has been subjected to severe criticism and his explanation of economic growth has hardly been accepted. What is mainly responsible for the criticism is his somewhat obscure terminology. He discusses thoroughly so-called preconditions, but he has not succeeded in explaining how these can be distinguished from the causes that result in a takeoff. One way of avoiding the Rostow dilemma was shown by Alexander Gerschenkron, who speaks of the "degree of economic backwardness." Economic growth, a takeoff, can be produced at many levels of economic development, and it is the degree of backwardness which will decide the factors that play the leading role.[2]

Other authors have also tried to force development into a system by speaking of a "big push," or "the early phase of modern growth," or "the critical minimum effort," or "basic conditions for economic growth," by which they have stressed different factors as decisive for producing rapid economic growth.[3] In all cases, however, it must be noted that the confusion in terminology has contributed to obscuring the aims of the two basic investigations which must be separated when studying the problems of economic growth. We take either a long view in studying economic expansion, i.e., analyze all the factors leading up to a stage where rapid economic expansion is possible, or a short view, i.e., concentrate on analyzing the changes and disregard how the structure develops, which in isolated instances leads to industrial revolution in the real meaning of the word. Hirschman's grasp of development problems is for an economic historian more satisfying than, for example, the stage-theories of Rostow, who concentrates solely on the investment sector and simplifies reality.

Another type of explanation is found in the more formalized theories that are based on, for instance, a simple multiplier-accelerator model where, with changes in the parameters, a certain pattern in the development can be arrived at.[4] A model of this type can be very instructive, but we must be certain that we can explain why changes occurred in production which, in its turn, generated a rise in income or the reverse, because in a multiplier-accelerator model there is a mutual dependence between production and income. It is not enough to argue that a change of this nature has occurred, for if the multiplier-accelerator has once begun to function it leads, according to the construction of the model, to economic growth (or fluctuations).

When we come to study the development in Sweden, it is also difficult to find *one* decisive cause of expansion. Studied closely, the problems are seen to be more differentiated, the causal connections more complicated, and the conclusions more guarded. In the following I will concentrate on analyzing the long-term changes and after that will dwell on the special situation in the 1870s and development up to 1914. This means that in the analysis I must import factors whose significance for economic growth cannot by themselves be determined or quantified.

Population Development

In 1800, Sweden had a population of 2.3 million. By 1830, its population had increased 23 percent and during the following thirty-year period, 1830 to 1860, it grew by 34 percent. The population then totaled 3.9 million. The increase was strongly differentiated. In eight counties the population increased by less than 30 percent; in seven, by more than 40 percent. It was greatest in the south and the west of Sweden and in Norrland; the eastern and central counties had the lowest growth rate. During the next forty-year period, up to the turn of the century, the increase was approximately as great as during the 1830–1860 period, i.e., 33 percent. Sweden now had a population of over 5 million. It thus had more than doubled during the nineteenth century. In the latter half of that century, more than a million people had emigrated. The emigration began on a small scale in the 1850s and reached its maximum during the 1880s. In addition, the population showed considerable mobility even before the emigration. The net migration, especially at times of bad harvest, amounted to several thousand per annum in some counties during the years 1830 to 1860. The internal population movements have not, as yet, been investigated, but it seems that the Swedish people were migratory long before the modern movements began. To how large an extent this contributed to the equalization of opportunities for employment and to the recruitment of workers for new industries is difficult to assess, but a mobile population must, reasonably, have been advantageous for raising the level of production and productivity and for preventing diminishing returns, which would have had an effect of decisive economic importance. The gross national product expanded also because of the movement of the labor force from low productive to higher productive industrial sectors. The transfer gains could be considerable.

When appraising the influence of population conditions on economic development, the displacements between different age groups must also be taken into account. A large increase in the nonproductive population in the pre-industrial phase must have contributed to retarding expansion in the national product. (Population development has been very little investigated in Sweden, despite there being, from an international standpoint, unusually complete material available.) A big increase in the population of people of working age, however, does not necessarily lead to greater production. In the pre-industrial phase, that increase could equally well lead to unemployment, more or less hidden, or to a reduction in wages, which could reduce consumption or savings and thereby investments. In an industrialized community, such an effect can also be produced, but there the durability of the depressive effect ought to be shorter. In Sweden, the number of those fit for work—meaning those at the ages of 15–64 years—

increased more than the total population during the 1830s, the 1840s, the 1870s, the 1890s, and the first decade of the twentieth century. Also during the 1850s, the increase was almost as large as the increase in the total population. We thus find that, during those phases when economic growth accelerated, the increase in the working population exceeded or almost equaled the increase in the total population. During the 1810s and the 1820s, as well as during the 1860s and the 1880s, when economic expansion was less accentuated, however, the increase in the number of potential workers was conspicuously slower than the increase in the total population. (See Table 2.) But if we consider not only the

Table 2. Percentage Change in the Size of Different Age Groups, 1800–1910

Decade	0–14 Years	15–39 Years	40–64 Years	15–64 Years	65 Years and Over	All
1800–1810	−0.4	+5.2	+2.6	+4.3	−7.7	+2.1
1810–1820	+10.4	+8.3	+2.3	+6.1	+13.8	+7.8
1820–1830	+22.6	+6.6	+5.6	+6.2	+9.3	+11.7
1830–1840	+2.9	+14.1	+11.3	+13.0	−2.0	+8.6
1840–1850	+8.7	+14.9	+6.9	+12.0	+12.0	+10.9
1850–1860	+12.7	+7.6	+17.4	+9.1	+19.8	+10.8
1860–1870	+9.7	+0.8	+17.4	+6.6	+12.6	+8.0
1870–1880	+4.8	+11.2	+11.4	+10.8	+18.7	+9.5
1880–1890	+7.0	−0.4	+2.1	+0.5	+36.7	+4.8
1890–1900	+4.5	+9.0	+5.5	+7.7	+16.9	+7.3
1900–1910	+5.0	+9.8	+6.9	+8.7	+8.4	+7.5

Source: *Sweden's Historical Statistics*, part I, Table A 16.

changes in the size of the age groups but also the proportion of potential workers in the total population, we obtain a rather different picture, although the main features, naturally, remain unchanged. From 1850 to the 1870s, the proportion of potential workers decreases, but after 1890 it increases. (See Table 3.) During the 1880s, the most extensive increase in Swedish manufacturing industry occurs, i.e., the number of workers rises more rapidly

Table 3. The 15–64 Age Group as a Percentage of the
Total Population, 1800–1910

Year	Percentage	Year	Percentage
1800	62.0	1860	61.2
1810	63.3	1870	60.5
1820	62.2	1880	61.5
1830	59.2	1890	59.0
1840	61.6	1900	59.2
1850	62.2	1910	**59.9**

Source: Jörberg, "Growth and Fluctuations of Swedish Industry," p. 20.

than the accumulation of real capital. It is evident that the changes in the composition of the population can have influenced the rhythm of economic growth, although at present it is not possible to assert anything about cause and effect in this process.

If we insist that this increase in population was sufficiently large to constitute an expansive power in the growth process, although not large enough to obstruct it, we touch upon the most important feature of the population problem in economic growth. In Sweden, as in other European countries, the increase in population was in general no greater than the expansion in production; before 1870 a rise in real income could occur despite a rather modest economic expansion in the beginning. We find that about 30 percent of the rise in Swedish national income can be explained by the increased population and the other 70 percent by greater productivity during the years 1872 to 1889, whereas the productivity expansion was an even more dominant factor up to 1912 and was responsible for over 80 percent of the measured rise in the national income.

The Transformation of Agriculture

During the introductory phase before 1870, Swedish society underwent a radical structural change. The relatively large increase in population may have resulted in overpopulation, and thereby also in a degree of proletarianization of the lower classes in the rural areas during the period up to 1840: the rise in national income was slower than the increase in population. The average productivity per person would, in other words, have fallen although it cannot be presumed that the marginal productivity was equal to zero. During the period 1750 to 1840, the number of farmers grew by about 16 percent, whereas the lower-class population increased by approximately 240 percent.[5]

At the same time, however, extensive land reclamation took place and thereby agricultural production also expanded. This land reclamation is usually explained by the fact that in 1830 an act permitting legal land parceling was issued. This was unquestionably a contributing cause of the land reclamation, but it does not explain why the farmers were so ready to parcel out their villages. For that, population development must also be taken into account. It was not the parceling-out movement that led to the population increase; it was rather the greater demand on the productive land in the old agrarian community, caused by increased population, that precipitated the parceling out. In those parts of the country that had a relatively slight increase in population, the parceling out came later than in the districts with a considerable increase in population. The same situation can be seen in Western Europe generally. In countries that had a rapid increase in population, e.g., England and Germany, land distribution took place; in France, with a stagnating population, this did not happen. The parceling out also necessitated considerable investments. New buildings, road construction, and fencing demanded heavy capital outlay over relatively short periods and, although much of the work was done by the farmers themselves and material was taken from their own forests, this new investment must have had an accelerating effect on the economy and have resulted in a definite multiplying effect. In addition, agriculture around

1850 became more capital-demanding. New implements, such as harvester combines, began to come into use and a more capital-intensive production must have led to an increase in both investments and income.

In this connection, the availability of capital for agriculture must be discussed. The work of parceling out and reclaiming land demanded considerable capital resources. If these had not been mobilized, it is probable that the remolding of Swedish agriculture would not have occurred during this period or, perhaps, not in the form that it took. What seems surprising is that the availability of capital in the rural areas appears to have been fairly good. The growth of the rural savings banks was, to some extent, a reaction against the savings banks in the towns, which refused to provide the rural population with facilities for deposits. In the opinion of the officials of the town savings banks, there were no investment possibilities for more money than could be saved by the small number of people in the towns. That this was a misconception is clear from the rapid growth of savings banks in the rural districts. The number of savings banks increased between 1834 and 1860 from 31 to 146 and their capital from 2.3 million kronor to 29.0 million kronor. Also contributing to investment activity was the development of mortgage societies. The first of these for the farming community was founded in 1836, and before 1850 most counties in south and central Sweden had their own. At the end of 1858, these societies had a foreign bond liability of 52 million kronor out of a total bond liability of 72 million kronor. This large importation of capital in the pre-industrial phase naturally contributed actively to facilitating the remolding of agriculture that took place.[6]

A further factor concerning the procurement of capital must be considered. About 1830 exporting of grain began on a small scale. It grew in importance and reached its maximum in the 1870s. The exports consisted mainly of oats, of which England

took the major share. There oats were used to provide the omni-
buses of that time with fuel (in the 1830s, London's largest transport enterprise employed more than 300,000 horses).

The expansion in the production capacity of agriculture thus
led not only to its becoming sufficient to support the growing
population, but also to a large surplus being made available for
export. Thus, the farmers had an important addition to income,
and through the multiplier effect this led to augmented income
formation in other sectors of industrial life. It helped to speed up
the demand on the home market for industrial goods. This
encouraged the beginning of a consumer-goods industry. Furthermore, the possibilities for loans on the foreign market were improved because the importing of agricultural products ceased to
be of importance in the 1830s. Continued agricultural imports
would have considerably checked the possibilities of borrowing
on foreign markets. The early economic development of agriculture may have been hindered by the relatively evenly distributed
production of different types of grain throughout the country,
which prevented production specialization and expansion of the
national grain trade. (Some irregularities in the distribution of
the resources would have increased trade, raised profits, and made
the share of trade in the economic growth more significant.)

Transformation of agriculture was unquestionably one of the
more important factors in the economic growth of Sweden. It contributed to the growth in capital and improved the opportunities
for rationalization in agriculture. Up to 1875, prices were rising
during the greater part of the period—with an inflationary peak
during the Crimean War and one at the beginning of the 1870s—
which ought to have made investments more profitable. The
credit institutions, created with agriculture as their best customer,
cooperated in channeling export profits to help enterprising
farmers.

All these factors combined can explain the transformation of
Swedish agriculture before the industrial transformation, and the

fact that these two changes did not occur simultaneously makes it easier to understand Sweden's economic growth. The industrial expansion occurred during an epoch when the problems of creating food supplies for the increasing nonagrarian population were largely solved. This is not meant to imply that agriculture had solved all its problems, only that the structural tensions had been reduced. About 1880, Sweden was again importing grain, and we get the impression that as a result of industrial development up to 1914 and emigration the agricultural labor force was diminished more rapidly than its productivity improved. The agricultural crisis during the 1880s and 1890s was perhaps not solely a reflection of changed conditions on the world market.[7]

History can be written in at least three ways: what has happened can be described without trying to explain the reasons for the development; the development can also be analyzed and attempts made to treat the underlying factors; or what might have happened had something else not happened instead can be discussed. This third method has long been cherished by historians because of the opportunities it gives for speculating without running any risk of proof to the contrary arising.

I do not intend to speculate in detail concerning the development that could have been the consequence of the stagnation of Swedish agriculture and its incapacity for yielding exports during the period before 1870. It need only be established that the transformation of Swedish agriculture took place before the Swedish industrial breakthrough. For a capital-poor country, such as Sweden was, this was crucial, because investments were largely concentrated in different sectors during different periods. This fact is important if one wishes to compare development in the underdeveloped countries of today with that of Sweden in those days—which has often been done. Today's problems are much more complicated, and an obstructive factor in the progress of the underdeveloped countries today is precisely the inability of agriculture to expand production in step with increasing population.

For Sweden this seems not to have been a problem. In other matters, too, resemblances to the problems of the underdeveloped countries of today are not particularly marked.

Agriculture has always had a low supply elasticity, which has frustrated rapid expansion. However, it is surprising to observe how rapidly Swedish agriculture responded to a heightened international demand during, for instance, the 1850s and the 1870s. It is not yet clear to what extent distribution of land through the parceling-out reform, land reclamation, or productivity improvement caused this supply elasticity, nor to what extent it was caused by unrational use of available resources, such as excess feeding of cattle, which with a strongly increased demand (e.g., at the beginning of the 1890s) could be modified. However, this capacity was an important factor in Sweden's economic development. Economic growth in Sweden depended not only on the industrial capacity of the country, but to an equal degree on its capacity to transform the agricultural sector.

One of the consequences of the development of agriculture was railway construction, which began during the 1850s. This was, to some extent, inspired by the demand of farmers for improved transportation to ports. The export industry joined in this demand, and during the 1870s, Sweden experienced a railway boom that has never been surpassed.

International Adaptation

Industrial development in Sweden up to the 1870s was to a considerable degree an adaptation to what was happening outside its borders and to a lesser degree an independent economic expansion. This was the case with the iron industry, which struggled with international competition and had to solve conversion difficulties in order not to lose contact with the international market. To an even greater extent, the expansion of the sawmill industry was, before the 1870s, a clear reflection of a larger demand from England and from those continental countries that were undergoing industrial development. The development of sawmill exports can be illustrated by a logistic curve. The inflection point is found in the 1880s; after that the rate of interest slackens up to World War I.[8]

The growth of the sawmill industry was stronger than that of almost every other area of economic expansion in Sweden before 1870. It can also be said to have had a decisive importance for the entire industrial development of the country. The multiplier-accelerator effect of the sawmill industry had importance not only for the capital-goods industry—which furnished the sawmills with machinery and in its turn led to an increased demand by the engineering industry for other products—but also for the consumer-goods industry, the boom in which can to some extent be seen as a reflection of the sawmill industry development.

The export industry thus came to be a driving force in the country's economic growth. The demand from foreign countries for Swedish products gave exporters and producers opportunities for expansion and enabled them to reduce their production costs. Investment activity influenced other industrial branches, whose production grew as the export industry expanded.

It was easier for the export industry than for the home-market industry to expand in a community such as the Swedish, with its low national income and poorly developed communications. The expansion in the export sector could take place before essential basic investments had been developed. Industrial expansion on the home market was delayed, being limited not only by low real income, but also by poor communications between regional markets. Investments in communications were therefore necessary in the initial industrialization phase in order to improve distribution facilities if an integrated home market was to be developed. However, because the demand for industrial products came from foreign markets, the industry could begin to expand before these investments were made. The industrial breakthrough in the 1870s coincided with rapidly constructed internal communications.

Because the export industry was first in Sweden's industrial development, it had no immediate need to compete with the home-market industries for labor and capital. Later, the competition between the two sectors became a stimulus mainly for the home-market industries, which urged innovations suitable for expanding their productivity. The expansion in the export sector therefore encouraged growth also in other sectors, partly owing to the bigger demand for export products having a multiplier-accelerator effect on other industrial branches and partly to "external economies."

Walter Hoffmann at the beginning of the 1930s investigated the distribution within a country's industrial structure of capital-goods industry and consumer-goods industry during the industrialization process.[9] As anticipated, he found that at the beginning of the industrialization phase, the consumer-goods industry dominated, but later its share was reduced and exceeded by the capital-goods industry. Hoffmann presumed that this development had general validity. As far as Sweden was concerned this "law" was not entirely correct. About 1870, before industrialization had seriously begun, the distribution between the two sectors was equal: both had approximately half of the production value in industry. According to Hoffmann's scheme such a distribution ought not to have been reached until considerably later. But the reason that Sweden fails to fit into the general pattern is easy to find. Swedish industrialization was a reflection of and an adaptation to conditions outside Sweden. The export industry was the dominant part in the capital-goods industry, and sawmills and the iron industry were responsible for the larger part of the production value of this sector. This resulted, in its turn, in an expansion in the consumer-goods industry.

The question then arises: why did the Swedish economy not

develop a structure similar to that of the raw-material-producing countries of today? Why did a "dual economy" not arise, with an advanced export sector and an underdeveloped home-market industry? Apart from historical analogies which are of dubious value, there are several factors that can be adduced in explanation.

Structure and Financing of Enterprises

One factor in Sweden's development has already been discussed. Not only industry but also agriculture had income from exports. This was advantageous for a balanced economic expansion. Another factor, also of considerable importance, was the emergence of an entrepreneurial class in Sweden. Industrial expansion brings with it, by definition, a high degree of investment. But investment is a subject that can be treated from different premises: (1) Who makes the investments? (2) How are the investments used? (3) What decisions lie behind the investments? All investments can also be classified as either private or public. In Sweden the state was responsible for the large basic investments in communications and education, and both these spheres of investment were essential for economic growth. In appraising industrial growth, however, interest must be concentrated on the private entrepreneur. A study of "entrepreneurial history" is of importance for the understanding of Swedish industrial expansion. "To study the entrepreneur is to study the central figure in modern economic history, and in my view the central figure in national economy," says, somewhat exaggeratedly, Professor Arthur Cole, who was one of the initiators of the Research Center in Entrepreneurial History at Harvard University.

The Swedish industrial entrepreneurs were recruited from a relatively small group. It is clear that the commercial houses, i.e., the wholesalers, founded most of the businesses in Sweden.[10] Most of the sawmills that were established, as well as enterprises in other branches, were initiated by merchants. From this small group were trained a large number of the entrepreneurs at the industrial breakthrough. These wholesalers, being both importers and exporters, had an international outlook. They saw the needs of the foreign market and reacted rapidly by founding or cooperating at the founding of the new export enterprises. The iron and timber industries had, at the beginning, the largest need for capital, because their plants were already of considerable size. In the iron industry, the promoting of new enterprises was slight. It was rather a modernizing of the old concerns that took place when the commercial houses with their capital resources came in as owners or reorganizers. In the timber industry, on the other hand, the merchants were also promoters of enterprises; in the engineering industry, too, the trading companies were there from the beginning. Within the latter branch, technicians were often initiators, whereas the commercial houses came in as financiers. Financing often took the form of short-term credits, for instance by promissory note guarantee, but in actual fact these were made long term by continual renewal, which was, naturally, a pressure on the liquidity of the enterprises.

The old idea in Sweden was that much of its working capital came from foreign countries. Professor Torsten Gårdlund's investigations of Swedish industrial financing have shown that this was not the case,[11] although foreign capital undoubtedly played a large role because it was probably in the form of marginal loans, which were of greater importance for the enterprises than their actual amount would lead us to suppose. Another factor in this connection, which Gårdlund does not discuss, is the importance of foreign short-term credits. It is clear, for instance in the sawmill industry and grain exports, that these credits played a large role.[12] The foreign trading houses made advance payments on coming deliveries with the result that the financing of the enterprises was facilitated; these short-term loans could be of considerable size. Without them, Swedish industry would not have been able to finance its operations as successfully as it did.

The reason that the commercial houses were able to engage themselves so strongly in promoting and financing enterprises was that, besides having sizable capital resources, their own trading yielded large profits. Up to the turn of the century, trading was for them still their essential business; after that their attention turned to financial operations. Their large profits resulted not so much from interest on the loans they made to industry as from the large commissions they were able to extract from sales. It is thus clear that merchants and commercial houses played a decisive role in spreading entrepreneurial operations in Sweden, and their attitudes toward these operations were more modern and the planning more far-sighted than those of most other leading entrepreneurs.

Sweden's old association with the European market, which mainly took place through the earlier exports of iron, became highly important because it enabled Swedish enterprises to recognize the possibilities for expansion and to use their foreign connections to relieve the country's capital shortage by allowing foreign buyers, through advance payments and short-term loans, to be responsible for a part of the operational financing.

In discussion of operational financing, incorporation must also be touched upon. Incorporation reduces the risks for individual financiers and simplifies capital accumulation (1) by facilitating the procurement of capital in such a manner that those who have capital become willing to invest, (2) by making it possible for smaller capital owners to contribute to productive investments, and (3) by the limited company form often being a condition for larger bank loans and for the issue of bonds. From the introduction of the limited company law in 1848 up to the 1860s, the attitude of the state toward the limited company form was restrictive and many applications were denied. After the 1860s, the attitude changed, and during the 1870s and 1880s, practically all applications were sanctioned.[13] However, the role of the state was to regulate, and it neither encouraged nor supported company formations. The number of new limited companies—whether they were newly formed enterprises or conversions of those already in existence—rose sharply during the first half of the 1870s, and the powerfully accelerated development during the 1890s resulted in the figures of the 1870s being for the first time exceeded. (See Table 4.) The increase during the twentieth century is due,

Table 4.   The Number of Newly Formed Limited Companies in Industry between 1866 and 1910

Years	No.	Years	No.	Years	No.
1866–1870	155	1881–1885	259	1896–1900	976
1871–1875	506	1886–1890	394	1901–1905	1,073
1876–1880	234	1891–1895	545	1906–1910	1,486

Source: Jörberg, "Growth and Fluctuations of Swedish Industry," p. 198.

above all, to the fact that small enterprises now also began to be operated in limited company form. Earlier it was chiefly the large enterprises which utilized the possibilities of safeguarding their owners from unlimited responsibility and which also had need for larger capital in their operations. It is not clear whether a rising economic activity is reflected in these figures during the twentieth century or whether a change took place in the attitude toward the limited company form. It is natural that the growth of Swedish industry meant not only that production grew and that the number of workers in industry increased, but also that a change occurred in the structure of production and ownership.

The limited company form was a driving force in Sweden's industrial development, at the same time as, during certain periods, it can be seen to be a consequence of this development. The limited company form created opportunities for more risk taking, and it is obvious that industrial production, to an increasingly high degree, occurred in enterprises that had the limited company form. In 1872, 45 percent of all workers were employed in limited companies; in 1912, the figure rose to almost 80 percent. (See Tables 5 and 6.)

Table 5.   The Percentage Increase in the Number of Industrial Workers in Limited Companies and Other Forms of Enterprises, 1872–1912

Years	Limited Companies	Other Forms	Years	Limited Companies	Other Forms
1872–1880	37.1	8.0	1897–1903	29.8	−4.2
1880–1889	82.6	49.8	1903–1912	24.1	−6.0

Source: Jörberg, "Growth and Fluctuations of Swedish Industry," p. 201.

Table 6.   The Average Number of Industrial Workers in Factories Owned by Limited Companies and in Other Forms of Enterprises, 1872–1912

Year	Limited Companies	Other Forms	Year	Limited Companies	Other Forms
1872	163	32	1897	101	33
1880	108	26	1903	82	29
1889	117	31	1912	75	26

Source: Jörberg, "Growth and Fluctuations of Swedish Industry," p. 202. The figures before 1897 do not include the sawmill industry or the iron and steel industry because of lack of statistical information concerning these branches.

The promotion of large-scale enterprises was facilitated also by the relatively new form of ownership. Alexander Gerschenkron has pointed out that the more backward a country is when it begins industrialization, the more likely it is that the first enterprises will be large. To some extent, this reasoning also applies to Sweden. The largest enterprises in Sweden had a greater share of the production in their segment of industry at the beginning of the 1870s than later. This does not mean that these enterprises were large from an international standpoint, but that in the main the number of enterprises was few and the range of products small, which thus made it easy for small enterprises to capture a large share of the market. This is in itself natural and not a peculiar characteristic of Swedish industrialization. In 1872, more than two-thirds of the workers in the Swedish industry were employed in enterprises each of which had more than 100 workers. This proportion fell during the course of the industrialization. (See Table 7.)

Table 7. Percentage Changes in the Number of Industrial Workers in Factories with Less Than 100, with 100–500, and with Over 500 Workers, 1872–1912

Years	Total	Less Than 100	100–500	Over 500
1872–1880	13.6	25.4	−1.6	25.9
1880–1889	66.0	51.9	67.8	97.0
1897–1903	19.1	25.5	13.0	22.8
1903–1912	16.3	12.8	17.8	22.1

Source: Jörberg, "Growth and Fluctuations of Swedish Industry," p. 150. The figures before 1897 do not include the sawmill industry or the iron and steel industry because of lack of statistical information concerning these branches.

However, the question is what amount of capital was required in the beginning in order to reach effective production. The size of the market naturally depends upon the demand, and the possibilities for development depend upon the slope of the demand curve. If the demand is strong or differentiated, a small capital investment may be sufficient to reach profitable production, and the enterprises may be relatively small without being less competitive than larger enterprises that can take advantage of large-scale operations. On the other hand, investments in, for example, railways must be made on a large scale. The initial costs are great, and not until the railway first comes into operation can income be realized. The fact that this capital-demanding type of investment was provided largely by the state freed the capital market in Sweden for less cost-demanding enterprises, which yield a more rapid profit.

This enterprise structure was advantageous for Swedish development. Many new articles of production were of such a nature that big investments were needed. These could only be provided by large enterprises. Because these latter were in the beginning often also without any competition worthy of mention, they could command high prices, and their increased profit was to a large extent diverted into new ventures. It is a characteristic feature of the large enterprises of that time that the owners' share of profits was often small compared with gross profits. At the same time, there was a negative factor in this development. Because communications were poor and the only available way for the enterprises to expand production was to find their markets nationally and not regionally, the enterprises were not quite able to utilize the advantages of large-scale operations. The optimum production size was, from an international standpoint, small. Also, the productivity in the larger enterprises was not higher than in the small. In many instances, the opposite was the case, particularly at the beginning of the industrial phase. The reason for this condition appears to have been the difficulty in organizing the enterprises in a rational manner and the lack of trained labor and technicians, which could have been a greater obstacle in the large enterprises than in the small ones.

A high degree of concentration does not necessarily mean that the leading enterprises had a dominant position on the market. The degree of market dominance depends on the size of the enterprises, on their product differentiation, on the existence of cartels, on enterprise integration, and finally, on the existence of international competition. In order to measure the importance of the concentration, it is not sufficient merely to measure the share of the enterprises in the national production; it is necessary to study the whole market.

A high concentration in the Swedish exports industry, for

example, did not mean that these enterprises had a dominant influence on the market. A high concentration has little meaning if the goods produced by the enterprise are easy to substitute for. There are, too, other factors. If demand increases rapidly, or if technical changes take place quickly, or if some form of product differentiation occurs, then under such conditions the dominance of the enterprises can easily be nullified. In this connection, it may be worthwhile to ponder the attempts of Swedish industry to master by cartels what the entrepreneurs considered to be a threatening overproduction. The forming of cartels need not become desirable only after overproduction has actually occurred; even when a balance exists between supply and demand, entrepreneurs might already feel themselves threatened. Cartels occurred prominently in the home-market industry; the agreements between the export enterprises were less extensive. Price cartels were predominant. However, proposals were made very early for more extensive cartels in, for example, the sugar industry; a sugar trust was discussed as early as the 1870s but was not introduced until 1907. Certain special enterprises in the engineering industry tried also to include enterprises in Norway in a cartel. Although this suggestion was not carried through, it was very advanced in form. The sawmill industry tried to forge an international link during the economic recession in the 1880s, when an attempt was made to interest both Finnish and Russian enterprises in making an agreement concerning restrictions in production. It is evident that in the branches of industry where production concentration was greatest, the possibilities for carteling were more easily accomplished. Home-market industries with a low degree of concentration were, for example, footwear and ready-to-wear clothing; to this group belonged also the engineering industry. In the latter, product differentiation was more important than forming cartels. (See Table 8.)

At the end of the 1880s, a protectionistic tariff policy was introduced in Sweden. Several authorities consider this to be a factor

Table 8.   The Three Largest Enterprises' Percentage Share of the
Production Value in Certain Industrial Branches, 1872–1912

Branch	1872	1880	1897	1912
Margarine			89	71
Flour mills	..	..	23	31
Sugar	54	59	43	98
Cotton	29	21	26	27
Wool	29	26	29	25
Leather	30	24	23	31
Footwear		95	36	17
Sawmills	..	..	11	7
Paper and pulp	50	20	15	13
Cement		100	84	72
Matches	59	56	57	82
Nonelectrical engineering	40	24	11	10
Electrical engineering		100	92	92
Iron and steel	..	..	23	24

Source: Jörberg, "Growth and Fluctuations of Swedish Industry," p. 170.

of importance for the growth of Swedish industry. It is possible
that home-market industries derived some advantage from this
policy. It gave enterprises a certain monopolistic position in the
home market, but prevented formation of international cartels.
However, it cannot be shown that this tariff policy was a decisive
factor in Sweden's industrial development. Because industrialization was rapid and because demand grew quickly, it was only during certain depression periods that tariff protection became useful.

Enterprise integration and fusions between enterprises were
hardly decisive for industrial growth. They were instead a consequence of technical development. When good communications
(both railways and post and telegraphs) were introduced, management could for the first time efficiently supervise an enterprise
that had several factories; it was not until the 1890s that such
developments began to appear generally in Sweden. It was the
same with cartels. Cartel organizations in which the members
could not easily communicate with and supervise one another

were of no value. Many enterprises found this out during the 1870s and 1880s, when quite a few cartels were formed but very soon ceased to function.

The Boom of the 1870s

The 1870s mark the beginning of Sweden's industrial breakthrough. As is obvious from the foregoing, by "breakthrough" I do not mean that industrial development appears for the first time. Industrialization had increased, although to a limited extent, since the 1830s. By "breakthrough" I mean a marked acceleration in development, a break in the previous trend; and furthermore, there were institutional changes and changes in production, so that we can speak of a new situation after this acceleration compared with what existed before. The boom period in the 1870s brought about these changes; therefore the industrial breakthrough in Sweden can be dated to this decade.

During the 1870s, extensive investment occurred in almost all sectors of industry, as well as in railway construction and house building. Agricultural exports increased strongly at the end of the 1870s. The production value of the capital-goods industry more than doubled during the boom period up to 1875; industrial investments increased more than 80 percent and national income more than 30 percent, measured in stable money value, during the first five years of the 1870s: an increase almost twice as great as during any following quinquennium up to 1914. Economic expansion was encouraged by a strong foreign demand for Swedish export goods, and expansion of export industries was greater than that of home-market industries. An inflationary rise in prices at the beginning of the 1870s created large profits, which to a considerable extent were used for further investments. The money market was, moreover, marked by low interest. This situation was typical of the Swedish capital market during the last decades of the nineteenth century and is explained by the fact that the expansion was "imported," i.e., the large profits from exporting were transferred to the capital market. (See Table 9.)

Table 9.   Percentage Annual Changes in the Value of Exports, Imports, and Industrial Production, 1869–1879

Years	Exports	Imports	Industrial Production
1869–1871	+20	+10	+ 5
1871–1874	+14	+27	+17
1874–1875	−9	−13	−5
1875–1877	+2	+7	0
1877–1879	−8	−14	−10

Source: Jörberg, "Growth and Fluctuations of Swedish Industry," p. 224.

The extension of the railways was unquestionably important for industrial expansion. Transport costs fell considerably, and the development of communications thus lowered expenses for industrial enterprises at the same time that it facilitated the marketing of products. Lower transport costs resulted in cheaper raw materials, which in turn reduced the prices of the products; this in its turn could contribute to a reduction in the costs of railway construction. Cheaper fuel for ironworks, for example, led to cheaper steel prices, which reduced the costs of rails and other railway material.

The railways in Sweden did not always run through already densely populated areas. The main line from Skåne to Stockholm traversed relatively underdeveloped and thinly populated districts. Large investments were therefore made in the new communities that developed around the railway stations, often outside old community centers. These investments contributed to the acceleration of economic development in the 1870s. They had a strong income-increasing effect on other sectors of industrial life. The railways themselves influenced relocation of the population from areas relatively low in productivity to more productive ones. The gains resulting from this may have been as considerable as the direct effects of railway investments.

The financing of the railways was handled mostly through state-arranged foreign loans. Thus, the supply of capital for other investments was not reduced. During the period 1855–1860, state grants toward railway construction amounted to almost 34 million kronor, but it was during the 1870s that railway construction was given a really considerable boost.[14] In that decade, railroads in Sweden were extended by an average of 14 percent annually, i.e., construction more than trebled during that period and railway trackage reached a total of more than 5000 kilometers, whereas the rate of extension after that up to 1914 was about 3 percent annually.

In the 1870s, then, decisive changes in communications took place. At the same time, however, structural changes occurred in investment activity in industry. Production became more capital-demanding, and because investments were especially large in capital-goods enterprises, there were repercussions in other sectors of industry. The iron and steel industry made large investments at the beginning of the 1870s. The Bessemer process was successful, and other technical improvements were adopted. These technical changes led to cheaper production and had therefore more profound effects on the production structure than price-reducing measures had in consumer-goods industries. It is true that they demanded relatively large nonrecurrent infusions of capital, and often investments that were larger than the immediate demand required; but this in its turn led to cheaper products and thereby increased the opportunities for investment in other industrial sectors, which used products from, for instance, the iron and steel industry.

The increasing mechanization within industry is reflected to some degree in the imports of coal and coke. These rose by 150 percent between 1869 and 1878, but by only 66 percent between

1880 and 1890. Although these imports also reflect the rapid railway extension during the 1870s, they nonetheless give an idea of the scope of investment and thereby the technical changes upon which the expansion was based.

The export sector increased its production almost in step with demand, but to judge from prices, production in the iron and steel industry was not quite in step with demand. Production stagnated, but prices during the years 1871–1873 continued to rise in the international market as well as in the Swedish. This development chiefly became noticeable in the iron industry because the investments there required a longer time before results could be realized and more capital was needed than, for example, in the sawmill industry, which, broadly speaking, managed to supply the increased international demand. The growth in the export sector changed the distribution of production factors and expanded productivity. The entrepreneurs there, to a large extent, used their augmented income for productive purposes.

The depression at the end of the 1870s was the first which obviously influenced the Swedish economy, and it was also the most severe up to 1914. Because of the close connection of Sweden's economy with the international market, we could expect that the business cycles in Sweden would be in agreement with the international ones—as by and large they were—but also that they would show a similar amplitude—which was not the case. Swedish economic development proceeded quietly with only slight fluctuations. Exports naturally fluctuated rather more than did production and had shorter waves than those of home-market industries.

It is difficult to establish the extent to which a strong increase in demand for agricultural products supported Sweden's economic growth during the industrial decline at the end of the 1870s. However, the industrial expansion that had begun earlier in the 1870s continued, with slight variations in percentage growth, up to 1914. This obviously refers to industrial development as a whole. The various industrial sectors showed a more

complicated development. (See Table 10.) Many countries have
passed through an expansion process similar to that of Sweden in
the 1870s. Not all, however, have been able to take advantage of

Table 10. The Annual Percentage Growth in the Production
Value of Swedish Industrial Sectors, 1867–1869 to 1912

Sector	1867–1869 to 1892–1895	1896–1912
Paper, pulp, and graphics	6.1	11.0
Gravel, stone, clay, and allied industries	6.0	5.3
Food (including tobacco)	5.1	4.0
Chemicals	4.5	7.3
Metals and engineering	3.7	7.0
Timber	3.7	2.0
Iron and steel	3.2	2.2
Textiles	2.6	5.6
Leather, hair, and rubber	1.7	10.0
Capital goods	5.2	6.2
Consumer goods	3.3	6.1

Source: Jörberg, "Growth and Fluctuations of Swedish Industry,"
pp. 61, 63.

expansion to continue building up their economy without, after
a longer or shorter time, having the expansion come to a halt.

Sweden's development differs very little from that common to
Western Europe. However, the Swedish expansion was of later
date and had a more rapid start than that of, for example, France
or Germany. The question is whether any causes can be found for
this development in Sweden which were lacking or less obvious
in other Western European countries. In relation to the rest of
Western Europe, Sweden was unquestionably a country that was
economically less advanced. It would thus appear that Sweden
had certain advantages for its further expansion. The availability
of capital exports from England and France to Sweden can be
pointed to as an example. The economic infrastructure and the
costly investments associated with it were built up with the aid of

foreign capital. This led to industry having greater opportunities for internal financing since the scarcity of capital was alleviated. We can also point to the fact that the wages of the Swedish workers were lower than, for instance, the German and considerably lower than the English, which from a competitive standpoint was to the advantage of Swedish enterprises even if it was not so for the workers. The most discussed advantage of a late economic start is that of being able to utilize the technical knowledge of more advanced countries. It is obvious that Sweden had some advantage from this circumstance. It imported a number of technicians, chiefly from England, who were employed in, for instance, the textile industry, engineering, and railway construction. When the Swedish rubber industry was projected in the 1890s, Russian experts were introduced. But the technical gap between any two European countries was much smaller in the nineteenth century than it is today between the underdeveloped and the advanced countries. The advantage to Sweden from the opportunity of importing technical knowledge could not have been of decisive importance for its industrialization. Nor can we argue that the rapid industrial development of the 1870s implies that Sweden was very much more retarded than any other country in Western Europe. National income calculations for this time are consistently unreliable and say very little about the general living standard. But if Kuznets's calculations can be believed, the difference between Sweden and Western Europe was slight in this respect, even though Sweden had lower national income per capita than most Western European countries.[15]

Sweden's rapid development in the 1870s thus cannot be ascribed mainly to its backwardness, but to other factors. The simplest available explanation is, again, its ability to satisfy the demand from foreign sources for exports from a limited sector of its economy. But this ability depended on the fact that it had, during the preceding decades, changed and stimulated its economic development in, for example, the sphere of agriculture;

that teaching and education had been assigned a relatively high status even from an international standpoint; that communications had been developed, although railway construction had its first large upswing during the 1870s; that its iron industry had been long occupied in channeling production into larger and more rational units; and that legislation concerning trade had been modernized and old decrees that regulated industrial life abolished. Only in the obvious fact that England, as the leading industrial nation, was of considerable help to all other European countries in their economic expansion can we find that Sweden profited largely by coming later to industrial devlopment.

The Development from 1880 to 1914

Sweden, after a rapid start in the 1870s, succeeded in continuing its economic expansion at a high rate. What factors contributed to this development? And is it possible to find that some differed from those that led to the general expansion occurring in other European countries during the same period?

Between the middle of the 1880s and the start of World War I, the volume of Swedish exports increased one and a half times. A certain transformation of the structure of exports occurred also. The share of the old staple goods was reduced. Grain exports ceased and were replaced by exports of meat and dairy produce, chiefly butter. Exports of paper pulp and paper, processed products of the timber industry, increased. A new raw material came on the market, namely iron ore, which together with the products of the engineering industry was responsible for the most rapid expansion. Iron ore represented the old type of Swedish exports, raw materials, whereas the engineering industry represented a new type, which demonstrated that Swedish economic development had reached a certain degree of independence. (See Table 11.)

One factor that to a high degree influenced the Swedish economy was the improvement in its terms of trade for almost the

Table 11. The Percentage Distribution of Swedish Exports by
Commodity Group, 1881–1913

Commodity Group	1881–1885	1891–1895	1901–1905	1911–1913
Timber	40.4	37.1	38.5	26.1
Iron and steel	16.2	9.5	10.2	9.3
Grain	11.7	4.7	0.4	0.3
Butter	6.3	12.0	8.9	6.0
Paper and pulp	4.6	8.3	12.9	17.6
Iron ore		0.4	5.0	8.0
Engineering products	2.6	3.1	6.7	10.5
Others	18.7	22.8	17.6	21.6

Source: G. Fridlizius, "Sweden's Exports 1850–1960," *Economy and History*, vol. 6 (1963).

entire period after 1860. During the early 1870s, the terms of trade were extremely advantageous for Sweden. Its export prices rose more than import prices until about 1875; they then deteriorated up to the depression of 1879. Thereafter a new improvement came about, and for a short period from the end of the 1880s, the advantage of export over import prices was very strong—about 20 percent. In this phase the cause was not the same as had operated during the 1870s, i.e., that Swedish export prices rose at a greater rate than import prices; rather it was that the import prices fell considerably whereas the prices of export commodities could be maintained.

Arthur Lewis has pointed out that terms of trade swung to the disadvantage of the raw-material-producing countries after 1883.[16] He says also that the reasons for this were increased production in these countries, immigration, reallocation of land, and capital investments, as well as reduction in the costs of transport. He is probably generally correct in this argument. However, we should remember that export prices were reckoned f.o.b. and import prices c.i.f. If transport costs fell considerably, as happened at the end of the nineteenth century, this did not necessarily imply that the prices which the raw-material-producing countries received were lower than earlier. Terms of trade may have been improved in the industrialized countries, thanks to lowered transport costs, which reduced the c.i.f. price. Terms of trade may also have been improved for the raw-material-producing countries for the same reason. To explain the absence of economic expansion in the raw-material-producing countries by referring to the fact that the raw-material prices fell in the industrialized countries is thus to identify only a part, and perhaps not the most important part, of a causal sequence.

In the 1870s Swedish exports consisted of about 50 percent raw materials; this increased during the 1890s when iron ore began to be shipped in larger amounts. Terms-of-trade improvement in Swedish foreign trade was true for both raw materials and manufactured goods. The raw materials that Sweden exported were predominantly of a type for which there was a big demand on the European market; they were in many cases essential materials for European industrialization. The improved prices for Swedish export goods naturally also meant that imports could be increased more than if there had not been improved terms of trade. The rising costs of imports could be met as well as installment and interest payments on the large loans that were taken for railway construction and other purposes.

Rising prices contributed to Sweden's economic growth both by facilitating capital accumulation and by stimulating social action. Falling prices had the opposite effect. In Sweden, prices were rising throughout the greater part of the nineteenth century. When prices fell, as happened after the depressions of the 1870s, 1880s, and up to the middle of the 1890s, the decline was less accentuated than in many other European countries. This may have contributed to Swedish economic expansion during the period up to 1914. Industrial profits were not satisfactory to the same degree during the 1880s as earlier or later, but measured according to volume, Swedish industry showed hardly any reces-

sion during this time. Whereas the investments of the 1870s, and
even more so of the 1880s, had an extensive nature, i.e., enlarged
the spheres where capital was employed, the development later
turned toward a more intensive use of capital per worker. The
degree of mechanization is the measure of the capital intensity
available. It shows little variation during the period, and one can
argue that the somewhat worse economic climate of the 1880s was
a driving force in the increased degree of mechanization. The
number of workers increased much more slowly than the amount
of horsepower used in all sectors of industry, but the increase in
horsepower per worker was slower duing the 1880s than during
the previous decade. It is hardly original to state that industrialization implies a substitution of machinery for labor. As a growth
factor, mechanization was important, and it was largely facilitated
by the fact that the prices for Swedish export products were maintained; the improved productivity enhanced the competitive
power of Swedish industry. Both mechanization and price development contributed to Sweden's rapid economic expansion.

Economic expansion in Sweden occurred at the same time that
all the countries in Western Europe strongly increased their industrial potential. (The shift of employment in Sweden toward
industry is shown in Table 12.) It was thus, in part, a reflection
of international developments, and for a country heavily dependent on its foreign trade, the abolition or reduction of tariffs and
other trade barriers was important. (Swedish timber exports first
attained really large proportions when tariffs were reduced and

Table 12. Percentage Changes in Population Employed in Agriculture
and Industry, 1870–1910

Sector	1870–1880	1880–1890	1890–1900	1900–1910
Agriculture	3	—4	—5	—5
Industry	30	31	37	24
Total population	10	5	7	8

Source: *Sweden's Historical Statistics*, part I (Stockholm, 1955).

later free trade was introduced in England and France at the middle of the nineteenth century.) During the 1880s, a protectionistic tariff policy was initiated in most European countries—including Sweden—as a consequence of, among other things, the poor competitive situation of European agriculture in relation to the United States and other transoceanic countries. The increased tariff protection ought therefore to have obstructed continued expansion during the 1880s and the 1890s. But just as it is difficult to establish the importance of Swedish tariff protection for Swedish industry, so it is difficult to measure the importance of increased tariff protection in other countries for the development of Swedish exports. Although it can be established that a certain redistribution of exports took place, this need not have been a consequence of increased tariffs but can be associated with the increasingly reduced costs of transport, which made Swedish commodities competitive in extra-European markets.

During the third acceleration period for Swedish industry, i.e., during the 1890s (see Table 13), the home market had a greater

Table 13.   Biennial Percentage Changes in the Value of Exports, Imports, and Industrial Production, 1893–1900

Biennium	Exports	Imports	Industrial Production
1893–1895	2.5	3.4	4.0
1895–1897	7.4	8.5	13.0
1897–1898	−4.8	11.8	9.9
1898–1900	6.4	8.5	8.7

Source: Jörberg, "Growth and Fluctuations of Swedish Industry," p. 186.

importance than earlier. The home-market sector expanded at the same rate as the export sector and was responsible for about half of the value of production before World War I—thus it had the same share as it had around 1870. The competitive capacity of

Swedish industry was sufficient to withstand the attempts of foreign countries to conquer the Swedish market; this was shown by, among other things, its ability before 1914 to begin competing in foreign markets with typical home-market products such as textiles and footwear. In addition an increasing proportion of capital-goods production remained within the country.

Erik Dahmén has said in his book *Svensk industriell företagarverksamhet* [Swedish Industrial Entrepreneurial Activity] that limited sales possibilities in the home market were a hindrance to Swedish industrial development before World War I. He points out that innovations within the sector might not have taken place because of a too-limited market and consequently too-limited returns on investment in new machinery or development of new techniques. This, in his view, was the situation in several branches of the engineering industry during the initial industrial phase in Sweden. During the 1890s, however, the engineering industry entered a new phase in which a powerfully expanding sector, based in some cases on Swedish inventions (separators, turbines, internal combustion engines, gas accumulators, and ball bearings), was directed to international competition; there was also a slowly growing sector directed to regional markets and only slightly specialized. The latter often consisted of small enterprises with low profits, partly because of lack of specialization and partly because of strong competition. Whereas exports of engineering products increased by more than 50 percent in each five-year period after 1889, imports increased scarcely half that amount. This means that the expansion of the Swedish engineering industry was sufficient to satisfy to an ever greater extent a growing demand by the home market as well as to increase exports.

A further example of the capacity of Swedish industry to supply its home market is found in the textile industry, especially the wool sector, which increased its production value from approximately 20 million kronor about 1890 to 70 million about 1910. At the end of the 1880s national production satisfied 65 percent of

Swedish consumption; immediately before World War I it was capable of supplying 80 percent of the home-market demand.

It was mainly during typical boom years that the spread of innovations was greatest; this also led to a considerable increase in number of enterprises. There was some difference in investment activity during the various business cycles. During the 1880s, which were thought to be a "poor" decade because of the then falling prices (although, despite this, increase in volume of production was considerable—about 5 percent per annum), investments were clearly extensive, i.e., the capital per worker rose slowly, the increase in investments being due to the rise in the number of workers; in the boom period during the 1890s investment activity was intensive, i.e., the capital per worker rose more quickly than the number of workers. A development similar to that of the 1880s occurred after the accelerated expansion of the 1890s, which was followed by a slowing down in investments within the larger enterprises. Investments that were extensive rather than intensive were made, which broadened the base of industrial development by establishing new enterprises.

It is obvious that the variations in exports are of utmost importance in explaining the fluctuations of Swedish industry. The income that exports brought in varying extent to industry reacted on the formation of income in the country by the multiplier effect of the export increase. Except for the depression in the 1870s, there were evidently only a few primary causes for the turn of the market within the country. The business cycle in the 1870s differed to some extent from the following cycles. The crisis at the end of the 1870s was naturally affected by the international depression. It seems also, however, to have been affected by the investment boom (broken by the economic decline); in many instances investments had proved faulty because of the inability of the whole economy to change within a short time from an agrarian to a partly industrial community. The hasty construction of new industries resulted in problems of balance. "The development blocs" were not ready; this resulted in industry's having difficulty settling those tensions which thereby arose. Other cyclical variations could to a large extent be explained by the dominant influence on exports by international business cycles and the further influence of exports on Swedish industry. The repercussions of the fluctuations were of comparatively slight importance as a hindrance to Sweden's industrial expansion. The economic declines, except for the depression in the 1870s, were mild. The explanation for this stability is naturally very complicated. I can only indicate certain points which evidently were factors moderating and leveling out the fluctuations of industry.

As a basis for reasoning concerning cyclical variations, expansive and structural changes must be emphasized. Industrial expansion during the second half of the nineteenth century and up to World War I resulted in a change in Sweden's economic structure. The share of industry in the national product increased, a change occurred in the nature of industrial production, and production techniques were improved. This is a normal industrial process and does not explain cyclical variations. International development facilitated Swedish industrialization by virtue of the fact that the demand for Swedish products, such as iron, timber, and paper, led to increased Swedish exports, and this resulted in increased opportunities for expansion in other industrial sectors. The expansion of the 1870s and the 1890s occurred during periods when there were strong rises in prices, which contributed to large profits for industry. This led to increased investments, which in their turn contributed to an acceleration rate of development. Industrial expansion was also distinguished by increased differentiation. New commodities, new methods, and new markets were created and helped to maintain expansion on a higher level even in those periods when the export industries were affected by international depressions. We can point to the breakthrough of the beet-sugar industry at the end of the 1880s; to the expansion of the ready-to-wear clothing industry, of the rubber industry, of the carpentry industry, of the paper pulp industry, and of the superphosphate industry in the 1890s; or to the origin of new products in the engineering industry, such as dairy machinery and internal combustion engines; to new ingot steel processes in the iron industry, which led in turn to a rapid expansion of iron mining and so on. When the market expanded, industrial production could increase, which naturally resulted in lower costs and also to a certain substituting of home production for imported goods. The protectionistic tariff policy of 1888 and 1892 may have contributed by creating the basis for home production of, for example, the footwear industry and the jute industry, although it is difficult to determine the influence of the tariffs on the development of production.

One of the obstacles to Swedish industrialization was the limited home market at the beginning of the period. Many of the enterprises created in the general optimism that existed during the boom of the 1870s must have discovered that the demand for their products was insufficient to enable them to operate profitably. Furthermore, poor communications were an obstacle to an integrated national market, and they hampered production development. Not until these obstacles had been removed could Swedish industry enter a self-generating phase. In the 1890s it reached the stage where its income-producing effect was so large that fluctuations in some sectors of industrial life including exports were of less importance. The demand by Swedish industry for Swedish industrial commodities played an increasingly important role. This demand naturally depended to some extent on the development of the export sector but the importance of the latter for income formation within the country was diminished because of the stability of the home-market sector. Industrialization resulted in an expanded production at the cost of imports. The expansion of the home-market sector, especially during the 1890s, was stronger than the increase in demand. Because the consumer-goods sector was less sensitive to business cycles than the exports sector, this increase in the degree of economic independence contributed to leveling out fluctuations and facilitated industrial expansion.

The stability which was established for the expansion of industry can also to some extent be explained by the investments that were put into railway construction and into housing during periods of economic decline. Also, agricultural exports were to a large extent of a countercyclical nature, and these exports amounted to about one-fifth of total exports up to the turn of the century. It must be remembered as well that almost three-quarters of the population of Sweden in 1870 and almost half in 1910 were supported by agriculture. This sector of the economy probably had a stabilizing effect on industrial production, because the demand from this segment of the population was largely unaffected by the fluctuations in industry. The introduction of protective tariffs in the 1880s may also have prevented a reduction in agricultural ·income, which would have affected farmer demand for products.

Industrial growth, however, was concentrated in a few well-identified boom periods (see Table 14), during which there

Table 14.   Percentage Changes in the Value of Exports, Imports, and Industrial Production, and in the Number of Workers in Industry, 1871–1909

| Years | Exports | | Imports | | No. of | |
	All	Industrial Products	All	Industrial Products	Industrial Production	Industrial Workers
1871–1874	+43	+51	+82	+87	+37	+15
1876–1878	−19	−18	−18	−22	−16	−10
1881–1883	+14	+12	+16	+16	+14	+7
1885–1886	−8	−10	−12	−11	−1	+2
1887–1889	+20	+27	+29	+29	+13	+23
1890–1893	+10	+8	−12	−17	+10	−1
1898–1900	+13	+18	+18	+14	+18	+8
1900–1901	−10	−11	−13	−12	−2	−1
1904–1907	+26	+24	+17	+24	+27	+8
1907–1909	−10	−8	−9	−14	−7	−5

Source: Jörberg, "Growth and Fluctuations of Swedish Industry," p. 338.

occurred an accelerated expansion in production and also in real wages for industrial workers. In the forty-year period up to 1910, the largest expansion in production occurred during the boom periods 1871–1874, 1898–1900, and 1904–1907; and the rise in real wages occurred during three periods: 1869–1875, 1881–1887, and 1892–1896.[17] The latter thus did not altogether follow the pattern for expansion in production owing to the fact that real wages did not always rise in step with nominal wages; this can also help to explain the relatively mild depressions during the 1880s and the 1890s.

These expansion periods coincided with international economic developments. But the fact that developments outside Sweden facilitated Swedish expansion does not explain how the Swedish economy could change and take advantage of the opportunities created. The role of agriculture has been emphasized here as well as the importance of the entrepreneurs and the fact that the state was responsible for basic investments—investments made with capital borrowed largely in foreign countries—which aided the formation of national capital and relieved capital scarcity. To this must be added technical developments leading to the establishment of a number of industries based upon Swedish inventions. Population diversification was also a factor which contributed to the change from an agrarian community to an industrial community. Emigration was probably not solely a negative element but may have contributed to simplifying the shift. The conclusion to be drawn from the foregoing discussion must be that the Swedish nation had a large capacity for change and showed a decided ability for creating a stable development.

Notes

1. *Report of Sweden's Economic and Financial Development during the Years 1834–1860* (Stockholm, 1863), the appendix tables; hereafter cited as finance committee's report.

2. W. W. Rostow, *Stages of Economic Growth* (Cambridge, Mass., 1960); W. W. Rostow, "The Take-off into Sustained Growth," in Rostow, ed., *Proceedings*

of a Conference Held by the International Economic Association (London, 1963); A. Gerschenkron, *Economic Backwardness in Historical Perspective* (Cambridge, Mass., 1963).

3. P. N. Rosenstein-Rodan, "Notes on the Theory of the 'Big Push,' " Center for International Studies, MIT (mimeographed; Cambridge, Mass., 1957); S. Kuznets, in Rostow, ed., *Proceedings*; H. Leibenstein, *Economic Backwardness and Economic Growth* (New York, 1957); H. J. Habakkuk, "The Historical Experience on the Basic Conditions of Economic Progress," in *Economic Progress* (Louvain, 1955).

4. E.g., J. S. Duessenberry, *Business Cycles and Economic Growth* (Cambridge, Mass., 1958).

5. E. Höjer, *Svensk befolkningsutveckling* [Swedish Population Growth] (Stockholm, 1959).

6. Finance committee's report, Table XXII, p. 83.

7. G. Fridlizius, *Swedish Corn Export in the Free Trade Era* (Lund, 1957). See also Jörn Svensson, *Jordbruk och depression 1870–1900* (Lund, 1965).

8. E. Söderlund, *Svensk trävaruexport under 100 år* [Swedish Timber Exports during 100 Years] (Stockholm, 1951).

9. W. Hoffmann, *Stadien und typen der industrialisierung* (Jena, 1931). English edition: *The Growth of Industrial Economies* (Manchester, 1958).

10. T. Gårdlund, *Industrialismens samhälle* [The Society of Industrialism] (Stockholm, 1942).

11. T. Gårdlund, *Svensk industrifinansiering under genombrottsskedet 1830– 1913* [Swedish Industrial Financing during the Breakthrough Period 1830–1913] (Stockholm, 1947).

12. Söderlund, *Svensk trävaruexport*, and *Skandinaviska banken 1864–1914* (Stockholm, 1964); see also Fridlizius, *Swedish Corn Export in the Free Trade Era*.

13. C. A. Nilsson, "Business Incorporations in Sweden 1849–1896," *Economy and History*, vol. 2 (1960).

14. Finance committee's report, p. 118.

15. S. Kuznets, "Quantitative Aspects of the Economic Growth of Nations, I–II," *Economic Development and Cultural Change*, vol. 5 (1956–1957).

16. W. A. Lewis, *Economic Survey 1919–1938* (London, 1963).

17. G. Bagge, E. Lundberg, and I. Svennilsson, *Wages in Sweden 1860–1930* (Stockholm, 1935).

Introduction to Chapter 5

The nineteenth century's dominant political and economic philosophy was liberalism. Very few historians would quarrel with that statement. However, when one tries to examine liberalism— its ideology, its social roots, and the political activities of liberal politicians—all sorts of difficulties arise. Indeed definition of the very word "liberalism" can be so difficult that productive research on the phenomenon can be seriously affected. The next essay is an analysis of the methodological problems arising from attempts to study liberalism in its social-political context. How one should approach the study of practical intellectual history has already been the subject of much discussion among Swedish scholars and Docent Göran B. Nilsson's ideas develop from their work as well as from his own research experience which has to a large extent focused upon liberal figures and movements at mid-nineteenth century. In general Swedish historians have shown a greater concern for methodological problems than their counterparts in Great Britain and the United States. Docent Nilsson's essay will give the reader not only an excellent insight into the question of how to treat intellectual history but also an example of how thorough Swedish historians are in their approach to methodological problems. Because Docent Nilsson wished to make a contribution to the current debate on how one should examine liberalism, he assumed that the reader had somewhat more than a beginner's understanding of the actual historical development of Sweden at mid-century. This assumption may prove to be slightly optimistic and the following comments should help the reader understand the general historical context of Docent Nilsson's analysis.

The hottest political question in mid-nineteenth-century Sweden was the representative nature of the Riksdag. Historically, the Riksdag had been made up of representatives of the four estates: nobles, clergy, townspeople (burghers), and farmers (peasants). Although the system of representation had been examined briefly during the writing of the 1809 constitution, the historical form was preserved. In 1830 the issue was raised anew by a concrete proposal for "national representation," i.e., abolition of the four estates, put forth by a provincial judge, J. G. Richter, and an estate holder, C. H. Anckarsvärd. According to their proposal, the largest portion of the parliamentary representatives would be chosen in a common election but with a very limited suffrage. The timing of this proposal suggests that the general political upsurge of the European middle classes had a counterpart in Sweden. The middle classes had increased their political power considerably through the July revolution in France (1830) and the parliamentary reforms in Great Britain in 1832. These general political developments in Europe obviously influenced the growing demand for reform of the Riksdag.

When Oskar I began his reign in 1844, there was great hope that a period of liberalism was at hand and that the Riksdag would be reformed. The question of representation was studied by a special governmental committee but its views were criticized by both liberals and conservatives. Under the influence of the revolutions of 1848, the general mood became more radical. Demonstrations were held demanding the vote be given to nearly all eligible males and the Riksdag was even presented with a royal reform proposal which was considerably more radical than anything that could have been imagined in 1847. However, by the beginning of the Riksdag's session for 1850–1851, the mood of the country had changed once more and the radical ideas of 1848 were no longer in vogue. Oskar's reform proposal was cast aside. During his entire reign, the representation issue remained unsettled. Only in 1865 under the leadership of Louis de Geer's government was the problem finally solved by the Riksdag. The four-chamber system was replaced by a two-house legislature in which the upper chamber was elected indirectly, primarily through a newly reformed local governmental body which guaranteed the complete dominance of a wealthy minority. The direct suffrage forms for the lower house gave rural political elements control of it. Many Swedish liberals did not themselves fully realize the extent of control that the agrarians could exercise over the lower house.

It is difficult not to see the changes of 1865 as a fundamentally conservative reform. The potential number of participants in the electoral process showed at least initially a slight decrease. The new urban groups found themselves by and large cut off from direct representation. True, the agrarians, particularly the large landowners, increased their influence at the expense of some of the more traditional holders of power. But the ever-increasing poor peasantry and rural workers were completely disenfranchised. The fear of the House of Nobles that the new reform would open the floodgates of revolution proved unfounded. Swedish political life continued after 1865 to be dominated by conservative forces.

In the two decades following 1865, the free-trade issue was at the center of the political arena. During the 1850s there had been a general European movement toward the establishment of free trade, which was a cherished goal of liberal economic thought. This movement had a direct influence on the Swedish development, particularly through Minister of Finance J. A. Gripenstedt. During the 1850s and 1860s Sweden reduced its tariffs dramatically and removed most of the domestic hindrances to an open market. During the 1880s reaction against free trade developed, primarily as a result of the protectionist trade policy adopted by Germany in 1879. Swedish free traders were forced to compromise under externally produced pressures.

In questions of foreign policy Pan-Scandinavianism was the critical issue. This movement was potentially a response to the growing power of Germany in the south and Russia in the east. But the liberals were divided. For many Pan-Scandinavianism was a matter of top priority whereas others saw it as political adventurism and wanted to concentrate on the economic and political development of Sweden. Pan-Scandinavianism was also complicated by the intentions of the Swedish royal house to use the movement for its own dynastic ambitions. When Pan-Scandinavianism was put to the test during the Danish-Prussian war of 1864, it fell of its own weight. The promise of the Swedish king to send Swedish troops to aid Denmark proved to be valueless and Sweden left Denmark to its own fate. The ambiguity and divisions within liberal ranks in Sweden over foreign-policy questions can also be found on similar types of problems in liberal circles on the continent.

Another area that typically represents liberal activity was that of domestic legal reform. By 1864 the legal principle of complete domestic economic freedom had been established. Every citizen had the right to choose his own occupation. Even women slowly began to receive a certain measure of legal freedom. In 1858 unmarried women were given the right to be considered legally responsible. In the matter of religious freedom, Sweden was considerably behind the times. It was not until 1860 that Swedes were given the right to resign from the state Lutheran church, but even then only if the state approved the new church to which the citizen wished to belong. At least legally, open atheism was not possible in Sweden until well into the twentieth century. Most of the restrictions against Jews were removed during the period between 1860 and 1873. Behind the movement for religious freedom were not only the liberals but also religious revivalism.

What characterized the period was a growing engagement of larger numbers of Swedish people in the public life of the country. Petitions, various forms of associations, and so on became all the more common in Swedish life. The municipal government reforms of 1862 typified this type of development.

There were, however, a number of important political decisions made in Sweden during this same period which lack any liberal overtones. An example was the support given by the Swedish government to the development of a modern railway system. At least in purely ideological terms the liberals should have opposed active governmental participation in such a program. However, because of the complicated nature of the issue and the need for foreign capital, many liberals accepted such activity. Railroad building divided the liberals badly but then so, too, were the conservatives split on the issue.

In very rough form one could make the following generalizations about liberalism in Sweden at mid-century: During the 1840s liberalism was primarily concerned with constitutional questions and was, particularly in 1848, quite radical; the 1850s can be categorized as a period that saw considerable success for liberal economic reform measures; the 1860s witnessed a culmination of liberal political and legal progress, especially with the parliamentary reform of 1865. For Swedish liberals, at least in political party matters, representation was the main issue that kept the group together. Once that had been settled, the liberals tended to look after their own particular economic and political interests and only a small, rather insignificant group continued the fight for further parliamentary reform. Parliamentary democracy would have to wait for a new political impulse before it could be established in Sweden.

5

Swedish Liberalism
at Mid-Nineteenth Century

by Göran B. Nilsson

Political ideologies including liberalism are traditionally studied in a way that could be called theoretical intellectual history. This method places great academic demands on both the researcher and the material he examines and thereby reduces the number of scholars and the issues under discussion. The demands of evidence, logic, consistency, and stringency made on the material eventually demonstrate interesting conclusions and results for the theoretical intellectual historian but seldom provide the basis for further research and interpretations. Changes in ideology are explained as the result of deus ex machina or infusion from other ideologies. Even if this characterization is exaggerated, the traditional methods of theoretical intellectual history are not satisfactory to the practical intellectual historian who seeks to study the application of ideological systems to life, to follow the changes in ideology as it responds to real situations, and to gauge the interrelationship between changing norms of society and the influence of a given ideology.

As a result the active politician often stands at the center of interest for a practical intellectual historian. For the theoretical

141

intellectual historian such persons have marginal interest, but the practical historian is interested in every individual or group that has had an influence on the development of the value structure of society. Do traditional research methods give answers to the questions raised by the practical intellectual historian? If not, what new approach can be developed? That is the main focal point for this essay. The concrete material used is Swedish liberalism at mid-nineteenth century.

I

The conflict between the theoretical and practical approaches to intellectual history occurs as soon as either tries to find a suitable definition of the term "ideology." There is general agreement that political ideology presents a system of rules for the way that individuals and groups relate to society. Inasmuch as one thus accepts the proposition that ideologies give rules for active and passive action, one also accepts the notion that value statements must play a role in every ideology. But no agreement exists on how important that role is. On the one hand, it has been maintained that the value element has very little significance since it is so generally inclusive that ideologies are reduced in practice to empirical statements (H. Tingsten). On the other hand, such exclusive weight is placed on value statements that ideologies are transformed into value hierarchies (R. Torstendahl).

It is clear that the former conception is most attractive for a traditional intellectual historian, while the latter gives more consideration to the practical intellectual historian's need to be able to deal with irrational ideas. But to take a stand for the one point of view or the other would be an undue simplification. Actually it is impossible to give a simple answer to the question of the role values play in ideologies, at least if the point of view that has been promoted primarily by Hans Albert and Ernst Topitsch (following Karl Popper) is borne in mind. The Popperians do not deny the importance of values, but point out that this impor-

tance can vary and be made to vary through the use of what
Albert calls immunization strategies. The purpose of immunization strategies is to protect an ideology against competition and
refutation in the social context where it has to work.

Value statements, however, are not always a protection against
empirical criticism, according to Albert, and he thereby turns
against a nihilistic value conception. His point of departure is the
observation that a value statement presupposes an empirical statement, *sollen impliziert können*. That is, one cannot raise ethical
demands that are not possible to realize in practice. But this opening for empirical criticism does not seem especially far-reaching.
It reduces the number of possible values but still leaves a great
freedom to discretion.

The importance of values is often reduced *in practice*, however,
namely when it concerns the usual contexts where the ideology
finds itself in a social situation of competition. The competition
then often leads to an effort to limit the number of basic values
to a minimum and/or to those which can be presumed to be or
to become comprehended by a majority of (potential) norm
givers. Bentham's theoretical construction based upon a supposedly trivial principle of happiness gives one example of this. "The
death of ideologies" in modern Western democracies can also be
seen as a result of this mechanism.

The death of ideologies is a sham death. This is a logical consequence of their function as prognostic instruments. The primary task of ideologies is to provide human beings with a rule of
conduct for action in a situation where sure knowledge of the consequences of a particular action is lacking. In this situation, ideologies function as an instrument—embraced with more or less
certainty—for selection among the apprehended alternatives of
action, in part through the selection of fundamental values but
often in larger part through the ideologies' claims of predicting
which effects the chosen alternatives will have. These prognoses
are based on causal analysis. Both this analysis and above all the

prognosis based on it are statements that can be controlled empirically, verified, or falsified. The conclusion is that ideology is sensitive to empirical criticism in its capacity as a prognostic instrument, in any case for *future* empirical criticism.

One example from the famine years of the 1860s in Sweden: Many liberals maintained that a strongly increased pressure on public poor relief was a necessary result of the right to poor relief that was written into current legislation. The right to poor relief—like other privileges—would lead to unhappy results, i.e., increases in public expenditures and in the number of people on relief. This causal analysis from a liberal ideology won wide acceptance but it proved not to function equally well as a prognosis. For when the famine years were past the demand on public poor relief decreased, although the old legislation remained; according to the liberal theory it should have continued to increase instead. The failure of the prognosis discredited the theory and the recommendation for new legislation based upon radical liberal principles which the Riksdag of 1869 had approved. Before a new law was promulgated in 1871, it underwent substantial modifications which were also accepted by many liberals from 1869.

The poor relief debates in Sweden in 1869–1871 give an example of how an ideology can be changed by the demands of reality, but they also illustrate Albert's analysis of how an ideology can protect itself against changes with the help of different immunization strategies. One way is to provide the original theory with auxiliary or helping hypotheses. In the poor laws case one could maintain—and some did—that the original theory certainly had to be modified through the assignment of greater weight to economic cycles; but even if one was willing to give a lower place to the importance of the right to poor relief as a cause of increased public financial burdens, it could be maintained that this right was still a sufficient *contributory* cause to justify more liberal legislation.

Ideologies have more effective methods to resort to in order to keep themselves intact, however. One can make the philosophical prognoses vague concerning results or realization in time and space. A known example is Marxism's prediction of the classless society's appearance and formation. It is not difficult to find less grand counterparts among Swedish liberals in the mid-nineteenth century: "the victory of the democratic principle and the republican forms allied thereto" was "the ultimate goal, though yet a century or two distant."

Another feature of the immunization strategy is the affection for selective information; that is, one holds onto the empirical statements that confirm the ideology's theory system and—consciously or unconsciously—disregards or refrains from seeking conflicting instances. In this connection one comes closer and closer to total isolation through transformation of the ideology's empirical statements to value statements that may finally be summarized in the saying "Father knows best." That is, the ideology's content is regarded exclusively as based on the authority of a leader or tradition. Here the value elements take the upper hand completely and reduce the ideology to blind obedience.

The strongly different conceptions about the role of values in ideologies are related to the fact that value elements play larger or smaller roles in different ideologies and within a single ideology larger or smaller roles for different individuals. The concept of ideology should therefore not be made strictly limiting. According to the importance of the value element in any ideology, one must imagine instead placement along a scale with one fixed endpoint, for the completely closed ideology (religion), and a continuum from there toward increasingly greater openness, that is, accessibility to empirical criticism. An absolute end-point in the other direction—a completely open ideology—naturally cannot be imagined. Even if one wants to place value on the metascientific (metametascientific, etc.) level, a value element must always enter in. The Popperians want to establish the value of a critical evaluation of values. And it can hardly have escaped the reader that the ideology which in terms of ambition if not actuality most nearly approaches the demand for openness is the Popperian view of science, fallibilism.

II

The traditional intellectual historian's demands for a definition of liberalism should, according to the reasons presented above, live up to high scientific demands, that is, show liberalism to be as open an ideology as possible. The values should be few and commonly embraced, the prognoses made precise and possible to falsify; the philosophical elements should be logically connected and not offer obvious contradictions; besides, the basic principles should be comprehensive enough to allow for a large number of positions in concrete contexts—all this without coming into conflict with the current use of language which at any one time characterizes professional thinkers' writings as liberal.

Stefan Björklund has recently tackled this difficult problem in an original way, which I cannot do justice to here. His ambition has been to create a definition of the concept of liberalism which can be applied in the study of this ideology in the historical contexts in which it has appeared, that is, in practice in the Western world after 1800. Björklund's results may be summarized in the following six criteria for liberalism: (1) The political organization exists in order to meet the needs of individuals. (2) All individuals have the same worth. (3) Since resources do not suffice to satisfy all individuals' needs, a conflict arises. (4) Individuals are capable of ranking their needs themselves. (5) If the needs of different individuals may freely compete in the political area, a harmonious weighing of different needs occurs. (6) If different individuals' needs may freely compete in the economic area, a harmonious weighing of different needs occurs (and resources increase most quickly).

Björklund's definition of the ideal type seems to meet the conditions that are placed on a definition of liberalism in traditional intellectual history (also called *theoretical liberalism*). In this connection, I see no cause to wish a revision of Björklund's fundamental clauses except on one important point, which concerns an exclusion of an element of the thought of the Enlightenment. A basic ideal of the Enlightenment seems to enter methodically into liberalism's varying forms of revelation in connection with the capacity of individuals themselves to rank their needs and thereby to work freely in the political arena (criteria 4 and 5). A prerequisite for the validity of these fundamental criteria of liberalism is that individuals be enlightened. This demand for enlightenment also gives a key to the study of shifts in liberalism between radical and moderate theoretical positions, which I shall return to in the next section.

As far as criterion 6 is concerned, enlightenment plays no role for classical liberalism, as Björklund has described it: in the economic area an invisible hand steers even the ignorant for the good of all. Thus a conservative politician can attach himself to liberalism's economic program without abandoning his low estimation of the individual's possibilities for free action in general. Criterion 5 in Björklund's definition can be spared revision if the liberal prerequisite is understood to be implied (which Björklund himself has pointed out): that the most enlightened opinion will assert itself in free competition of opinion. On the other hand, criterion 4 should be retouched to read as follows: The individual can be enlightened and is then capable of ranking his needs.

III

The traditional intellectual historian's conception of liberalism must be taken into consideration by the practical intellectual historian who investigates Swedish liberalism in the mid-nineteenth century. This is necessary simply because the political actors in his viewfinder made claims to represent a rationally qualified ideology just by annexing the designation liberal. Since this is not a unique circumstance, it is therefore obvious that an ideal-type definition of theoretical liberalism, such as Björklund suggests, fills an important need for the practical intellectual historian. He needs to have access to a national measure, a standard, against which he can view the particular variation of liberalism he is considering.

Another question that might be asked is whether it is possible to give a sufficiently systematic presentation of theoretical liberalism among the Swedish liberals in the mid-nineteenth century. The lack of professional thinkers is a hurdle that has caused Rolf Torstendahl to limit himself to trying to establish the value hierarchies of individual politicians without making any claims to a systematic connection.

I have a more optimistic view and believe that it is possible to use as a starting point the statements of ideologically conscious and ambitious politicians and writers and develop a generalized picture of theoretical liberalism as it was understood by these groups at this time. One reason for this optimism is that the liberal politicians were not as theoretically naive as Torstendahl seems to believe. Another reason is that the political groupings at this time were firmer than was thought earlier, which gives the political leaders' statements greater authority and scope.

For the present my judgment can only be put forth as an assertion. The sketch of theoretical liberalism in Sweden in the mid-nineteenth century to be given here cannot fill especially high scientific demands. But the presentation, despite its impressionistic character, should serve as a point of departure for the following discussion of the usefulness of the ideology concept of traditional intellectual history for the practical intellectual historian.

In Swedish society at the middle of the nineteenth century, liberalism was usually understood as a realization of the principles of the French revolution: freedom, equality, and fraternity. Thus far, liberalism did not diverge noticeably from Björklund's definition. The demand for equality, the realization of the principle of personhood, meant far-reaching changes in the political system. The monarchy should give way to a republic, constitutional governance to parliamentarianism. The influence of elitist (aristocratic, clerical, bureaucratic) groups on the political process should disappear in favor of the competent individual's right to participate politically on the local, the regional, and the national levels. So too privileges and regulations in the economic area should disappear—here the liberals had to overcome aristocratic opposition and also democratic opposition from the privileged craftsmen and the workers groups that considered themselves disadvantaged by free trade and economic freedom.

Both in the political and the economic sense, liberalism championed a freedom *from* and not a freedom *to*. Freedom was to be brought about by the removal of the *legislated* regulations. On the other hand, there was still a willingness to accept "natural" inequality, which in a liberal society was presupposed to give "education and wealth" a favored position. It was assumed that the leading role in society should and could be taken over by the middle class, which was identified with the people, or in any case with the people's "core."

The demand for social equality in the unequal liberal society would be met by the principle of fraternity. One aspect of this was a decrease in the physical suffering that the society was allowed to cause the individual, a "humanization." Another aspect was an increase in voluntary contributions which would ease the effects of economic inequality. The better situated should help their "brothers in the laboring class" in the short run through redistribution of economic resources (poor relief, health care, and other forms of charity) but also in the long run through spiritual and material contributions toward self-help: resocialization work, founding and support of insurance funds, production and consumer organizations, and so on. Although liberalism

was individualistic it by no means denied the need for cooperation between individuals, but this should be voluntary. The
voluntary association should replace the legislated guild.
In all of these connections, the liberals demanded a wide-reach-
ing and well-maintained popular enlightenment. Popular education was of course a prerequisite for the realization of equality
without regard to sex, race, or class, at least in the future.
The future would be better in all respects. The ideas of development and progress, as Björklund has shown in another connection, were intimately tied to the period's "bourgeois liberalism."
They could also be used to give liberalism an immunized sense of
conviction. For the battle against the arch-enemy conservatism
was not "a battle between such parties as are in part right and in
part wrong; it is a battle between views which belong to a vanished time and views which are the products of a higher time."
Liberalism itself was a fruit of development toward the better.
But this development was also toward scientifically rational truth,
toward systematism. And progress should also be applicable to
religious questions. Christianity needed a liberal reformation to
make Christianity's view of man as optimistic as liberalism's.
Religion must be expanded even if there was a danger that confused and intolerant sects would profit from such a development.
The liberals did not wish to acknowledge the occurrence of
constant disharmonies in society. Their unbounded faith in the
individual's goodness led them for the time being to believe all
problems of the future could be cured, all wants supplied. Only
when prognoses failed to eventuate was it necessary to change
to the more pessimistic conception which is seen reflected in
Björklund's definition.
Theoretical liberalism in the middle of the nineteenth century
in Sweden, as it has been described here, was more or less logical.
A peculiarity which cannot be related to the Björklund definition
was liberalism's strong nationalistic emphasis. Nationalism was
often understood as a fundamental liberal clause. One explana-

tion is that the national liberation movements at this time most often had liberal ideas written into their programs. A more tactical explanation lies in competition with the conservatives, who accused the liberals of unnational and shallow rationalism. The liberals could then defend themselves by proclaiming their Swedishness, a Swedishness that was more extreme than the conservatives', since the national ideal was older and taken from the peasant society, which the absolute rulers of the seventeenth century had ended.

At face value, nationalism posed a danger to the consistency of the liberal system. It is revealing that the little radical-liberal Riksdag party in 1871 was split on a nationalistic issue, defense. The demands of a strong national defense came into conflict with both the peasants' demand for equality and the demand for equality reforms in general. As Nils Elvander has shown, nationalism became a plank of conservatism in the future and, it may be added, an ideological bridge for old liberals.

So much for the liberal ideology among mid-nineteenth-century politicians in Sweden. But the picture would be essentially false if one did not pay attention to the great variations in this philosophical system. In part these resulted from the presence of philosophical elements from competing ideologies. But an even more decisive cleavage between the liberals seems to have been caused by their different conceptions of how far the principles of equality should be extended, not as a program for the future but in the current situation. Theoretical liberalism presupposed that all enlightened individuals could lay claim to the blessings of equality. But clearly views diverged markedly on the question of how far enlightenment could be regarded as having spread at the moment. The radical liberals were optimistic on this point, the moderate liberals pessimistic.

This relates to a problem discussed by Björklund—how it is that points of view considered liberal at the middle of the nineteenth century were not considered liberal fifty years later. An unsatisfactory answer to this question, which Björklund gives, is that little by little the content of the concept is changed, although it retains a family resemblance. It is possible, however, to give another analysis of the apparent relativity of liberalism, namely, that the societal norms existing at a certain time must be considered. He who demands an extended application of the principle of equality at any one time appears as a liberal—radical or moderate, depending on how far he wants to stretch equality beyond what then exists. Such a description gives the concept of liberalism the desired constancy. But it is important to be aware of how the criteria of liberalism change as societal norms change: a person who is theoretically a moderate liberal at one time may, after a development which brings, say, dictatorship or a democratic breakthrough, then represent, without any change in ideology, a radical liberalism or a pragmatic conservatism.

IV

In applying Björklund's definition of theoretical liberalism to a restricted time and space, I have tried to work within traditional intellectual history's compass and methods. But despite the attempt, albeit sketchy, to do justice to these methods, the problem remains for the practical intellectual historian that this definition of theoretical liberalism is not adequate as a working instrument for his purpose of studying the role of ideologies in changes in the society's norm system and the impact of these changes on the ideologies themselves. In word and deed liberal individuals and groups with political influence act in a way which not at all or incompletely corresponds to the theory. The practical intellectual historian clearly needs other methodological tools.

In part these can be found by clarifying the bothersome terminological muddle that is inherent in both mid-nineteenth-century language use and later academic discussion. The word "liberal" has appeared in at least three different meanings. First, it has been used as a classification for those espousing a form of theoretical liberalism. But the term "liberalism" has also been annexed in Sweden, as in other places, by political parties and therefore has served as a name for members of a political group. Third, later research has placed very great weight on attitudes toward the dominant issue in Swedish domestic politics during the middle of the nineteenth century, representation. Anyone who in this matter asserted the principle of combined election (in contrast to class election) has been regarded as fulfilling a sufficient criterion for liberalism. Some have gone even farther and let the connection to specific reform proposals on representation determine the classification of a person in question as liberal.

Even if these four meanings of the term "liberal" coalesce for a relatively large number of persons, the exceptions are sufficiently important to result in unsatisfactory consequences for analysis of liberalism's political manifestations. This has certainly been the case with ideological and political group associations. Rolf Torstendahl, in an investigation of the Riksdag politician F. F. Carlson, has shown that it is dubious if this mixed ideologue can be classified even as a moderate liberal. Politically, however, he undoubtedly belonged to the grouping in the clerical estate that was called "the liberal side." Conversely, the leading politician in the burgher estate's conservative faction, Mayor C. J. Stolpe, made reform statements that have led to his classification as liberal.

It proves to be even more difficult to take a politician's positions on representation as indicative of what his classification should be, ideologically or politically. Not only was the representation question complicated and difficult to solve; it lent itself to public positions that promised little risk of being realized in practice. Even more important, the principle of combined elections was not sufficiently discriminatory to rule out important moderate conservatives. I have tried to show in other contexts that moderate conservative groups could associate themselves with the changeover from the four-estate Riksdag to the two-chamber system executed in 1865–1866, a reform that met opposition from radical liberals, among others. According to the often used terminology, the former are characterized as liberals and the latter as conservatives!

These terminological problems should be easy to solve. It is not particularly toilsome for the scholar to make clear to himself and his reader in which meaning he uses the word "liberal," be it as the name for an ideological position or the label for a political group association. The third and fourth meanings of the word, dependent on support of the combined election principle, must be discarded.

V

The main problem of explaining theoretical liberalism's imperfect manifestations remains. It cannot be solved only through consideration of unforeseen difficulties within the area that play a role in the transformation from theory to policy, and they do not even need to be regarded as a disadvantage for the politician, since they give him something that may be called ideological room for maneuvering.

Björklund has given as an example the well-known ambiguity in the concept of freedom and how different interpretations resulted in the variations of liberalism, old liberalism (negative freedom, freedom from), and social liberalism (positive freedom, freedom to). The ambiguity was brought to the fore during the time under consideration in Sweden not only on the economic but on the political level. An individual's freedom of political action in the personal, the communal, and the state spheres could give contradictory results. Theoretical liberalism made claims of coping with this problem but in reality neglected it.

A similar problem concerns the ambiguity in the concept of the individual: who is meant, those now living or future (for conservatism, even past) generations? The indiscriminate cutting of forests in the middle of the nineteenth century serves as a specific example of contradictory individual rights. On this environmental issue theoretical liberalism gave no clear answer. And if one wanted to stress the rights of coming generations, this could reflect either social liberalism or social Darwinism, as Björklund's definition shows.

At least as interesting as these internal ideological difficulties are the extra-ideological issues, the appearance of more or less systematic ideas which are not covered by theoretical liberalism. That there are a lot of such ideas is a trivial fact, which, however, argues against the view that ideologies should fully encompass societal action.

One type of such ideas outside the frame of ideology, which I shall not discuss more extensively, is that of silent assumptions. These are more or less conscious ideas, which are so commonly embraced that they do not have any ideological interest and therefore are generally overlooked. This does not prevent them from being made timely in special situations, when they reveal themselves in a super-ideological character. A well-known case concerns war and other crises, which bring to the surface the assumption that the existence of the political organization is guaranteed. When this existence is felt to be threatened, many are inclined to let vital parts of any ideological program temporarily give way to the ideal of national unity. For Swedish liberalism during the mid-nineteenth century this occurred during the Crimean War and in connection with the February Revolution of 1848—especially on the latter occasion was there an ideological split among the liberals, when the more radical saw the crisis as an opportunity to carry out quick social transformation.

Extra-ideological elements, which the practical intellectual historian has cause to keep in mind more constantly than the theoretical historian, may be grouped under two main headings: means argumentation and interest argumentation.

VI

It may seem surprising that the means argumentation is called extra-ideological. Theoretical liberalism, according to both the more general definition which Björklund has proposed and the more specific one that has been given here, not only propounds a program of ends but also states the means for realizing them. Such an ends-means program may only be carried out, however, in a society where unlimited power, currently and in the future, is at the ideologue's disposal. In practice this is usually not the situation, of course; in the case of Swedish liberals, their ideology often found itself in competition with other ideologies, which forced an extra-ideological means argumentation.

For the usual situation, theoretical liberalism gives nothing like clear recommendations on which means should be resorted to for the execution of its program, or of how quickly it should be realized. The choice lies between the poles of revolution and of reformism. In determining the choice, theoretical liberalism gives little guidance. We cannot investigate here which philosophical systems do give such guidance, but the importance of the issue is demonstrated by Rolf Torstendahl's study of F. F. Carlson, a politician who had elevated political compromise to an ideology and was willing to waive his liberal ideas for its benefit.

In the investigation of liberalism's concrete manifestations, it appears clear that more or less long-range considerations, strategic and tactical, influence its selection of means. Strategically, we must take into account the possibilities and resources within the existing system for the ideology's representatives to execute changes in order to realize their theoretical program in the shorter and longer run.

Such possibilities and resources were not lacking for liberalism in nineteenth-century Sweden. The political system accommodated possibilities of change through the Riksdag, and in two of its four estates, the burghers and the peasants, there were good possibilities for liberalism to assert itself. Besides, from the 1830s the press had made ever stronger claims as a third branch of government in functioning to protect a wide-ranging legal freedom of speech and press.

The press became all the more powerful in the middle of the 1800s, and by the end of the 1850s one could speak of a pluralistic liberal press monopoly. This was connected to the growth of economic resources in the underprivileged middle-class groups in society, resulting from the beginning of industrialization and the increasingly effective productivity in agriculture, and to increased popular education. Material and intellectual resources were thus created that supported the purchase and reading of newspapers with liberal ideas.

Even more directly did liberalism benefit from the development of material and intellectual resources: the dominance of the old elites was broken. The noble and clerical estates in the Riksdag were still composed in large part of individuals who were dependent for their careers on favorable relationships with those in power in the government. But in the burgher and peasant estates, there was greater independence. In the former, economically well-situated factory owners, wholesale merchants, and lawyers appeared as liberalism's spokesmen. The peasant estate was also influenced by increased economic independence, which allowed more active and independent political engagement than before, and made the peasants less easy to corrupt by material temptations; but increased education was also a factor: it became more difficult to dupe peasants, who, as an underprivileged middle-class group, easily gravitated to liberal ways of thinking.

In the long run, the opportunity for liberalism to grow in power was increased because of the weakening of the two higher estates. After the abolition of the Institute of Entail in 1809 and after new ennoblement as good as ceased after the 1820s, the noble estate inevitably weakened. A striking sign of this was its continued loss in numbers in the Riksdag: a quantitative loss that was not balanced by any qualitative strengthening. The clerical estate had even earlier been the weakest link in conservatism's chain and grew still weaker; the priest's true calling was not that of politician, least of all in times of religious division.

When the government was forced to seek support in the Riksdag and thereby take more notice of the lower estates after 1858, liberalism's opportunity to serve as a norm-determining ideology was greater than ever before. The time 1858–1866 was a dramatic chapter in the history of the "old" liberalism, climaxed in 1865–1866 when representation reform was accomplished and the four estates were replaced by a two-chamber Riksdag. But this did not prove to be the beginning of even more substantial gains for theoretical liberalism, as the radical liberals had hoped. Their "new liberal" party got little support in the new Riksdag and they presented their ideas from the 1840s in vain. In the future, national politics came to revolve around the issue of equality for a limited social group, the peasants. Only in the 1880s did conditions become favorable for the creation of a radical liberalism. But the main ideological competition was then no longer conservatism.

For the radical liberals of the mid-nineteenth century a means program that worked within the framework of the existing political system appeared all too slow and unsatisfactory. They were therefore willing to try means which utilized the liberal press's resources. But the press was used less to influence the Riksdag's politicians than to mobilize the politically unprivileged or underprivileged groups in the society. The radical liberals tried to engage in extraparliamentary activity which would lead quickly to liberal goals; this took more permanent form in movements like the reform association after the 1848 February Revolution in Europe and the "popular meeting" at the end of the 1860s, and more temporary form in a stream of petitions, ranging from the 1834 appeal for reform in representation to the demand for more equal suffrage in the middle of the 1860s.

The radicals were regularly disappointed in the effectiveness

of these extraparliamentary methods but equally regularly they
began anew in the hope that popular education would make the
next attempt more successful. The spokesmen for extraparliamentary activity among the liberals seldom espoused revolutionary
aims. During the period after the February Revolution radicals
could, to be sure, through the press and the reform associations
propose a kind of revolution. But they meant a political revolution "without bayonets and citizen blood, only through the power
of the general way of thinking." Similar statements made in the
1860s were no more precise. It may be conjectured that the concern of theoretical liberalism—even in its radical form—for
humanity was a hurdle blocking its pursuit of its goal. In any
case, the campaign for a bloodless revolution failed and brought
upon its supporters the derisive name "revolution sheep."

In connection with means, the name "radical" has been used
here for politicians who advocated a quick and *relatively* ruthless
execution of their theoretical program. Their liberal opposites
may be called "moderates." The antonym pair radical-moderate
can also be applied to the theoretical program itself: in radical
liberalism the principles of equality and freedom are carried to
greater length and have more far-reaching implications than in
moderate liberalism. In the literature these two meanings have
not been separated, which has led to a confusion in terms that is
illustrated schematically below. The risk of ambiguity is smallest

Type	*End*	*Means*	*Generalizing Definition*
1. . . . . . Radical	Radical	Radical liberal
2. . . . . . Radical	Moderate	Moderate liberal
3. . . . . . Moderate	Radical	Moderate liberal
4. . . . . . Moderate	Moderate	Moderate liberal

in type 1; a radical theory, according to the analysis given here,
presupposes demands for sweeping changes in the existing social
system and thereby most often leads to embracing radical means.
The fuzziness in terminology becomes far more disturbing where

moderate liberalism is concerned. As is shown, the term "moderate liberal" covers shifting constellations in the end-means relationship. The name can designate an individual or group (whether drawing-room liberals or end-conscious strategists) willing to compromise in the execution of a theoretical program. The term can also be applied to those whose ends are not purely liberal but who want to execute them without compromise.

To distinguish these two types (2 and 3) from each other would be desirable but is impossible to do without a thorough study. On the other hand, it appears justified and possible to eliminate the term "moderate liberal" in type 4, which demarcates a group of individuals on liberalism's outer fringe. They may be either "conscious" mixed ideologues and compromise politicians like F. F. Carlson, or "unconscious" interest-group politicians of the type exemplified by the peasant estate. In the latter case, the term "crypto-liberal" seems better. In the former, the designation "moderate liberal" can advantageously be reduced to "moderate," a term which also can be used for corresponding borderline cases on the conservative side.

Discussion of tactical means must depend on individual analysis rather than generalized definitions and need concern us only briefly here. The tactical considerations which often cause problems for the intellectual historian are those where the person in question is forced to make a choice *within* the framework of his program's goals. He may waive one fundamental goal in order to realize another. Since most liberals in Sweden took the moderate, long-range, and willing-to-compromise path, tactical decisions were an everyday occurrence. During Oskar I's so-called liberal period, many liberals were inclined to tone down republican and parliamentarian demands and prescribe illiberal measures against conservative opponents. In the representation reform of 1865–1866, the government's recommendation was wholeheartedly supported by most liberals despite an awareness that the victory was pyrrhic.

A further influence from the extra-ideological realm, already touched upon, concerns both the theoretical program and the means to carry it out. I refer to the form of egoism that is usually called interest.

VII

A strict distinction between ideas and interests has long been made. This contrast has often been used as a pretext for devaluing the importance of ideas in a society's formation and change. The role of ideologies is understood as purely decorative, a respectable disguise for the real driving forces, crass material interests.

The importance of special interests cannot be denied. On the other hand it is not productive to draw a sharp dividing line between ideas and interests. Interests must be understood as one form ideas take. This suggestion may affront those who hold that interests are an implacable manifestation of material factors beyond the control of human consciousness. That there may be such factors will not be denied either. But the decisive point is that interest, in the normal use of language, never has an absolute meaning. What lies in an individual's or group's interest is a matter that is determined by the individual's or group's *subjective* understanding. A trade union that demands a 25 percent pay raise can justly be said to act in the members' interest. But the same judgment can with the same justice be pronounced if the same trade union in the same situation demands a 15 or 35 percent pay raise, or shortened working hours, or increased vacation, or what have you. Identical material conditions lead to nonidentical manifestations in human affairs.

A definition of the term "interest" according to current usage might be this: the understanding of an individual or group on which method of conduct will lead to a short-term increase of the individual's or the group's material (economic, etc.) or spiritual (power, etc.) resources. Thereby one can make a vague but not immaterial delimitation between the terms "ideology" and "interest" as different types of ideas according to the scheme below.

	Span		Demand for Rational Consistency
	In Space	In Time	
Ideology . . .	autonomous society	long range	greater
Interest	part of society	short range	lesser

From this it appears that interests differ from ideologies in making less strict demands on extensiveness and rationality. If one couples this with the observation that greater strictness in these regards has a higher status value in a civilized society, a natural consequence is that interest-serving politicians have the ambition of appearing as ideologues, and conversely that politicians have the ambition of presenting ideological opponents as interest-serving politicians. (In the Swedish peasant estate, to be sure, the opposite was long true.)

The practical intellectual historian, then, cannot be content with charting the manifest philosophical content of a politician or a political group. He must routinely undertake a delicate resource analysis: to what extent *could* the expressed position be motivated by interests? Interests have been treated here as a less complicated variation of ideologies; anyone who wants to assert the primacy of interests may freely regard ideologies as a form of long-range egoism (compare the expression "be in someone's *true* interest"). The main thing is that they be seen as types of ideas and not as something separate.

The concept of interest has naturally had importance for the formation of liberalism's theoretical as well as practical programs. This is epitomized in the term "bourgeois liberalism," as the period's theoretical liberalism has often been named. The strong emphasis on the importance to liberalism of the middle class in society could easily have resulted in a false identification between the middle class's interests and liberalism's ideas. But even where means are concerned, there is reason to bear in mind the interests that have constancy through time. Swedish liberalism that took the reformist path had to work in a Riksdag divided into four groups, with clear differences in social composition and thereby in interests. Liberalism's forms in the different estates also showed characteristic differences, which made it justifiable to speak of noble liberalism, clerical-estate liberalism, burgher-estate liberalism, and peasant-estate liberalism.

If any example is required, the representation issue is pertinent. The noble liberals demanded, for the benefit of "education and wealth," far-reaching limitations on the program of theoretical equality. The burgher estate's liberals had cause by reason of their interests to be more generous but they too put limits on equality through voting qualifications based on income and total value. The peasant estate's interests, finally, dictated a still more democratic suffrage program.

Interests played an important role in the formation of liberalism and in the changes it underwent but also were responsible for losses of support once one or another goal had been accomplished. This hardly needs clearer illustration than radical liberalism's temporary demise shortly after the execution of the representation reform. It had satisfied powerful interests which earlier had thrown their weight behind liberalism.

This essay has had the purpose of making it clear that the practical intellectual historian cannot let himself be content with the traditional intellectual historian's conception of ideologies, although he should not disregard it either. The study of politically active groups' ideologies, i.e., practical liberalism, must take into account empirical events and ideas outside the framework of theoretical liberalism, events and ideas which influenced it. That the theoretical goals thereby often have played a subordinate or coordinate role is a fact that perhaps is regrettable but cannot be passed over. It is important to investigate when and why this has been the case even for those who believe that logical and consistent ideologies should have the greatest importance in the formation of the social life.

Introduction to Chapter 6

The conventional treatment of modern European history normally reserves a small section of one chapter for "demographic" changes in the later nineteenth century. Under this euphemistic rubric fall such items as the population explosion, the movement to the cities, and the great emigration from Europe. The authors of such works do not intentionally wish to slight these developments; the problem is simply that they are so difficult to write about in a concise and meaningful manner that, in despair, they are relegated to an insignificant position. Indeed the examination of social history is in general a much more difficult task than studying political and economic changes. Documentation, methodological problems, and simply the additional demand on a historian's time make this form of historical literature far less common than others. Yet social history must be understood if we are to get a clear perspective on our own situation. Among the most critical social developments in late-nineteenth-century European history were the great migrations.

The importance of migration to recent European history can hardly be overstated. Since 1850 certainly well over 50 percent of all Europeans have been directly involved in some form of migration. There was of course the spectacular emigration between 1820 and 1924 of over 50 million Europeans, including over one million Swedes, primarily to North America. But of even greater significance has been the internal national migration—the movement of Europeans from one area to another within their own country, particularly but not exclusively from rural to urban areas—and inter-European migration. The change from an agrarian to an industrial society encouraged and, in some cases, forced Europeans to leave their traditional homes and to establish new patterns of life. The migratory process is a fascinating one, combining so many of the important historical problems of the period: the impact of technological and industrial change, the population explosion, the breakdown of rural society, urbanization, cultural assimilation, the creation of new cultural forms, the Europeanization of many areas outside Europe, and so on.

Historical treatment of migration has been somewhat narrow. Great stress has been placed on emigration, on certain aspects of the growth of cities, and on cultural interchange. Migration as a whole has rarely been examined by historians. The process of urbanization has been of greater interest to sociologists and geographers than to historians. Recently, however, there have been efforts to combine the more traditional historical methods with the techniques and results of other social sciences. These efforts are beginning to produce stimulating results. The following essay by Sune Åkerman, which is a product of these newer methodological approaches, examines the migration process in Sweden over the past 150 years, seeks to illuminate the factors that have caused it, and analyzes the effect of migration on Swedish society.

Typically, migration for Swedish historians has been seen primarily as a problem of emigration. The Swedes have long been concerned about the meaning and impact of the mass exodus from their country, particularly that of the last twenty-five years of the nineteenth century. Contemporary organizations dedicated to halting the emigration were created in many parts of the country. A great, comprehensive study commissioned by the government was done in the first decade of the twentieth century in an effort to understand the phenomenon. Since then, there has been evidence of continued fascination with the problem, including a whole spate of best selling novels and popular films. Only in the past few years has the emphasis within historical research in treating migration moved from a purely emigration-oriented approach to research that puts emigration into the larger migration process. Docent Åkerman's observations about the relation of the great emigration to the internal migration process should prove very stimulating.

6

Swedish Social Development from 1840 to 1970 as Reflected in Emigration

by Sune Åkerman

During the eighteenth and the early nineteenth centuries, mercantilist legislation effectively stopped emigration to the New World from Sweden as from so many other countries. The absence of emigration thus was the result of an active isolationist policy and did not reflect actual social conditions that might of themselves have produced emigration. The situation is similar to that today in numerous Communist countries that have successfully blocked voluntary population movements across their borders. Sweden's main exception to such policies during this period was its attempt to colonize New Sweden on the Delaware River. This emigration, although interesting in itself, will not be treated in this essay, even though it is an excellent example of how emigration reflected important political as well as social and economic elements in a society. Instead this essay will focus upon the great population movements of the nineteenth and twentieth centuries.

The development of commercial ties, which began especially in the 1830s, was related to Swedish emigration to the United States in the early nineteenth century. At this time the United States rescued the Swedish iron industry, which had a market crisis after 1815. There was no longer the same need for Swedish bar iron and steel in England as before and New England emerged as a welcome new market during this critical period for the Swedish iron industry. Business contacts and study trips led to emigration of some members of the gentry class, although the numbers were not significant.

But the great mass of people was very little affected. Of greater importance was the emigration which began in the 1840s and which in part reflected the special religious conditions in Sweden. The all-powerful state church had already been shaken by separatism to some extent during the eighteenth century, but it was only toward the mid-nineteenth century that "Reading," a low-church protest against the hierarchical organization and ritual of the state church, really took hold.

The religious emigration is perhaps best and most dramatically exemplified by the very special form of sectarianism represented by the Jansonites. This sect was forced to emigrate after fairly severe persecutions at the end of the 1840s. It later built a colony in Bishop Hill in western Illinois and there tried to create a so-called state of God. Typically, the Jansonites came from areas with large numbers of Readers, especially in Hälsingland and Dalarna. Other sects, such as the Baptists and Mormons, which came into conflict with the religious authorities were also recruited from these areas for emigration. The Mormon group had a special tie to western Sweden, for example Dalsland, from which a very early and well-organized Mormon emigration took place.

These groups became objects of direct persecution in Swedish society. Hence they were not typical of the mass emigration to follow, although other examples of political persecution will be cited later in this essay. On the other hand, they represented an important precursor for the future, namely a mobilization of people outside of the strictly institutionalized society. The forms Reading took were a challenge to the whole structure of established society in the religious field.

The majority of the Readers belonged to the small landowning segment of the agricultural population and could thus almost be characterized as a lower-middle-class stratum. A large part of the growing emigration in the 1850s and 1860s came from just this social level. But it would be misleading to look for the cause of emigration in religious conditions except when this is clearly documented. The crisis of the state church was matched by a crisis within the whole agrarian society.

The rapid population growth which began at the end of the eighteenth century meant that large parts of the agrarian population were proletarianized. This development could be counteracted in various ways. The division of farms into more units was begun early and was facilitated by the fact that land redistribution was largely completed by the middle of the nineteenth century. Larger contiguous holdings could be divided more easily among several families and be worked more effectively than sharply splintered strips of land in the common fields of a whole village. This division of land was called "homestead splitting" and a heated political discussion broke out at the time on how far it should be carried out. In certain provinces such division of property was carried to great lengths. Another possibility was the cultivation of new land. Rather extensive marginal lands were put under the plow during this phase in southern and central Sweden. At the same time, the colonization of Norrland's interior began; it was not concluded until well into the twentieth century. To a certain extent, birth control was another alternative. It may seem anachronistic to discuss the use of birth control in the middle of the nineteenth century, but it appears that family planning was practiced locally even in the mid-eighteenth century. This should not be totally unexpected; we have long known that family planning may have been practiced in certain regions of France at this time.

The rising tide of emigration among farmers shows that homestead splitting, new cultivation, and family planning by no means sufficed to stop the process of proletarianization. On the contrary, conditions deteriorated. It seems to have become more difficult to cross the important social line between propertied and unpropertied, while more and more people were forced into the unpropertied class. The gulf between rich and poor grew. Land values rose continuously in the middle of the nineteenth century, and this further hindered the prospects of those who wanted to acquire a farm of their own. There were also tendencies toward a stronger stratification within the class of farm owners between the rich and those who had very limited property.

Emigration discloses more clearly than anything else how critical conditions had become. In the first waves of emigration in the 1850s and 1860s there were a considerable number of farm owners and members of their families who clearly found the situation in Sweden untenable and who were attracted by the possibility of obtaining land in the United States. Many sons and daughters of farm owners, faced with the threat of further swelling the group of unpropertied and thereby moving downward socially, became emigrants. It is particularly noteworthy to see landowners emigrate to such an extent; this category typically is one of the least migratory. It is also revealing that the actual proletariat hardly entered into this first emigration at all. The most badly off were clearly so oppressed that they could not extricate themselves from their situation. It is probable that psychological conditions as much as economic ones were responsible for their inertia, especially later when ticket prices for the Atlantic crossing were driven down to a comparatively very low level.

The dramatic emigration peaks in 1868 and 1869 illuminate how a large body of people reacted to specific pressure. In many parts of Scandinavia during those two years, there were two extraordinarily bad harvests in a row. The result was that more than 70,000 people emigrated from Sweden at one fell swoop. It still was not the most severely proletarianized people, who literally were in danger of starving to death, that emigrated. But for

the smallholders and their families and those in other similar
categories, there clearly was a crisis of confidence in the agrarian
society. We still do not know enough to be able to say definitely
how the famine emigration gathered speed and why it reached the
extent and had the structure it did. But many contributory factors
can be distinguished.

It might be asked how such a transatlantic emigration could
occur at all in so-called stationary European "peasant societies,"
such as Sweden presumably was. How could information spread
under such conditions and how could a pattern of migration be
established? On closer study it becomes clear that it is very deceiv-
ing to work with stereotypes of European conditions like those of
Oscar Handlin in his well-known book *The Uprooted*. In Sweden
we do not find a stationary agricultural society whose narrow
horizons coincided largely with parish boundaries; this was at
best only a memory in the 1850s. On the contrary, Swedish society
was marked by a great mobility in which the points of contact
with other people and other geographic environments must have
been many and varied.

It is not possible to assert, as Robert Wiebe has for the United
States at this time, that the labor market disintegrated into a
number of small, isolated islands which had little exchange with
"society at large." A revealing feature in nineteenth-century Swedish society was labor migration, which extended over both long
and short distances. The long-distance migrations are especially
interesting for us. These show that important labor markets had
almost a national character and that in part they had an inter-
Nordic character. In the same way, the in-migration to the cities
was also not limited to a narrow surrounding area. In the case of
Stockholm, for example, one can speak without exaggeration of
the whole country as a source of migrants even if the greatest
migration exchange occurred within the Lake Mälar area.

More than anything else migration intensities reveal how mobile the "old peasant society" was at the beginning of the mass-em-

igration period. Migration was not equally important in all parts of the country. Eastern Sweden, especially the Lake Mälar area, had the greatest intensities, while western Sweden and Norrland had the lowest. It was later that industrialization led to migration of a somewhat different type and of a more sweeping nature.

It is important to note that the pattern of migration also reveals an inertia against changing one's environment. Even the labor migrations clearly indicate this. The labor migrants preferred to return to their place of origin each year, although the major part of their income and the largest part of their working time was spent in industrial areas or some other environment with better possibilities for earning a living. There was as well an inertia against migration across what we have come to call the rural-industrial barrier. This means, for example, that the recruitment area for the labor force of a beginning industry was largely not the nearest surrounding area and its agricultural population. Instead, in the early stages other, already somewhat industrialized employees moved from farther away to such an industrial environment. Only in a later phase can we find contacts between the immediate surrounding area and the industrial center.

In 1870 there was every reason to expect that emigration would remain at the high level it had achieved or even increase. This did not turn out to be the case at all. A thorough change now began in Swedish society, which it is not hard to trace: industrialization had entered an intensive stage. Thereby was introduced a fourth component, along with homestead splitting, new cultivation, and family planning, to counteract emigration. Even in its beginning phase industrialization showed how effectively it could work against emigration. Later there was a race between the ability of Swedish industry to grow and absorb surplus farm population, which is analyzed by Lennart Jörberg elsewhere in this book, and the expelling forces at work in agriculture. A balance was not reached until the 1920s.

The road was long. During recessions like those in the 1880s, the early 1890s, and the first years of the 1900s, emigrants were recruited to an increasing extent from the industrial and urban population. We have no really satisfactory statistics concerning the emigrants' occupations but this much is sufficiently clear. It may seem obvious that an increasing proportion of city dwellers and people engaged in industry in the whole population would lead to a strong increase in urban and industrial emigration. There is still reason to look closely at this situation, which seems to be more revealing of psychological changes in the urban migrants than of anything else. It was not primarily short-term residents in the city environment who were, so to speak, pushed out of it. The emigrants had most often remained for a rather long time in urban surroundings and they were by no means completely unskilled workers. Although they outwardly were rather well-adapted individuals, they still opted for emigration to America. It seems as if the first rural-to-urban migration created ambitions which could not be satisfied in the new environment. To return to agricultural work clearly did not appear to be an attractive alternative for these emigrants.

The interesting thing is that even at those times when there was a scarcity of agricultural workers, as in the beginning of the 1900s, the urban industrial workers who had a hard time finding employment preferred to emigrate. In addition a large part of the emigration from agriculture seems to have occurred more as a result of maladjustment to the rural labor environment than because of difficulties in finding employment. Suffice it here to refer to the special conditions which prevailed in agriculture, with its domination by masters, long working hours, and relatively modest pay.

The migrations of women become especially significant in this connection. That they meant an emancipation from the working conditions within agriculture is documented both by oral tradition and by statistical material. In many cases, this emancipation seems to have occurred in two stages: first a move to the city, in which women dominated, and thereafter a continued migration, to the United States.

If we examine the structure of emigration in more detail, we can also find certain characteristic social conditions and attitudes reflected in emigration. For example, it was not unusual for destitute people and those who were an economic burden to church congregations to be helped to emigrate. Perhaps this could be called a final solution of the poor relief problem. This traffic was not as great in Sweden as in Switzerland, for example, but there are many instances of parishes in various parts of the country engaging in this practice. Another interesting form of emigration was that resulting from conflicts over the right to organize. Beginning approximately at the turn of the century we can find a series of such emigrations, in which people who had been blacklisted by employers were forced to leave the Swedish labor market. There were also many examples of working friends in such cases helping the blacklisted person with a ticket to America and other expenses that accompanied emigration. Here emigration can be said to reflect a continuation of the social and political awakening exemplified by Reading at the middle of the nineteenth century.

Emigration had been characterized from the beginning to a rather great extent by whole families moving together and in this phase the average age was also considerably higher than it later came to be. In the twentieth century we are mostly concerned with single emigrants, and people in the 20–30 age group dominate very strongly. Many of these emigrants have planned to work for some time in the United States or Canada and then return home. In other words, the frequency of return has become considerably greater than before; here we can discern an equalization between the economic levels of the sending country and the receiving country. The turning point occurred at the end of the 1920s. Since then, Sweden has primarily become a country of immigration after earlier having been drained of more than a million people.

The most important emigration in the contemporary period has been connected to an earlier immigration of foreign labor or political refugees. We can observe such a counterstream in conjunction with the end of World War II in 1945, when most of those who had taken refuge in neutral Sweden during the war moved on. A considerable refugee immigration to Sweden took place later, especially during the 1960s. The emigration that we can observe from Sweden in recent times is, then, a reemigration and has many important features in common with the mass emigration which occurred earlier. Sweden has become part of a new labor market which covers large parts of Western Europe and also adjacent areas of Africa and Asia. The population exchange has become especially great between the Nordic countries since the passport requirement was eliminated in 1953.

A special and much-discussed new stream of emigrants has been made up of researchers, a phenomenon usually called a "brain drain." This emigration in its way reflects on conditions at Swedish universities and, at the same time, it is an excellent example of migration's streams and counterstreams. The net emigration of scientists and academically educated personnel has been rather inconsiderable. A large number of those who figured in the statistics later returned to Sweden and thereby furnished the society with new experiences and intellectual resources.

In this short kaleidoscopic essay have been discussed historical conditions in Swedish society that in part are sharply reflected in external population movements. It is also possible to analyze the changes in phase we can observe in emigration as a closed system. Certain features in emigration seem not to be especially dependent on historical events and conditions. That people at different social levels are pulled into emigration in a certain order illustrates a more general hypothesis concerning the dissemination of information. Ideas and actions seem often to spread from an urban milieu to a rural one, and we can also see that higher social levels are affected earlier than lower levels and that the former act as agents of information. The growth of the emigration curve as a result of close personal contacts is confirmed by a number of studies. It is also clear that emigration conveys certain distinct features in the social structure of the sending country to the new receiving country. This is a matter that will not be further commented on in this essay. That the emigration of men has been greater than that of women throughout the whole period reflects women's continuing underprivileged position in the society under discussion.

It would be interesting to make an intellectual experiment in which we had only emigration statistics as the documentary source for the development of Swedish society over the last hundred years. We would then be in the position that medievalists often find themselves in. How would we interpret this social development? Historians and some sociologists have not sufficiently utilized emigration statistics to illuminate the psychological development of nineteenth-century society. Migration should be used as a tool to help us understand psychological and other factors which otherwise are almost impossible to reconstruct. The preceding quick sketch gives an idea of what results can be achieved if one approaches emigration in this way. The observations made possible by studying changes in the structure and volume of migration must naturally be supplemented constantly by use of other source material. It is regrettable that researchers have shown far too little interest in what has happened to individuals in connection with the great revolutionary changes in society during the last 100 or 150 years, such as urbanization and industrialization. Emigration was only a part of this transition from a rural society to an urbanized and industrialized one. If it is not possible to go out and interview people about their conditions and reactions, a penetrating analysis of mass data of the type discussed here would give considerable insight into the changes that affected the human environment during the latest great social transformation.

Introduction to Chapter 7

One of the most characteristic developments of nineteenth-century life in Europe was that an increasing portion of the population participated actively in the political process. Historians normally associate the growth of political participation by the masses with the spread of industrialism. Undoubtedly in many European countries such a relationship existed but a generalization of this kind underestimates the importance of a growing political awareness that actually occurred before any large-scale effects of industrialism can be found. In Sweden for example, long before industrialism had begun to make important inroads in the economic and social patterns of the country, there were clear indications of increasing popular involvement in the political and social life of the country. The manifestations of this involvement are generally referred to by Swedish scholars as the "popular movements." The political awareness and participation stimulated by the industrialization process after 1870 built upon these already established popular movements. The following essay by Docent Sven Lundkvist is a pioneering examination of the specific role played by the popular movements on the social scene between 1900 and 1920. The period that Docent Lundkvist treats is that in which the popular movements had their greatest impact. However, as social-political phenomena their origins are of an earlier vintage.

The three major popular movements were religious revivalism, the prohibition movement, and the labor movement. Religious revivalism was the oldest of the three and began shortly after the end of the Napoleonic wars. This revivalism was to find outlet both within the established Lutheran Church and in the form of a free church movement. It was this latter development that was to be of greatest significance after 1860. However, as early as the 1830s initial inroads by Methodist groups had been made. Similarly the prohibitionist movement began in the 1830s but it was not until the 1870s that total abolition of alcohol was advocated. The last of the popular movements to develop, although the one that has had the greatest impact on Sweden, was the labor movement. "Workingmen's associations" and at least one union existed by the late 1840s but they functioned more as friendship societies than as modern trade organizations. Only in the 1870s did the modern union movement begin and in 1889 the Social Democratic party was founded by union members. The central trade union organization, LO, was created in 1898. Because of the impact the labor movement later had on modern Sweden, there is a temptation to assume its primary importance from its inception, disregarding the significance of the other popular movements. To make this assumption would lead one to misinterpret the dynamics of Swedish political life between 1890 and 1920.

By the time the industrial worker began his struggle to achieve democracy, equality, and justice, the other popular movements had already been active in demanding many of the same or similar changes in Swedish social, political, and economic life. This commonality in goals was to a certain extent due to the conservative nature of Swedish society, which forced groups agitating for change to find common ground if they were to have hopes of achieving their ends in a nonrevolutionary manner. Additionally the pattern of industrialization in Sweden led to continued close contact between industrial workers and underprivileged rural elements in Swedish society. Indeed many of the more important early attempts to organize industrial workers in order to improve their conditions were made by other popular movements or by concerned liberals. The labor movement, when it became a strong organization on its own, carefully nurtured its ties with other reforming elements of Swedish society. In this way, the labor movement in Sweden, particularly the Social Democratic party, avoided the experience of its sister party in Germany which was isolated from nonlabor elements of German society. Docent Lundkvist's findings clearly demonstrate how interrelated the Swedish popular movements were with one another.

7

Popular Movements and Reforms, 1900-1920

by Sven Lundkvist

During the early twentieth century a broad spectrum of social-political movements, commonly called the popular movements, had a strong impact on Sweden. While the country's population increased from 5.1 million to 5.9 million in the years 1900–1920, the major popular movements—the revivalist or free church movement, the temperance movement, and the labor movement—grew from about 450,000 to about 840,000 adult members (those above the age of fifteen; to these figures should be added the many members of youth organizations, especially in the free church and temperance movements). Each of the three had approximately the same number of members in 1920. Because of a large turnover in membership, it can be assumed that the numbers involved were actually greater than the figures above indicate. A large part of the population of Sweden in the early years of this century could be counted as popular movement members or as indirectly associated with popular movement activities through family ties.

NOTE: This essay is based on my forthcoming book *Politik, nykterhet och reformer: En Studie i folkrörelsernas politisk verksamhet 1900–1920* [Politics, Temperance, and Reforms: A Study on the Political Activity of the Popular Movements, 1900–1920].

However, there were significant regional variations; the popular movements were especially strong in central and northern Sweden.

A steady increase in membership occurred in the free church movement during the years up to 1910, but thereafter a decline set in. The temperance and labor movements grew during the whole period; the rise was relatively constant for the former, while the latter experienced periods of sharp increase or decline. Most of those who joined the three movements belonged to the lower strata of society. Representatives of the middle class were found primarily in the free church and temperance movements, where by achieving positions of leadership they played a more important part than their numbers would have suggested.

Each movement had its own definite goals. The free church movement wanted to bring individuals to lead a Christian life and thereby to establish a Christian society; the temperance movement wanted to save individuals from the baleful effects of alcohol and society from the problems engendered by intoxication of its citizens; the labor movement wanted to create tolerable living conditions for its members, as well as to give them influence and power, and it believed society should control the means of production. Although the movements had different aims, they all agreed that society must be reshaped. The methods advocated varied: the early labor movement spoke of revolution; the others depended on peaceful means. As time went on, any thought of revolution was relegated to the background, except in certain acute labor crises.

In order to influence legislation, it was necessary for the movements to elect their own representatives to various governmental bodies, from county councils to the Riksdag. The right to vote was critical. Only an extension of suffrage to include all adult men and women could give the popular movements influence in proportion to their numbers. On this point, the movements found a basis for practical cooperation, since their different objectives could all benefit from universal and equal suffrage. The free church movement, with its large component of women, was especially vigorous in demanding for women the right to participate in deciding how society should be governed.

The appeal for suffrage was not supported with equal force in all the movements, nor were other common goals. In fact there were regional variations within the same movement. Local organizations had divergent traditions and perceptions. Sometimes leaders had interests that prevented their wholehearted support for specific demands; in some areas agrarian participation exercised a conservative influence. Along with regional variations in policy went regional variations in strength and support, not least within the labor movement, which was weak in many areas for a large part of the period under discussion. The political influence of the movements was strongest in central Sweden and Norrland and in parts of Småland. Within the free church movement, it appears that the greatest activity in elections was localized in Svenska Missionsförbundet (the Covenant Church of Sweden), while within the temperance movement the International Order of Good Templars (IOGT) and Svenska Blåbandsföreningen seem to have been most active.

As early as the 1880s, the free church movement was represented by almost 30 members in the Second Chamber of the Riksdag. Until the turn of the century, no significant changes took place, but then the number rose so that, in 1911, 51 of the Chamber's 230 members were directly associated with the free church movement; there were a number of sympathizers and allies besides. The temperance movement came later, but by 1911 there were in the Second Chamber 144 absolutists, that is, those who advocated a total ban on consumption of alcohol. At the turn of the century, the labor movement (Social Democrats) had one member in the Second Chamber; at the end of 1911, 87 members. The spring election of 1914 was something of a catastrophe for the free church supporters: their representatives decreased from 51 to 37. The temperance supporters also decreased. Only the Social Democrats held their position and even increased in numbers somewhat. The decline of free church members continued after 1914. On the other hand the temperance supporters increased their number in 1917, so that their strength returned to approximately what it had been in 1911. The figures given here represent a separate count of the free church supporters, absolutists, and Social Democrats respectively; since a delegate to the Second Chamber could be a member of all three movements the total popular movement membership in the Second Chamber was less than the sum of the figures for the free church supporters, the absolutists, and the Social Democrats. The proportion of absolutists was highest within the Social Democratic party, somewhat lower among the groups on the right. The picture for the free church movement was different: the greatest number of its members were within the Liberal camp, the next largest number on the right, and the smallest among the Social Democrats. In the First Chamber the three popular movements did not acquire strength sufficient to direct its decisions before 1920.

The majority-vote electoral system in use until 1910, with its single-member constituencies, favored the movements' political activity. An election could be directly and noticeably influenced if a sufficient number of votes could be mobilized, and the apparatus for doing that could be simple. Central directives could reach out into all parts of Swedish society through the strong local organizations of the movements, and personal influence in turning out all sympathizers could easily be applied. The local organizations of the movements often set up joint committees that nominated and campaigned for candidates. The local election supervisors, especially IOGT's, had considerable strength and could work effectively with small means. The local press also was important: through it the movements could spread their messages to the different voter groups. Studies of election statistics document the political influence of the movements: in many locations where the popular movements had high membership the voter turnout was heavier than average. With the adoption in Sweden of proportional elections, which required the formation of parties, the conditions for political activity of the movements were changed. Since the labor movement already functioned politically within the Social Democratic party, it could continue as before, but the other movements had to decide if they wanted to create their own political parties or if they preferred to join already existing parties. Between 1908 and 1911, discussions on forming new parties took place within both the free church and the temperance movements, but the decision in both ultimately was that in the future each member should be allowed to work within the party whose program best corresponded to his own ideas. The various parties thereby received a considerable infusion of experienced leaders, partisans, and voters. The largest number joined the Liberal and Social Democratic camps, the latter gaining in favor as the decade wore on. After 1910, the cooperative bodies of the movements primarily directed their efforts toward propaganda and pressure instead of acting as election organizations as before.

After 1910, then, the history of the popular movements becomes in part an account of a struggle for power within the political parties, particularly those on the left. And in the decade of the 1910s, with which we shall be primarily concerned here, the temperance question came to impinge on a number of the most important issues of the period. There were two focal points in the debate over temperance: the implications of a local veto and the financial impact of government-controlled sales of liquor.

Proposals for local veto gave decision-making power to all adult men and women, who by majority vote would determine whether spirits would be sold within their township. This contrasted with the regular election system in which there was a restricted electorate. In addition to its influence on prohibition, local veto was regarded by many as a first step toward achieving universal suffrage.

The establishment of dry communities by local veto would deprive the state, towns, county councils, and rural economy associations of considerable sums. In a budget of approximately 200 million crowns for the period from 1901 through 1910, not less than 15–20 percent of the state's total income came from the sale of intoxicants. During the same period, between 7.4 percent and 12.1 percent of the urban townships' income and between 2.6 percent and 5.5 percent of the rural townships' income came from this source, as did between 25 percent and 36 percent of the income of the county councils and approximately 70 percent of the income of the rural economy associations. Certain cities depended on this source for 40 percent of their incomes, and in some cases, considerable funds accrued to the cities in the form of taxes from the distillery companies, rents, and so on. Large economic interests were at stake, and adoption of local veto was regarded in leading conservative circles as a dangerous possibility. An informal study of the townships' position on the local veto, which had been made in 1908 by the temperance organizations, indicated a majority in favor. In an unofficial referendum taken immediately thereafter, 56 percent of all the men and women in the country over the age of eighteen expressed their approval of total prohibition. A local veto would be economically ruinous in many townships, and total prohibition would necessitate a number of large new sources of income for the state if existing obligations were to be met, not to mention increased spending for defense and social reforms.

The results of the Second Chamber election in 1911 made it evident that the Liberal and Social Democratic programs appealed to the new voters enfranchised that year under proportional universal male suffrage. The Liberals emphasized a parliamentary form of government, a revision of the defense system, and local veto; the Social Democrats demanded a decrease in military burdens, sweeping social reforms, "energetic temperance legislation, leading to statutory prohibition of intoxicating beverages," abolition of the duties on food, and so on. The temperance issue was clearly interwoven with defense and social reforms.

Conservatives were troubled by the outcome of the election and the voting trends it revealed. In the previous ten years, their numbers had decreased from 137 to 65 in the Second Chamber. Leading Conservatives believed that the decline in popularity of their party was largely the result of strong anti-defense sentiments among the people, and they took steps to change public opinion. During the next years, the defense issue became dominant in political discussion. King Gustav V dictated to the protocol of the King's Council his disapproval of the defense policy of the new Liberal government, headed by Karl Staaff. The conservative press began to criticize the government and its actions vehemently. The defense issue became extremely important even in the rural newspapers, where pro-defense feeling had previously been weak. At approximately the same time, the traveling scientist Sven Hedin wrote his celebrated brochure, *A Word of Warning*, and two different collections to finance armorclad ships were begun.

Lines had been clearly drawn in the budget committee of the 1911 Riksdag. The Conservatives wanted to maintain and strengthen defense with all available means—for them, defense had priority over social reforms. The Social Democrats wanted to cut defense expenditures for general doctrinal reasons and to free funds for social reforms. The Liberals, on the other hand, wanted both defense and necessary reforms, necessitating a balancing of goals and resources.

A number of reform recommendations were current. General old-age insurance had been under study since 1907. The costs for such a program would be considerable. The government's proposition in April 1913 gave the costs for the state as 4.7 million crowns in 1914 and projected an annual increase, so that for 1930 the costs were estimated at 23.4 million crowns. The government received sizable sums from the Norrbotten mine fields and from various specific taxes, like a tax on tobacco and a stamp duty. But with the passing of the old-age pension in 1913 these funds were in large part used up. Other necessary reforms involved township taxes and care of the poor. Another reform of great interest was of course temperance.

The two chambers of the 1909 Riksdag had agreed on a study of the economic role of the intoxicating beverage industry. The 1913 Riksdag freed the townships, county councils, and rural economy associations from direct dependence upon revenues from liquor sales, the reform costing the state 13 million crowns per year. The funds which had previously gone to different governing bodies were now to go to the state, which would be allowed to keep 39 million crowns per year; amounts above that sum were to go to a fund for social purposes. It is interesting that public elementary school teachers were to receive large parts of their remuneration from the income from sales of intoxicating beverages.

The allocation of part of the income from intoxicating beverages for reforms of various kinds was greeted by the cultural radicals with joy, and Conservatives too saw various benefits in this strengthening of the public treasury. Total prohibition, which would eliminate an important source of public income, became their common enemy. Even in temperance quarters there was hesitation about pressing for immediate total prohibition.

The spring election of 1914 saw a reversal of the previous trend against the Conservatives. Their representation in the Second Chamber increased from 65 to 85 members. This increase was at the expense of the Liberals, who dropped from 101 to 71. The Social Democrats rose from 64 to 73.

At the end of May 1914 the Riksdag appointed a special parliamentary committee to consider the defense question. On June 2, the vice-speaker of the Second Chamber, Daniel Persson af Tällberg, requested that a special parliamentary committee should also be set up to handle temperance motions. The Liberal and Social Democratic parties had presented motions that supported local veto and sales reforms. The Second Chamber approved Tällberg's recommendation and invited the First

Chamber to concur in this decision, thus putting the temperance and defense issues on the same level. The First Chamber, however, rejected the recommendation.

The new Hammarskjöld government took up the temperance issue in a proposition on July 24. Local veto was abandoned, as well as the sales reform recommended by a temperance committee set up by the Riksdag in 1911. The proposition occasioned a very bitter debate. The Second Chamber opposed the government and instead opted for local veto and the other regulations recommended by the temperance committee.

The work of the special parliamentary committee on defense went slowly during June and July. The Conservatives were afraid that the defense question would be overshadowed by temperance. A compromise was sought that would couple the two issues. A prominent Conservative, Sam Clason, wrote in a letter to Queen Viktoria in the middle of July: "For the present, a number of leftists dare not take the government['s recommendation], but if they could say to the voters that they had won something in the temperance question, then they could defend their crossover to the government's defense program." Clason therefore recommended that the Conservatives, in order to retain the initiative, should let the government present a temperance proposition including even some form of local veto. This was a line similar to the one advocated by the finance minister, Axel Vennersten. The two Conservative leaders, Arvid Lindman and Ernst Trygger, feared that such a recommendation would split the right. The debate between Vennersten and the two Conservative leaders became extraordinarily sharp; those on both sides threatened to resign their posts. On July 17, Vennersten gave in, however, and local veto was not included in the government proposition of July 24, although the finance minister added in the protocol that he would have nothing against a modified form of veto.

With the outbreak of World War I the opportunity for the left to couple temperance with defense negotiations in the Riksdag had disappeared. Thereafter the Liberals accepted almost without deviation the Conservative line on defense. The electorate, however, did not give its unqualified support to the government's defense program. In the September 6, 1914, election the Conservatives declined somewhat or just held their own in almost all areas, and the Liberals lost more ground. The Social Democrats gained strongly. The Liberal losses and the Social Democratic gains came primarily in Norrland and central Sweden. In five months an important reversal had taken place in Swedish politics. The spring election had made the pro-defense Liberals move to the right. The fall election indicated support for reforms and dissatisfaction with the defense agreement and its consequences. In this situation, the Social Democrats reaped success.

A regional analysis shows that the dissatisfaction with the Liberals was great within areas traditionally dominated by strong popular movements. In the spring election, many temperance advocates and members of free churches had held fast to Staaff's party, but in the fall election, there was a step to the left. A more radical program was demanded.

The electorate had made its voice heard in the fall election. Unity on defense was qualified. The Conservative line had not won general support despite the Liberals' acceptance of it. Instead the Social Democrats' position on defense had demonstrated great attraction for voters. Intimately coupled with defense in the public view was the matter of reforms, primarily temperance. The desire for reforms had persuaded many to leave the ranks of the Liberals. They were not satisfied with what they considered to be negative action; they wanted a positive solution to national problems.

The defense and temperance propositions were formally decided in the Riksdag on September 12. The former was passed; the latter fell because of Conservative rejection in the First Chamber. Ernst Trygger's criticism was characteristic of the Conservatives' view: "For us local veto is not a temperance question but a purely political question, a means of altering the bases for communal suffrage in general to the detriment of the country, and we have made it absolutely clear that we cannot go along with the coupling of the temperance issue and questions foreign to it."

Local veto reappeared in the 1915 and 1916 Riksdags but fell both times on the rejection of the First Chamber Conservatives. Karl Staaff attempted to use the strategy of threatening tax increases in negotiating with the First Chamber over local veto, but after his death in October 1915 his successors let the initiative drop. At the end of April 1917, the committee on supply presented a compromise recommendation on the temperance question which sacrificed local veto in order to obtain a new sales reform. This recommendation was dictated by the Conservatives within the committee. The Social Democrats and a number of Liberals entered reservations. The First Chamber voted in accordance with the committee's recommendation. The debate was more heated in the Second Chamber, and recommendation for returning the proposal to the committee was carried there. During the next days, however, a decided shift took place in the ranks of the Social Democrats, which led them to accept the committee recommendation for sales reform but no local veto.

To understand why this happened it is necessary to take account of the mood in Sweden following the Russian Revolution. On April 28, the Social Democratic leader, Hjalmar Branting, had put a question to Prime Minister Carl Swartz on the desire of the government to assist in undertaking a constitutional revision aimed at general and equal suffrage for men and women. He cited the Russian Revolution as the beginning of a world revolution and declared that developments in Sweden must come into harmony with it. On May 7, the Social Democratic Riksdag group announced that it favored the establishment of a special parliamentary committee to follow the developments within the international labor movement. The First Chamber showed evidence of alarm and fear. On May 20–23, the Social Democratic party leaders discussed the possibility of a revolution in Sweden. Many voices were raised in favor of a revolution, but the leaders of the trade union movement were strongly opposed.

The shift within the left on the temperance issue should be seen against this background. It was especially marked among the Social Democrats, many of whom were actively engaged in the events of the day. They expected a rapid and drastic change, in which the First Chamber would be swept away; the issue of local veto seemed unimportant in this context. General and equal suffrage would soon be introduced in any case. But the expected quick change did not come. The revolutionary mood receded as quickly as it had come. On June 5, the prime minister answered Branting's interpellation and a long debate ensued, in which Branting took the floor several times. It became clear that his earlier hopes for rapid change had disappeared. Branting now indicated that a long road must be traveled before the goal of equal suffrage was reached. In June the First Chamber Conservatives were no longer afraid of revolution.

With the acceptance of the temperance compromise, local veto disappeared as an issue. In the future, temperance became a purely social problem and the suffrage question was approached directly. At the ordinary 1918 Riksdag, no real results were achieved in suffrage despite the installation of a Liberal–Social Democratic government in September 1917. Only at the extraordinary Riksdag during the late fall of 1918 could the government, under the influence of the great revolutions in Europe, pass a constitutional revision giving equal and general suffrage to men and women. This constitutional revision was carried out with strong support from the popular movements. Not only the labor movement but the temperance and free church movements were deeply involved. A driving force behind the reform was the ecclesiastical minister Värner Rydén, a Social Democrat and zealous temperance advocate. The minister of war, Erik A. Wilsson, a Liberal and leading free church supporter, was another popular movement leader within the government who espoused constitutional revision.

In summary it is clear that the three largest popular movements were strongly in favor of reforms. The reforms stressed depended on which movement was concerned, but they had a common basic interest in suffrage. This interest in reforms was absorbed by the leftist political parties: the Social Democratic party became a suffrage party, and the Liberals were forced to take account of reformist demands. At the same time, it is apparent that the political parties forced members of the movements onto paths different from those on which they started. This was clearly the case with free church supporters on the edge of the right, for example: in joining the Conservatives they had to abandon their original goal of local veto because the party leadership did not share their attitude.

It is not possible to delimit precisely what this or that organization contributed in the give and take that resulted finally in democratization of the Swedish body politic. There are a number of historical topics that have not been studied closely; until further data are available there will be uncertainty in any judgments on the political contributions of the popular movements. For example, the role of farmers needs examination. Although the number of Sweden's industrial workers increased between 1900 and 1920, the majority of its population was still involved in agriculture. Even in 1920, 44 percent of the population was occupied in agriculture against 35 percent in industry and crafts. The political development among farmers is not easy to interpret: about 1910, they seemed to turn to the right, while in 1914 they went to both the right and the left. Many of them, especially in central and northern Sweden, voted for the Social Democrats. In 1917, the conservatively oriented groups were collected in the Agrarian party and the Farmers' National Association, but there remained a strong political mobility within the ranks of the farmers. A number of comparative investigations are also needed, primarily of the other Nordic countries. They would help establish why, for example, the Swedish free church movement did not have greater influence on politics—in certain other countries, religious questions have been major subjects of controversy—or why the temperance movement became so strong in Sweden and had such political consequences. It would then be possible to judge what is general and what is unique.

Introduction to Chapter 8

After the reforms of 1866 the demand for parliamentary and democratic reform subsided. The main issues in the Riksdag were ones concerning economics, defense, and the special privileges of certain elements of Swedish society. The upper chamber was dominated until the late 1870s by the aristocracy, wealthy businessmen, and members of the bureaucracy, whereas the lower chamber was controlled by agrarian groups. The political struggles of the period mirrored the interests of these groups and often took the form of conflict between urban and rural interests. By the late 1880s the most controversial issue had become the free trade–protectionist question. Representatives of business had by this time become important figures in Swedish political life. During the heat of the debate on protectionism in 1887 the king, Oskar II, dissolved the Second Chamber on his own initiative, an act which demonstrated that the royal house intended to keep as much power as it could. The controversy over protectionism eventually led to a division in the older political groups and to the formation of new political alliances. The 1890s was a period in which the political groups that had so long dominated the Riksdag were able to reach compromises on almost all the questions that had caused so much controversy in the previous decades. However, at the very time when these old elites were finding common ground for compromise, new groups demanding major social and political reform began to make themselves heard.

Initially there had been a few Swedes who had been very disappointed with the conservative nature of the Riksdag reforms of 1866. Only 5½ percent of the males over 25 had been given the right to vote and as late as 1896 only 6 percent of the Swedish populace could participate in the Swedish electoral process. Between 1865 and 1890 most of the other Western European countries had extended the franchise to include all males over a specific age. By the early 1890s progressive elements in Sweden, the radical liberals, the Social Democrats, other popular groups, organized themselves into a movement to establish universal male (later female as well) suffrage and parliamentary democracy. This movement organized "people's parliaments," petition signing, and even a brief general strike in 1902. By 1900 the pressure to take some action on suffrage was unavoidable. The question remained what specific solution to adopt.

At the same time as the political debate became more heated, a new form of social-economic crisis developed: the conflict of the labor market. The growth of the trade unions with their determination to improve the conditions of their members combined with the desire of the employers (who after 1907 were themselves organized in a central body, the SAF) to limit the power of the unions and to keep wages at "competitive" levels led to an increasingly violent labor market struggle. The lines between the opposing groups in the political debate did not correspond precisely to the lines between the groups contending the economic question. Additionally, a question which at least in its origin was completely outside Swedish control—the dissolution of the Swedish-Norwegian union—reached a climax at the same time, 1905, when suffrage reform could no longer be postponed, and the economic conflict moved toward a major blowup. The years between 1905 and 1914 were ones of great crisis. The following essay, by Docent Bernt Schiller, is a study of the initial outcome of these conflicts and an examination of the interrelationship between the political and economic struggles.

8

Years of Crisis, 1906-1914

by Berndt Schiller

In Swedish history, 1905 stands out as the year when the union with Norway was dissolved, but it was also the year when the country received its first Liberal government and when the big industrial employers accepted the first collective bargaining agreement. The union crisis marked the end of one historical era; the other two events laid the foundations for a new political and industrial phase.

Suffrage and parliamentarianism were the catchwords which dominated the political arena. But more was involved. The whole political structure was affected when common people and workers in the country and the cities under Liberal and Socialist banners attacked the positions of those who traditionally held power. This struggle is easiest to follow as a political battle between the right and the left over the control of government and this will be a main theme in this chapter. Equally important changes took place in the industrial sector. The curve of industrial production, which had begun to point steeply upwards especially during the 1890s, continued to climb. New industries contributed more and more to the industrialization of Sweden. The Lappland mine fields were exploited; paper pulp factories grew up alongside earlier sawmills; the now famous products of the engineering industry, such as telephones, ball bearings, separators, AGA lighthouses, and turbines, sold more and more on the world market; a domestic industry for the manufacture of clothing and shoes continued to develop. Within industry, a reorganization of conditions of ownership occurred in order to bring about larger units and broader raw-material bases. The entrepreneurs were well aware of their importance for the national upswing and demanded that society show consideration for the needs of industry. When workers in quickly growing numbers joined the trade union movement the entrepreneurs found themselves forced to form their own battle organizations—employers' associations. The economic conflict of interest over wages and working conditions became a political contest between capital and labor through the close connection of the trade union movement with the Social Democratic party. The struggle between employer and worker associations is the second main theme in the following pages.

The course of events is described below as an internal Swedish one; counterparts elsewhere have had to be disregarded. Yet it must be recognized at the outset that neither Swedish industry nor Swedish politics enjoyed any autonomy from world developments; the effects of the international recession of 1907–1909 and of the increasing great power conflicts before the outbreak of war in 1914 were acutely felt by Swedes. The conditions that led to the two major crises in Sweden during this period, the general strike of 1909 and the castle courtyard coup in 1914, were created beyond the nation's boundaries.

The Struggle for Suffrage and Labor Conflicts

The leader of the Liberals, Karl Staaff, was a lawyer by profession. During his years of study at Uppsala University, he had belonged to the radical student association Verdandi and had known Hjalmar Branting, who later became head of the Social Democratic party. The literary portraits of Staaff indicate that he had few intimate friends, was stiff in social situations, and had a rough manner, but his simple straightforwardness made him a "popular" leader. The government formed by Staaff at the beginning of November 1905 differed in several respects from earlier Swedish governments; it was a pure party government, it exercised a continued real leadership over the Liberal caucus in the Riksdag, it had a national organization, and it based its existence only on the popularly elected Second Chamber. The government had been formed for one purpose: to carry out the Liberal suffrage program. When the Riksdag voted down this suffrage proposal in May 1906, the Liberal government resigned. During Staaff's first government, the basis for one conflict was laid and another was sharpened. A personal enmity arose between Staaff and Crown Prince Gustav and the gap between the right and the left in Swedish politics was widened owing to the events surrounding the government's fall.

In composition the Swedish Riksdag stood out at this time as one of the most reactionary of European parliaments, surpassed only by the Prussian Lantdag. This was due to the very limited suffrage in Sweden and the strict regulations on eligibility for election. The First Chamber was an upper house, where government officials, landed gentry, and big businessmen dominated. The Second Chamber, despite the election regulations in effect, had a more popular character not only because it was directly elected but also because of its composition of middle-class men from the cities and countryside. The Liberal suffrage recommendation proposed general and equal suffrage for men in elections to the Second Chamber. The elections would remain determined by majority vote. The First Chamber would be left unreformed. The chambers were equal according to the constitution, but if the Second Chamber were elected under universal suffrage it would in practice come to surpass the upper house in importance, like the lower house in Great Britain. This was admitted frankly by the prime minister in the debate in the First Chamber: "It is the duty of the Second Chamber or lower house to see that the clock runs; in the great political questions, the First Chamber or upper house must see what the clock has struck." The rejoinder from the opposition was that the First Chamber should see to it that "the clock runs correctly, correctly according to its understanding."

The government proposition was defeated in the First Chamber by an overwhelming majority on May 14, 1906, but the Second Chamber passed it on the evening of the following day. The prime minister then made a speech in which with great force he posed this question in conclusion: "Shall royal power with popular rule or royal power with upper-class rule prevail in the kingdom of Sweden? " The foreign minister and war minister handed in their resignations to protest the prime minister's statement. "This is a declaration of war, and I don't want any part of such political struggles," the foreign minister explained. He had, he said, only then realized that this government had a different character from earlier ones. The conservative press accused the prime minister of having stepped down from the high position of his office in order to act exclusively as a partisan and agitator. Within the left, Staaff's words were taken up as a call for battle. At an audience with the crown prince, who in practice functioned as regent in place of the aged king, Staaff asked to be allowed to dissolve the Second Chamber. If the popularly elected chamber, after an expected big election victory for the left, could reconfirm its vote for the Liberal suffrage proposal, the First Chamber would be forced by popular opinion to capitulate. The crown prince asked for time to consider the matter. After the cabinet meeting a week later, the king, in the presence of the crown prince, informed Staaff curtly that he could not approve a dissolution of the Second Chamber. Staaff presented the resignation of the Liberal government immediately.

A new prime minister was already waiting in the wings to take possession of the stage. During the week that had passed, the crown prince had assured himself that a new government would be on hand. The offer had been made first to a moderately conservative farmer-politician, Alfred Petersson af Påboda, whose recommendation for proportional elections to the Riksdag had been the counterproposal accepted by the First Chamber instead of the government recommendation. He said no, but joined the government as minister of agriculture. Factory manager Arvid Lindman was then asked to form a new government and he immediately accepted. Lindman was not one of the foremost conservative politicians in Sweden, but he soon would make himself known as an energetic and agile leader for a modern form of conservatism. In a dictation to the cabinet protocol, the king wished the new government "prosperity and success." Because of the position he adopted more than because of his words, the king was henceforth regarded as allied with the right. "That is how strong the power of attraction is between groups that belong together socially," *Social-Demokraten* wrote. A radical rural paper noted that the question of monarchy or republic "has become a timely issue." The paper in the capital that was closest to the fallen government wrote, "The royal power sows wind; it is well if it does not reap storm." On the other hand, various conservative newspapers approved the king's actions and accused Staaff of having tried to subvert the constitution.

The newly formed government was a coalition of moderates and conservatives with Lindman and Påboda as leaders. The moderate Påboda group had its strongest support in the Second Chamber in the Ruralist party and the National Progressive party. Lindman and other conservative ministers were close to the First Chamber. From the beginning, conflicts between the farmer Petersson from Påboda and the businessman Lindman from Iggesund factory took the form of a personal rivalry over leadership of the government; they also reflected a peasant's mistrust of company conservatism. Like its predecessor, the government came into being in order to carry out a suffrage recommendation; unlike it, Lindman-Påboda succeeded.

The government proposition included proportional elections to both chambers. Suffrage would be universal and equal for men at elections to the Second Chamber; at township elections, which determined the First Chamber's composition, a graduated scale would limit any individual to no more than forty votes. The moderate-conservative government offered as much as the Liberals had on elections to the Second Chamber, but also proposed a considerable democratization of the township elections and thereby indirectly of the First Chamber. For many moderate farmer members of the Riksdag, the possibility of increased township influence was appealing. The recommendation's relatively radical character had repercussions as far to the left as in the Social Democratic party. After the fall of the Liberal government in May, a general strike by the labor movement in support of suffrage had become a possibility but at a general strike meeting in April 1907, the debate showed how the government had snatched away the political prerequisites for a strike.

While the government proposal was attractive to moderate middle groups, it was nonetheless a conservative solution of the suffrage question. Proportionalism guaranteed considerable conservative minority representation in the Second Chamber, and the forty-grade scale for voting continued a conservative majority in the First Chamber.

In order to enact its proposal, the government had to entice twenty-one members of the Second Chamber from the majority that had voted for the Liberal election proposal the previous year. Påboda worked for this through his contacts with the farmers on the Liberal party's right flank. The Liberal farmer leader Persson af Tällberg introduced a motion that further "improved" the government recommendation by introducing remuneration and reducing the eligibility requirements for the First Chamber. Lindman's contribution consisted of the not inconsiderable political feat of persuading the First Chamber to swallow Tällberg's additional conditions in the final round under the threat of the government's resignation. The solution of the suffrage question had shown that in a battle between the right and the left, the farmer groups in the political middle played a decisive role. On an issue which for decades had been pursued by the left and which was the primary point on the Liberal party program, farmer support had allowed solution by a moderate-conservative government according to its prescription: universal suffrage with conservative guarantees.

At approximately the same time as the Lindman government took the lead on the suffrage question, the employers seized the initiative on the trade union battlefield. At the beginning of 1907, the Swedish Employers' Confederation (SAF) directed an ultimatum on "the freedom of labor" to the Swedish Confederation of Trade Unions (LO) under the threat of a lockout.

SAF had accepted a collective bargaining agreement in principle the previous year on one condition: "freedom of labor" had to be written into all contracts. This meant the right of the employer to direct and assign work and to freely hire and fire workers regardless of whether they belonged to LO or other organizations, or were unorganized. The provisions on the freedom of labor were incorporated into the statutes of SAF under paragraph number 23 (later §32). As in other countries, freedom of labor became the first commandment of the employers' organizations.

When the freedom of labor was ushered into practical politics during 1906 and brought a number of conflicts with LO, a crisis arose in SAF. Should it continue with §23 unchanged? The SAF directorate was shunted aside by a coup and specially deputized men were given the assignment of negotiating a compromise with LO's leadership. In the so-called December Compromise, freedom of labor was accepted in return for recognition of the right to organize and protection against firings directed at exercise of this right. The acceptance and immediate execution of the compromise created strong antagonism within SAF. A group of industrial leaders saw the settlement as a detestable concession, and they threatened a lockout against LO. SAF's connections with both the First Chamber and the government were intimate. The political repercussions of a general labor conflict were discussed. SAF's chairman defended the December Compromise with references among other things to the fact that a conflict would jeopardize the suffrage issue. Christian Lundeberg, the majority party's leader in the First Chamber, a factory owner, and also a member of SAF, was critical of the December Compromise and also of the suffrage proposition. In his view, a general labor conflict could have positive political results by opening the eyes of the people. It is hard to judge if political considerations played a role for SAF's leadership, as some alleged. It seems to be clear, in any case, that the Lindman government and the majority of conservative newspapers wanted a peaceful solution of the conflict between SAF and LO. On the other hand, the ultraconservative press supported the combative industrial leaders. After new negotiations an agreement was reached without a lockout.

The strains SAF had been subjected to forced a comprehensive reorganization. The old leadership was replaced, and power in the organization was concentrated. The jurist Hjalmar von Sydow became both chairman of the board and executive director. Organizational and economic resources were strengthened. SAF became a power equal to LO. In the collective bargaining agreement the employers had maintained their foremost condition— freedom of labor. Everyone knew that what had occurred was the beginning of a tug of war in the labor market.

The next phase came during 1908. Once again, freedom of labor or §23 was at the center of the battle. SAF and the Shipowners' Association had agreed to force through this provision in the contract being negotiated with the harbor workers and thereby break the monopoly which the Transport Workers'

Union had achieved, especially in the Norrland harbors. The battle was long and hard. In order to bring an end to strikes which were gradually extended, the employers imported strikebreakers from England. Severe disturbances resulted. In Göteborg a riot broke out, and in Malmö a receiving ship was blown up by some Young Socialists and one English strikebreaker was killed and several injured. The king visited the injured men in the hospital in order to express his sympathy. The bourgeois press condemned the anarchist propaganda carried on by the Young Socialists, who shortly before had formed a separate party after their leaders were expelled from the Social Democratic party.

At the same time as the attack in Malmö took place, all the employers' organizations in the country had joined together and proclaimed a general lockout. In response, innumerable workers' meetings demanded that labor leaders call a general strike. A general work stoppage thus threatened the country. In this situation, the government intervened forcefully. A special conciliation commission was appointed under the leadership of a prominent diplomat. The interior minister, who before his appointment as minister had been mediator at the negotiations on the December Compromise, exerted pressure on both sides. Even the king engaged himself in the critical final phase. The LO then accepted the arbitrator's suggestions and by strong pressures broke the transport workers' resistance. The last hurdle to an agreement was the employers. In an almost couplike manner during the night of July 17, the arbitrator gaveled through a proposal whereby the general lockout was called off at the last minute.

Both the trade unions and the political leadership on the union side had opted for a peaceful solution. The LO representative assembly had taken a stand against a general strike and forced the transport workers to make concessions. The Social Democratic party leadership had noted how the labor conflict prejudiced the preparations for the Second Chamber election at the beginning of the autumn. Branting feared that a labor conflict, with attendant stoppage of wages, would weaken the Social Democrats' position in leftist cooperation with the Liberals in Stockholm because the construction workers would fall below the so-called tax line.*

On the employers' side, the willingness to accept a general strike had been considerably greater. A united front of employers had been reached on the principle of freedom of labor in the harbors. The organizations were well equipped and the declining business cycle, which had become more and more apparent during the previous six months, gave them more trumps in their hand. The inclination on the labor side for peace in all probability would not have been sufficient to prevent an outbreak of battle. Only the government's intervention accomplished that.

The government's action had been consistent with its desire not to have a major labor conflict at the time of the suffrage proposal's presentation in 1907. The suffrage recommendation would now surely be accepted on a first reading, but a second reading had to take place in 1909 after the new elections in 1908, as provided by the constitution. The need for continued support for the suffrage proposal contributed to holding the government factions together.

Many employers were strongly critical of the government's intervention. AB Separator's executive director accepted news of it as mournful tidings which brought tears to his eyes. In a letter to the conservative politician in the First Chamber who was Separator's chairman of the board, he wrote: "It is rather quiet and peaceful in the business so that we have a lot of time to grieve over the way in which HM's government interests itself in the country's industry. Once again the Socialists have received powerful help from the government and the injury this will cause is, to my mind, *incurable*. . . . Such a propitious opportunity to strike a blow that would bring a long-lasting peace and a healthy fear in those who would overthrow society will never return!" On the

* Eligibility to vote depended on payment of taxes.

labor side, the transport workers especially—the losing party in the agreement—expressed bitterness over the outcome. Others regarded it as acceptable or in any case necessary. The Young Socialists denounced it as treachery dictated by fear of losing Riksdag seats.

The press, from moderately conservative to Social Democratic newspapers, expressed a more or less clear approval of the conclusion of peace. The newspapers farthest to the right and farthest to the left condemned it.

The parties carried on intense campaigns before the Second Chamber election at the beginning of September 1908. The prime minister himself went out as party leader in a way that previously had not been customary. His interior minister attacked the trade union movement in a speech at the dedication of a new power station and issued the call for battle: Solidarity against socialism! But a short time later, the government's agriculture minister stood in his native parish's church and attacked an ultra-right candidate hostile to reforms. Påboda explained that the Swedish farmer class was called on to be a conciliatory and mediating element between the extremes. The agriculture minister, as spokesman for the political center, turned against the "big employers and company stockholders." The leftist parties, Liberals and Social Democrats, went to the polls advocating parliamentarianism and opposing the power of the upper classes.

The government was defeated in the election. The Social Democrats quadrupled their representation. The major parties' position in the Second Chamber for the 1909 Riksdag as a result

Party	Seats Held	Loss or Gain
Conservative groups	91	−17
Liberals	105	−4
Social Democrats	34	+21

of the election is shown in the tabulation. Election participation was 61 percent. The two cooperating left parties had 139 seats in the popularly elected Second Chamber against the government's 91. Karl Staaff proposed to dislodge the government. For that purpose the technique of directing an interpellation to the prime minister on an important political issue was used. The left's interpellation concerned the rights of the Riksdag relative to the administration. Påboda opposed the answer the prime minister intended to give. Lindman then urged him to leave the government. Two ministers joined with Påboda and resigned. All were replaced by conservatives. At the debate that followed the prime minister's answer, both of the opposition leaders declared that "the government lacked the chamber's confidence," whereupon a demonstration by the majority of the chamber's members followed. But the prime minister had been able to entice to his side the conservative farmers in the Second Chamber. Although the farmer representative Påboda no longer sat on the ministers' bench, the left's demonstration was met with a declaration of confidence in the government by the conservatives, in which the farmers in the Ruralist party and the National Progressive party concurred. Påboda had not given up his effort to represent a farmer center in Swedish politics, however. The question of the farmers' political home was not decided. Within the Liberal party, Staaff had reason to keep an eye on them.

The government dismissed the left's parliamentary maneuver in the Second Chamber and continued, with farmer support in that chamber, to sit as a purely conservative government.

The General Strike

While the political situation was undergoing "the Påboda crisis," the clouds of a new major crisis began gathering over the labor market. After the dramatic agreement on July 18, 1908, the employer organizations had directed new threats of lockouts at LO, whose board, with a majority of the trade unions behind it, persuaded various labor groups to bow to the employers' demands. This policy of concession aroused more and more displeasure among the trade unions. The discontent was effectively fanned by the Young Socialists, who agitated for syndicalist tactics and a revolutionary general strike. The Young Socialists numbered only several thousand members, especially among masons, mine workers, and unskilled and factory workers, but their propaganda in the prevailing situation had a wide dissemination.

A number of labor conflicts broke out in the spring of 1909 that concerned wage issues in certain cases in national agreements. The labor unions' demands for wage increases collided with the employers' demand for keeping the status quo or decreasing wages. A strike at Skutskär's paper pulp factory occasioned a proclamation from SAF in July on an extended lockout. The LO leadership found it impossible to persuade the trade unions to go along with SAF's demands presented under the threat of a lockout. It was equally impossible to wage a long and hard battle on a limited front. In that situation the national secretariat found itself forced to suggest a general work stoppage, not only against SAF but against all employers in Sweden, to begin on August 4, 1909. Exemptions from the strike were suggested for workers at socially important companies and for workers with strike prohibitions in their contracts. The decision-making body within LO, the representative assembly, did not go along with exempting workers prohibited by contract from striking. The general strike proclamation exempted only workers in health care, animal care, gas, water, and electrical plants, and sanitation workers.

In the proclamation the trade unions themselves were entrusted with formally making the decision whether or not to strike. The pressure to participate in making the decision was extremely strong. The streetcar men, who had a contract with a strike prohibition, gathered at a meeting the night of August 3 in Stockholm. This was their reaction, according to one report: "The atmosphere was indescribable. People got up on chairs and made speeches without asking for the floor. Those who voted against were called traitors, the association's board was characterized as cowardly, etc. A suggestion for a resolution on surrendering half of the day's income during the strike days to the strikers was greeted with whistling." In this kind of atmosphere, it was decided to disregard the contract, and the streetcar director was telephoned in the middle of the night and informed that he should not expect any streetcar traffic when the morning dawned.

The bitterness over the exemptions was as strong in some quarters as the enthusiasm over the general strike proclamation was universal. The workers in a small community in Hälsingland expressed it this way: "Our opponents have never shown any consideration for us. Therefore we don't owe them any in return." Protests over the exemptions streamed in to the strike leadership both before and after the outbreak of the general strike. According to Hjalmar Branting, the LO leadership had shown wisdom and power by making exemptions from the general strike and not provoking the important middle layers of society. The spokesmen of these middle layers in the liberal press warned labor's leadership against measures that were directed at the society as such. In the face of the general strike the liberal newspapers' opinions came close to those of the conservative press.

It proved to be difficult for the LO leadership to maintain the exemptions. The employees at Stockholm's gasworks stopped work, despite attempts by the national secretariat to persuade them to remain on the job, when the authorities refused to draw back their military units. The gravediggers at the New Cemetery, whom no one had thought of exempting, heeded the summons to strike but they let themselves be persuaded to return to work. Later during the general strike it seemed for a time as if the secretariat would change its mind and give the sanitation workers permission to strike. In response to a rumor that a Liberal arbitration initiative was being prepared, however, the secretariat immediately returned to its original position. When the workers asked that the pit coal mines in Skåne be flooded, LO's chairman,

Herman Lindqvist, threatened to resign if this was authorized; the strike at the mine pumps was rejected by LO's representative assembly.

One problem for the LO leadership was what to do about the trade unions that did not belong to the confederation: typographers, railway men, and so on. A decision on principle was made not to encourage them to participate but, if they asked, they would be invited to heed the strike proclamation. Such a tactful temperateness did not suit the common workers when they gathered for their strike meetings. A large meeting at Lilljans in Stockholm accepted the following resolution: "Comrades! We are now in the third day of the general strike and no change in the battle situation has occurred. . . . One means to carry on the battle with greater strength is work stoppage by railway men and typographers. This meeting therefore directs a comradely appeal to the country's railway men and typographers to stand on the sidelines in the battle no longer but to join the ranks. May the trains stop, may the newspapers cease to come out. The working class's combined action demands this. Railway men, typographers, we appeal to your solidarity in the conviction that our exhortation will not resound unheard." The meeting's chairman was indicted by the authorities and the bourgeois press, even radical newspapers, took the resolution as proof that the general strike was hostile to society.

Several days after August 4, the board of the Typographers' Union announced that it was joining the general strike under pressure from its members. All differences between conservative and liberal views on the general strike ceased in the face of the typographers' strike. In the provisional editions of newspapers which soon began to appear, there was total agreement that the general strike must fail before any intervention for peace could be allowed to occur. A bourgeois united front had appeared.

The railway men decided after a general vote within their association to support the strikers with money only. The national secretariat tried to prevent all attempts to get the railway men to participate in the general strike. Strike appeals from the workers in Ystad and from a board member of the Social Democratic party were repudiated. The LO leadership's action seems peculiar, in view of the common labor ideology that a communications strike was especially important in any general labor dispute. The Lilljans meeting's resolution reflected this ideology. An investigation of what the trade union movement's leaders intended by their proclamation on a general work stoppage contributes to our understanding of their position.

For a statement on the general strike's purpose to have value as a source, it must be from the time immediately before the strike. Such a statement exists: a letter from the trade unions' general commission in Germany to the German trade unions' representatives, which reports a statement Hjalmar Branting made on behalf of LO at a meeting with the German commission. Branting had said that a general strike in Sweden would be aimed at exerting such pressure on society that the Swedish government would be forced to intervene after a short time. The general strike was thus from the beginning not intended as a long-drawn-out war of starvation but as a lightning blow. The sudden shock that the society was to be subjected to was intended to persuade that society to intervene and force through a peace agreement acceptable to the workers. The society as such would not be threatened by the strike's taking on a revolutionary character. Therefore LO's leaders wanted to conduct the battle humanely and grant exemptions for the workers in the most essential functions of society. As noted above, the secretariat originally also wanted to exempt workers with a strike prohibition in their contracts; thus it did not propose that either typographers or railway men would participate. The typographers could not be stopped; when the railway men decided against participating, the national secretariat refused to try to persuade them. In its view a strike on the Swedish State Railways would have meant a direct attack on the state, which would then have entered the fray on the same side as SAF.

If it were not to invite a futile discussion on how a general strike is to be defined, it would be tempting to say that LO's leaders in 1909 did not originally suggest a general strike. After LO's decision was made, the work stoppage became greater than intended. When the strike proclamation reached the masses, it was greeted as the call for a general strike for which they had been waiting for years. The general strike ideology was an effective force here. The exemptions were at the same time too few and too many: too few to prevent liberal opinion from moving to the right in support of the employers—primarily because of the typographers' strike, but also because of other real or imaginary breaches of contracts. At the same time, one exemption too many was made: the railway men. During the prevailing economic crisis, there were large supplies of wares ready to be carried out of the country by train and boat. In a short strike, free railway traffic and shipping played no role, but in a long battle they became important. The general strike in Sweden in 1909 turned out to be long, probably the longest anywhere in the world.

The government never intended to try seriously to stop the outbreak of the strike. Lindman remained passive in accordance with the desire of the employers. But this desire was shared by the greater part of the bourgeois society. Not until the end of August did the Liberals propose arbitration to the government, at the same time stating that the general strike must then be regarded as unsuccessful. They were met by a categorical no. On September 6, LO was forced to call off the general strike. Only then did the government declare that there was no longer any barrier to arbitration to try to bring the sides together. For nearly five weeks all industrial production and part of the local transportation system had stood still. Almost 300,000 workers had participated in the strike.

Soon after the outbreak of the general strike, the director of

SAF, Hjalmar von Sydow, had begun to work out the employers' conditions for peace. They would constitute a major contract between SAF and LO and contain a collected codification of the principles of agreement which SAF had consciously fought for since 1907, often with the threat of a lockout as a weapon. These principles were either taken directly from Danish models (the Danish September Agreement of 1899) or indirectly from the Swedish engineering industry's agreement of 1905. That the Swedish employers followed the Danish line meant that, internationally, they allied themselves more to developments in Great Britain than to those in Germany. They had won the victory in the general strike and now wanted to force through a single all-embracing contract system. The principles were to be these: freedom of labor, non-union-member foremen, and the right of sympathy expressions (the right to strike and lockout for the purpose of expressing sympathy, despite valid contracts). Through uniformity in the contracts, which would include all entrepreneurs in the same industry in the kingdom, the employers wished to create a "straight line" against the workers and prevent the trade unions from gradually trying to move forward on the issues of wages and other working provisions.

LO preferred not to confirm the workers' defeat. Therefore no peace was ever concluded after the general strike. The central leadership for the main labor organizations did not agree on a major contract until almost thirty years later. What made it possible for LO to avoid signing an agreement signalizing defeat was SAF's tactic in the conflicts that continued even after the general strike itself was ended. When the workers could hold out no longer, the employers allowed them to return to work on the condition that they would not belong to LO as long as the disputes went on. LO gradually lost half its members in this way but also to a corresponding degree did not have to pay out benefits to striking workers. LO just withdrew from the battle without having accepted the employers' conditions. Lockouts continued formally although work gradually returned to normal.

One exception was the ironworks, where the trade unions' stamina was such that a real conflict continued far into the late fall. Certain individual employers resorted to desperate measures like evicting the workers from their company-owned housing. These actions made a bad impression on public opinion and the bourgeois opposition toward the labor conflict began to dissolve. In the end, SAF was forced to cancel the lockout at the ironworks in the middle of November.

It is difficult to determine with certainty the general strike's effect on bourgeois opinion. Every indication is that it was considerable. A move to the right appears both in the press and in individual statements. For the Liberal party, encompassing both a moderate and a radical wing, the shift in opinion must have been bothersome. It had to retain its hold on the farmer wing and, with it, the moderate urban Liberals. Discussions about forming a center party had taken place between Påboda and Tällberg, but the plans had been dropped because the right would gain most from a new center party. It must be understood that Påboda could not count on any support for a new party from the conservative farmers in the Second Chamber, who now followed Lindman. Forming a farmer center party would then have meant a weakening of the Liberal party.

Karl Staaff recognized the danger to his party, and in a widely noted speech in Eskilstuna at the end of October he sharply attacked labor's leadership for encouraging the breaking of contracts during the general strike. The speech had two purposes. The speech was intended to forestall a loss of moderate Liberals, preferably sacrificing instead some unsatisfied urban radicals to the Social Democrats. Furthermore, the speech was designed as a contribution to the dialogue between Liberals and Social Democrats: the Social Democratic party must restrain anarchistic tendencies and reestablish cooperation among the leftist groups before the next Riksdag.

The main issue at the 1910 Riksdag was the government's proposal for labor contract legislation. During the general strike, the government had dissolved the contract law committee that had been formed earlier and forced out a proposal for a law on collective agreements, individual labor contracts, and labor courts. In various places in the proposal, the principles of SAF were incorporated. What LO had avoided at a high price during negotiations in the fall of 1909 might now come through legislation. With the general strike still fresh in memory, bourgeois opinion across a broad spectrum regarded legal regulation of the labor market as necessary. Would the moderate wing break away from the Liberal party to give the Lindman government a majority in the Second Chamber as in the suffrage question? In contrast to 1907, Påboda now hoped that the Tällberg group would "hold straight" and not fall into Lindman's arms. In letters to Tällberg he warned of the dangers of contract legislation passed under the influence of temporary agitation.

The Liberal party was not opposed to contract legislation per se, but it wanted extensive changes in the government's proposal. A Liberal farmer representative demanded that mass lockouts should be prohibited. For agricultural employers it was an asset without value because it could not be used in agriculture. But the right to join a labor conflict in sympathy would result in the rural workers becoming the labor union movement's most protected vanguard. Agriculture would pay the costs of battle for industry. The interests of the Liberal farmers coincided with the main Liberal argument that the general lockout, if it was legally sanctioned, would preserve the industrial employers' advantage, while its curtailment would create a balance of power between the sides on the labor market. The end result was that the two chambers of the Riksdag arrived at contrary decisions and thereby the law was defeated. Support of Liberal farmers for the government, which had forced through the suffrage proposal in 1907, failed to appear. Lindman had not raised a question of confidence this time; the government remained.

SAF had intended to cancel the lockouts formally remaining if the government proposal passed. Now the lockouts continued until December 1910. SAF tactics, allowing the workers to return to work after withdrawal from LO for as long as the conflict lasted, had let LO escape from a basic contract. To what extent did the same tactics, especially the evictions, cause a swing in public opinion that made it possible for the Liberals to prevent the passage of contract legislation? Scholars have not yet found the answer in their research, but the question is worth asking.

Suffrage, general strike, contract law—conflicts over right and might in the political and industrial areas had succeeded one another. At every crisis the outcome had depended on a change of allegiance: in 1907, the Liberal farmer wing's shift to the right; in 1909, a movement in the same direction by almost all of the Liberal party to create a temporary bourgeois block; in 1910, a movement backed by the Liberals with restoration of the old boundary line between right and left in Swedish politics.

The Defense Battle and the Castle Courtyard Coup

An investigation of national defense had been going on since 1907. It drew serious political attention to the defense question for the first time in 1910, when the three Liberal members of the commission resigned in protest against a conservative proposal for building three ironclad vessels immediately, before the work of the investigation was done. The Lindman government forced through the decision on building the ironclads in the so-called joint vote with the help of its majority in the First Chamber. This occurred in the spring of 1911 and defense became a major issue in the fall election.

The election was the first one to the Second Chamber that

would take place under the proportional method and with general suffrage for men. Major changes in the composition of the chamber were expected and did not fail to appear, as shown in the tabulation. Election participation was 57 percent. Other

Party	Seats Held	Loss or Gain	Percentage of Vote
Conservatives	64	−29	32
Liberals	102	0	40
Social Democrats	64	+29	28

major changes are reflected in these figures besides the shift in absolute numbers. The rural-urban proportion within the parties shifted strongly because of the new method of election. The Conservative party gained in the cities and the Liberal party, which previously had approximately as many city as rural representatives, was transformed into a party that was three-fourths rural although still led by urban representatives.

The total Riksdag majority at Lindman's disposal for votes on financial questions was lost through the decrease in Conservatives in the Second Chamber. Lindman immediately realized that it was impossible for him to continue to govern and that Karl Staaff must form a new government. The king came to the same conclusion gradually and reluctantly.

Staaff demanded the king's promise that he be allowed to dissolve the First Chamber in order to let the suffrage reform work there and in this way obtain a joint voting majority. The pattern from May 1906 was repeated: Staaff asked, the king wanted time to think—to consult with the men behind the throne, i.e., the foremost Conservative leaders—the king answered Staaff. After several rounds in this pattern, the First Chamber's dissolution was granted during the fall. The Conservative majority in the reformed First Chamber continued but was strongly reduced: Conservatives, 86; Liberals, 52; and Social Democrats, 12. The Liberals' election platform had included a proposal for systematic defense adapted to the country's economic capacity. The new Liberal government appointed four civil defense committees: on financing, on the balance between the army and the navy, on possible savings, and on training periods. The decision on the building of the ironclads which had caused the protests earlier was annulled by a decision in council two weeks after the appointment of the committee. The king dictated his views, differing from those of the government, to the council protocol. The royal power stood on the side of dominance by the upper classes as Karl Staaff put it. But the king's position was also in accord with European political changes.

The tension between rival power groups, the Triple Entente and the Triple Alliance, had grown, as had the tempo in the arms race. In 1911, the second Morocco crisis occurred; in 1912, the First Balkan War; in 1913, the Second Balkan War. International developments prompted unease about peace and increased interest in defense. The postponement of the building of the ironclads triggered an attempt to raise the necessary money through voluntary contributions. The collection, organized by men close to the established Conservative political camp and even supported by pro-defense Liberals, was soon successful. The government swallowed its pride and accepted the ironclads. The climate for agitation on behalf of defense was favorable, and Sven Hedin's pamphlet *A Word of Warning* went out in an edition of millions. It frankly played on fear of the Russians and painted a picture of Cossacks around the statue of Karl XII in the Royal Garden in Stockholm. Part of the propaganda consciously depicted the king in opposition to the government. This was very badly received in officers' circles and several controversies with the military ensued. On the other hand, during the visits the king began to make to the regiments around the country, he could count on ovations that often resembled those the kaiser received in Germany.

In demonstrating against the government on the defense question, the king publicly gave expression to a policy different from that of the government. Gustav V was asserting a personal royal power despite the demands of the Liberal government and the left for parliamentary rule in which the government alone made decisions and bore political responsibility. The prime minister wrote several lines which give a picture of a difficult case of adult education: "G V unreasonable, went in circles. Erupted: You want me to be a shadow king, etc. I again lectured: he must, in accepting a Liberal ministry, give it the same freedom as one whose views he shared. Again pointed out the political responsibility." The parliamentary doctrine was rather new even to some within the left, however, and Karl Staaff could complain as late as the end of 1913: "A strange inability to correctly comprehend the quadrangle's [the castle's] constitutional position comes out in our own papers at times. Yet perhaps not so strange, for we have had such historians and teachers of political law that God have mercy on this country." From the beginning, the government's battle over the defense issue was simultaneously a battle for parliamentarianism.

But the Staaff ministry could only mount skirmishes. Its parliamentary strength after the left's election victory in 1911 would not support anything more, especially since its position was slowly weakened. In the defense investigations even some men of the left shifted to the view that defense should be strengthened. The urban Liberals were moving away from the party's line, while many rural Liberals, among them Tällberg, retained their old unwillingness to increase defense burdens. The split in the Liberal party grew. The king began to speculate about the possibility of replacing the Staaff government with one made up of pro-defense moderate Liberals or a nonpolitical government. But dissension prevailed even behind the throne. Defense propagandists like Sven Hedin and some officers called for action and thereby inspired the queen to push the king on with her stronger will. The leader of the Conservatives in the First Chamber, law professor Ernst Trygger, was prepared to lend his support and the king found his relations with Staaff's government increasingly intolerable. The former government head, Arvid Lindman, and his former ministers, however, advised decidedly against action. According to their view, Staaff should be allowed to continue until he had presented his proposal on defense. If the proposal turned out to be insufficient, as was to be expected, the pro-defense Liberals would secede and the Liberal party split. On the other hand, if a crisis was forced with Staaff, the Liberal party would rally around its leader.

The difference in opinion between Ernst Trygger and Arvid Lindman was not only over what was the correct tactic for the right in the situation at hand but also over leadership of the Conservatives and over Conservative policies. Trygger represented an agrarian and bureaucratic ultra-right against Lindman's adaptable moderate conservatism. They had opposed each other in 1907, on the suffrage question when Trygger did not want to abandon the First Chamber's old position; in 1911, when Trygger wanted Lindman not to yield to the election results; and in 1912 and 1913, when Lindman and his supporters tried to maneuver Trygger from leadership of the united Conservative parties in the First Chamber, after Lindman himself had taken over the chairmanship of the united Conservative parties in the Second Chamber and in the national organization. If the king's desire to drive Staaff out was fulfilled there would be an opportunity for Trygger to become head of the Conservative government and thereby win a strengthened position in the competition with Lindman.

The next move in the political game was Staaff's. It could not be long in coming. The threatened split among the Liberals demanded a unifying cry for battle. Staaff tried to give it in a speech in Karlskrona on December 23, 1913. In it, he recommended a strengthening of defense through a substantial rearmament including more ironclads. He also pleaded for a lengthened training time. He said, however, that the question of length of training for a major part of the conscripts—the infantry—should not be decided before the fall election in 1914, in consideration of the promises that had been given the voters in 1911. The increased costs of defense should primarily be borne by the higher income earners through a progressive tax. The speech aroused opposition within his own party's anti-defense phalanx at the same time that it was proclaimed completely unsatisfactory by the right.

On the same day that Staaff's Karlskrona speech was published in the press, the newspaper *Uppsala* and some Stockholm papers called for a farmers' march. The initiative for a farmers' march had been taken by two politically unknown men, a member of the landed gentry and a wholesaler in Uppland. The idea was that Sweden's farmers should declare themselves willing to bear increased defense costs. This declaration would be made personally before the king, for which purpose a march to Stockholm would be arranged. The idea of a farmers' march, like the collection for ironclads, soon resulted in a strong response. Participation was greatest from Uppland and the central Swedish provinces; the relatively distant Skåne, however, turned out large numbers. The social and political composition of the farmers' march has not been investigated. Some statements, perhaps colored by propaganda, appeared that asserted on the one hand that many marchers were not farmers at all, and on the other hand that the march was composed of farmers who only wanted to see the capital cheaply and didn't know what was involved. The composition of the farmers' march is of interest not only because it constituted an enormous demonstration outside of the usual political forms of expression but also because subsequently the farmers tried to create their own political organizations between the existing right and left parties in Sweden. In December 1913, a first constituency association for an Agrarian party was formed in Skaraborg County's southern constituency and, on the anniversary of the farmers' march, the Farmers' National Association appeared, which counted many of the leaders of the farmers' march among its initiators. In the beginning the Agrarian party was closer to the Liberal Coalition party's moderate farmer wing; the Farmers' National Association was closer to the right in composition and views. Both the established right and left in Swedish politics tried to prevent the appearance of these new farmer parties in the center. The new parties were in part an expression of the view that farmer interests had not been protected, and that corporate interests and city radicalism were seen by the farmers as serious threats.

The climax of the farmers' march on the king was to take place at the royal castle's courtyard on February 6, 1914. About 30,000 marched to the castle under flags emblazoned with the arms of various provinces. Forty thousand farmers and 70,000 nonfarmers had given their support to the aims of the farmers' march in writing. In speeches in the courtyard, its spokesmen demanded that the defense question be solved without delay and in accordance with the recommendations of military experts. The king's answer, which Arvid Lindman and his friends tried in vain to moderate, was a response not only to the farmers' march but also to Staaff's Karlskrona speech: "To be sure, those people who entertain the opinion that the question of training time for the infantry should not be solved now are not lacking in our country, but I by no means share this opinion; on the contrary, I have the same view as you have just expressed to me, namely that the defense question in its entirety should be considered and decided now, without delay and without interruption." The king's answer also contained a statement that he was not willing to disregard the recommendations of military experts. The king had publicly repudiated his government.

The farmers' march touched off the political crisis that had been approaching. In the Riksdag, the left demonstrated against the monarchy, and a workers' march with about 50,000 people expressed its support for the government two days later. Since, however, the king could not be persuaded to take back his words to the marching farmers or to promise not to make personal political statements in the future, the government submitted its resignation.

The king now called on the moderate Liberal secessionists and assigned the task of forming a new government to Governor Louis De Geer the Younger. After two days he had to give up his assignment. What Lindman and others had predicted had happened. The king's coup against Staaff had united the Liberal party. A moderate Liberal government definitely had no chance now. Trygger was willing to take over, but Lindman succeeded in blocking his plans and instead launched a civil servant government under the leadership of Hjalmar Hammarskjöld. The new government's first measure was to dissolve the Riksdag and declare new elections.

The Decline of the Liberal Party

Several days before the farmers' march, the critics of increased defense costs, including Tällberg, had held a discussion meeting with about sixty Liberals. The party leadership was not invited. Several days after February 6, a preliminary cabinet session was to have been held to decide on a government proposal. It is not certain that unity within the government would have prevailed. Then the castle courtyard crisis intervened and pushed constitutional considerations into the foreground. The unity created among the Liberals by the king's action could not be maintained. For the election moderate urban Liberals in Stockholm formed the association Liberal Friends of Defense. They turned not only against the Liberal proposal on the defense issue but also against the party's cooperation with the Social Democrats. The approaching election drew Liberals generally to the right, as in the general strike, especially within bourgeois social groups. In the pre-election debate the Liberals advocated parliamentary rule, while the right put "defense first." The Social Democrats opposed increased defense burdens. A slanderous campaign supported from the court was directed against Karl Staaff, painting his government as republican and traitorous. In general the election campaign was pursued with unprecedented virulence from both sides.

The election, which took place in April, was the first major defeat for the Liberal party; the results are shown in the tabulation. Election participation was 70 percent. Hammarskjöld

Party	Seats	Loss or Gain	Percentage of Vote
Conservatives (including 7 seats for Liberal Friends of Defense)	86	+22	38
Liberals	71	−31	32
Social Democrats	73	+9	30

remained as prime minister. Despite the big Conservative election victory, the defense issue was still unresolved when the Riksdag again met. The government proposal supported by the Conservatives still was opposed by a majority in the Second Chamber.

The outbreak of World War I on August 1, 1914, saved the government. In an open letter to the prime minister, Karl Staaff declared that the government could count on the Liberal Coalition party's support for its proposals. The situation at the time encouraged the Liberals to "sacrifice their views," Staaff wrote. Many Liberals, however, felt that such capitulation was uncalled for. Tällberg and some thirty others abstained from the final vote in the Riksdag; the Social Democrats also opposed voting to support the government.

At approximately the same time, the ordinary Second Chamber elections were held. The Liberal party was paralyzed and the voters continued to turn their backs on it, as shown in the tabulation. Election participation was 66 percent. This time it was the Social Democrats who took over the seats the Liberals lost. From having been the largest party in the Riksdag and the holder of

Party	Seats	Loss or Gain	Percentage of Vote
Conservatives	86	0	37
Liberals	57	−14	27
Social Democrats	87	+14	36

the power of government, the Liberal Coalition party had during 1914 first been driven from power by the courtyard coup and then lost forty-five seats in two elections and became the smallest party in the popularly elected chamber. Two almost equal Conservative and Social Democratic blocs now faced each other. Where had the Liberal voters gone? In the Lake Mälar region, which had provided the majority of those taking part in the farmers' march, the Liberal farmers went over to the right. Among the capital's bourgeois voters, the Liberals also suffered large losses to the right. In the Norrland counties, where the Liberals' earlier strong position was demolished, the small farmers and workers joined the Social Democrats. After the battles of 1914, the Liberal party was no longer the same party it had been. It had lost large parts of both its right and its left wings.

Summary

How can the decade between the dissolution of the union in 1905 and the outbreak of world war be characterized? The answer, as this survey has tried to indicate, depends on the aspects chosen for emphasis. If one chooses to stress conditions and events other than those singled out here, the picture can be a somewhat different one. In the history of Sweden which Ingvar Andersson began to write immediately before World War II and which was published in Sweden after the war, the assessment of the period is this: "The tradition of the 'Middle Way' and cooperation was secured then, although under virulent and bitter struggles that were further sharpened by the lack of familiarity with a modern party system, by the unnecessarily long delays of certain impor-

tant reforms, and by the workers' strong distrust of the historical
bases of Swedish society. But with few exceptions these battles
were conducted with the general welfare as a guiding star and
with marked feeling for the value of things uniquely Swedish."
Following the political and industrial battle lines of the period—
as here—does not lead to the same final judgment as Ingvar
Andersson's. We have instead been able to observe a continued
sharpening of the conflicts between right and left in politics,
between employer and worker in industry. The representatives
of the "middle way," the moderate groups in the middle, were
drawn into a tug of war. In the suffrage reform in 1907, when
both moderate-conservative and moderate-liberal center groups
worked together, the "middle way" and cooperation would leave
their mark on politics. On other occasions, the right or the left
split the center groups or pulled them over to one side. In 1909,
the center groups joined in the general bourgeois protest against
the general strike and thereby made possible the government's
policy of nonintervention. In 1910, on the issue of contract legislation, they were split on either side of the line between right and
left in Swedish politics. During the battle over defense, Karl Staaff
in his Karlskrona speech tried to unite all of the Liberal party
on a middle course, but pressure from right and left was too great.

Of the three great conflicts during the decade, one—the suffrage
battle—was settled by compromise, while two—the general strike
and the defense battle—brought victory for the employers and the
conservative political groups in Swedish society respectively. At
these three points, the Liberal party's unity was broken or threatened and the left suffered defeat. The right, through an active
policy, successfully maintained its political and economic position
of power. To a certain extent, this fact has been lost sight of in
judging the period before World War I. It has been handy to
disregard conservative successes when looking backward after the
breakthrough of parliamentarianism and democracy at the end
of World War I. Such a view is anachronistic. If the Central

Powers had been the victors in 1918, the political entrenchment made by the conservative suffrage reform in 1907 would have remained well defended for a long time. The conservative economic entrenchment, fortified through the victory in the general strike, held its position even longer than the political one.

What was it that made conservative power in Swedish society superior, that brought suffrage on predominantly conservative terms, collective agreements on the employers' terms, and military defense according to conservative demands? In part, there had been a willingness to adapt the conservative values to a changed society, to accept part of the opponents' demands. Organization was also important—in the close-knit employers' groups and in fewer and more effective political parties supported by a national organization. Then, too, modern tools of communication were utilized in order to propagandize for the cause. We must note as well the offensive spirit and mobility that distinguished men like Arvid Lindman and Hjalmar von Sydow, perhaps the decade's most successful representatives of a modern conservatism and employer policy respectively. Finally, the conservative gathering of strength took place under favorable inner and outer circumstances. The growing strength of the labor movement had begun to be seen as a threat by many in the middle groups of society and made them incline toward a new grouping into bourgeois and socialist groups. The conditions and events originating outside of Sweden—the international recession and the outbreak of World War I—decisively influenced the two great crises during the decade, the general strike and the defense battle.

Introduction to Chapter 9

The economic and political crisis of the period between 1906 and 1914 had led not to a compromise between the right and left but to a victory for the conservative forces. The collapse of Karl Staaff's government in February 1914 and the appointment of Hjalmar Hammarskjöld as prime minister left little doubt of the continued strength of the traditional forces in Swedish society. The new government represented the interests of the royal house, big business, and the supporters of a strong defense policy. The forces of the left—the Liberals under Staaff and the Social Democrats—were in considerable disarray. The previous seven-year period had hardly been one of great victories for them. Although the two parties had continued to increase their combined strength in the Riksdag, they still faced the problem of how to translate their electoral successes into parliamentary ones. How they would have reacted over the long run in peacetime to the Hammarskjöld government is a fascinating question but can only be speculated about. The beginning of the Great War in August altered the situation dramatically.

The experience of World War I was of critical importance for the shaping of modern European states, even for the nonbelligerents such as Sweden. The political constellations that had existed before the war were rent asunder by the pressures of the period and a new political ordering was created. In Sweden the initial response to the war was a plea from the government for a united effort to maintain Swedish neutrality. The domestic conflict was to be forgotten in the face of the external threat. In fact this was what happened until early 1916. The left, fearing a Swedish alliance with the Central Powers, supported Hammarskjöld even though they resented his imperial manner. By 1916, however, the left could no longer accept the prime minister's neglect of parliament or what they considered to be a disastrous economic (trade) policy. The spring of 1916 witnessed the renewal of domestic wars but with a strange new twist. The left parties received important support for their attack on Hammarskjöld from certain elements of the business community including the foreign minister, Knut Wallenberg, because these groups also objected to Hammarskjöld's trade policy. The economic pressures of the war had created strange political bedfellows. The Conservative leaders wavered in their support of Hammarskjöld and he fell from office in March 1917. The Conservatives took direct responsibility for the government. They were determined to avoid the establishment of parliamentary democracy based on universal suffrage but within eight months parliamentary democracy was an established fact and the basis for a major suffrage reform had clearly been laid. The great pressures which produced this striking turnabout were primarily external and created a highly inflammable political situation in Sweden.

For Europe 1917 was a year of political upheaval. The most significant event was the Russian Revolution which gave great hope to the democratic forces all over Europe. Conservatives found themselves in a very exposed position and felt obliged in many cases to beat a tactical retreat. One of the primary causes of the political upheavals was the economic dislocations produced by the war. Particularly in northern and Eastern Europe hunger stalked the land. Food riots had precipitated the Russian Revolution. Food shortages and riots occurred in Sweden, too, in April and May 1917. Would the "Russian disease" spread to Sweden? Professor Carl-Göran Andrae in the following essay examines how the Social Democratic leadership in Sweden tried to cope with and use the events of 1917 for their own purposes. Food shortages and potential political revolution were not the only factors to consider; there was always the outcome of the war and how it might affect domestic developments in Sweden.

9

The Swedish Labor Movement
and the 1917-1918 Revolution

by Carl-Göran Andrae

The Russian Revolution in February–March 1917 was given a great deal of space in newspaper columns in Sweden. Because of its geographic position and its status as a neutral country, Sweden served for several days as almost the only source of news about the events in Russia. Commentaries in the press varied according to a newpaper's political color. The conservative and pro-German press followed the events with unease, because of fear that the "Russian disease" would spread to Sweden, but also with a certain skepticism, because it was believed that the revolt was nothing but a coup d'état staged by the politicians of the Entente. In the liberal and Social Democratic newspapers, the revolution was greeted with joy, not least because the burden of the Russian czardom had now been lifted for the Entente's supporters in Sweden, who saw the Western Powers as guarantors of the perpetuation of democracy in Europe. As to hopes for further developments in Russia, views were sharply divided between the center and the left, especially the extreme left, the opposition wing within the Social Democratic party, which would soon break away as an independent political party.

While the events in Russia in the spring of 1917 caused a sensation in the Swedish press and directly influenced political developments in Sweden, the revolution in October–November passed almost unnoticed, because the Swedes were completely occupied with their newly appointed government, which for the first time included a number of Social Democrats, an event that Swedish historians have called "the democratic breakthrough." It was essentially only Leftist Socialists who placed any great importance on the Bolshevik takeover of power in Russia. But Swedish opinion was by no means unaffected by the revolutionary events in Europe during the period immediately following. During the crisis European society experienced near the end of World War I, the political tension in Sweden reached three peaks: the first came fairly soon after the Russian Revolution, when, in the middle of April and in May 1917, riots began in Swedish cities; the second occurred in connection with the Finnish Civil War in February–March 1918; and the third came in November of the same year under the influence of the German collapse, when the Social Democratic Leftist party issued a manifesto: "Forward for the Socialistic Republic!" These three periods can also serve as examples of how public opinion can be created within the working class: in April 1917, there was a spontaneous outbreak of discontent among workers occasioned by a shortage of food; in February 1918, there was a reaction by the labor movement to a very strong shift in bourgeois opinion in favor of intervention on the White side in the Finnish Civil War; and in November, finally, unease among the workers was largely a result of the Socialist leaders' own agitation. I shall dwell here on the first and last of these occasions, because the shift in public opinion came to revolve around one of the central political issues of the time—a constitutional reform that would give universal and equal suffrage even in township elections, eliminate the voting requirement of paid taxes to the state and the township, and allow women the same political rights as men.

Let us first consider the situation in April 1917. A bad harvest and the English trade blockade had resulted in severe shortages of food, which approached famine for the lowest classes. The general discontent was expressed in enormous "hunger demonstrations" in which thousands of workers participated. The workers' movement had begun in the city of Västervik under the strong influence of some radical syndicalists there. The resolutions that were adopted at the first demonstrations set the style for all the resolutions that followed. Their contents were colored by syndicalism, with demands for "direct action" instead of central negotiations with the employers. In May, these demonstrations were followed by a new type of action, "inventories." Groups of workers and workers' wives investigated to see whether potatoes were hidden in storekeepers' shops or farmers' cellars. A few cases of plundering of bread shops and forced purchase of bread without exchange of bread coupons also occurred. In Stockholm, in Göteborg, and on the little island of Seskarö outside of Haparanda, there were direct encounters between the workers and the police, and troops were called out.

But military demonstrations disturbed the authorities more than anything else. At the same time as the workers' demonstrations, soldiers had begun to express their discontent with the poor meals they were receiving. At the end of April at many garrison locations around the country, the men marched through city streets in closed ranks but without any officers, to emphasize their solidarity with the demonstrating workers. It would subsequently be impossible to use military units as security forces in any civil disturbances, and thus the army, the ultimate support of the sitting government, was neutralized. The conscripts' demonstrations were the result of propaganda by the Social Democratic Youth League, originally tied to the Social Democratic party but at this time a hotbed of opposition to the old-line party; the League was to be the core of the new Social Democratic Leftist party, formed in May 1917. On April 20 in Stockholm, these young people set up the Soldiers' and Workers' Society; the name alluded to the powerful Workers' and Soldiers' Council in Petrograd which had been formed several weeks earlier. It was no coincidence that young people came to play such a prominent role in the disturbances. They had been especially hard hit by unemployment and it was they who first had to submit to extensive military service. According to the Social Democrats, the increased influence exerted by the radical labor movement could be explained by the large proportion of young and unorganized workers among the thousands who joined the demonstrations; they would be ripe for the syndicalists' propaganda. That is not the whole explanation, however. During the revolutionary period that prevailed, even the workers within the reformist labor unions felt the new leftist currents, all the more because the Leftist Socialists had formed a "union opposition" that would act within the framework of the reformist labor union movement, which included the overwhelming majority of the organized workers in the country.

How did the leading politicians react to this situation? Hjalmar Branting, the Social Democratic leader who had returned in the middle of April from a visit to revolutionary Russia, tried to take leadership of the wave of demonstrations. He supported the demands for improvements in the food situation, but in place of the extensive economic demands which the demonstrators had presented at the instigation of the Leftist Socialist groups (such as restoration of workers' wages to the 1914 level and introduction of the eight-hour day) he stressed the need for universal suffrage in both general and township elections. Despite his dominant position within the Swedish labor movement, Branting did not find an audience receptive to his policies. The demonstrators preferred listening to the promises of a program of action for easing their problems immediately rather than supporting a distant parliamentary reform that could only in the long run mean an improvement in the position of the working class.

Branting had greater success in the Riksdag, when he addressed a question in the Second Chamber to the prime minister: with regard to the present situation, was the government prepared to take the initiative in a reform of the Swedish constitution? The Conservative government was split on this question. With May Day approaching, a number of security measures had been instituted by the government. The garrison troops in Stockholm were exchanged for regiments from the countryside, whose forces of farm boys were regarded as more reliable. The internal security service was strengthened and emergency units held in continuous readiness to cope with any disturbances. Several members of the National Youth League had secretly, but with the tacit approval of the government, begun to organize a civil guard of "reliable and courageous" persons. Within the government, however, there were also strong forces working for acquiescence in the demands for reforms. In almost incessant cabinet meetings during the entire month of May, the prime minister's answer to Branting's interpellation was discussed: how far could the government go in complying and how great was the danger of revolt if the demands were rejected?

The Social Democratic leaders, alarmed at the possibility that they were losing their hold on public opinion, formed the 1917 Workers' Committee on May 7, with representatives of the party government, the Riksdag caucus, and the Swedish Confederation of Trade Unions. The committee's purpose was to unite the Swedish labor movement and present reformist demands vigorously. But the committee could not produce unity even among its own members. The politicians, who quite naturally were most sensitive to shifts in public opinion, wanted to support an extensive program of action clearly answering the demands of the demonstrators. Insistence on action came especially from the younger politicians who were involved in the battles with the Leftist Socialists. To do nothing in this situation, not to seize all means available to the working class—including preparation for a general strike—would be, they said, to neglect "a historic opportunity."

In opposition to these young Social Democratic activists stood the representatives of the union leadership on the committee. In the Confederation of Trade Unions, the events of 1909 and their consequences for the movement were still fresh in memory; all previous experience encouraged the union leaders to proceed with the greatest care.

Zeth Höglund, leader of the Leftist Socialists, urged a general work stoppage on the same day as the prime minister was to answer Branting's question in the Riksdag. On the night of June 4, the Leftist party distributed thousands of leaflets to all the working places in Stockholm calling on the workers to gather in front of the Riksdag building. This appeal was heeded by thousands of workers and bloody skirmishes between the workers and the mounted police occurred. The mass of people, violently driven from Gustav Adolf's Square, moved toward the People's House, where speakers from various political camps tried to make themselves heard above the noise. Branting's position was not an easy one. He had been able to direct a very strong attack at the sitting government through his interpellation, but he had no desire whatsoever to take over the responsibility of government at this time, considering the food situation and the upcoming fall elections. Appearing before the agitated workers at the People's House, he therefore deliberately exaggerated the vague concessions that had been made in the prime minister's answer to the interpellation and declared that the fall elections would decide the constitution issue. The idea of refraining from all demands for the present and putting their hopes on a distant election victory did not appeal to the workers, and Branting's speech was met with boos and whistling. The representatives of the Social Democratic Leftist party were, on the other hand, received with cheers when they spoke for immediate action. Branting thus was repudiated in his own political stronghold—and victory could be seen within reach of the radical left wing. But there was no appeal at the People's House for a general strike to focus attention on the workers' demands. Instead the Confederation of Trade Unions was urged to support such a strike. No response came from the union leadership. On the following day, crowds of workers marched to one of the largest meetings ever organized in the capital: about 10,000 people gathered in Hornsberg's field in Södermalm. Again they did not dare go all the way and proclaim a general strike on their own. Instead, on the initiative of Zeth Höglund, it was decided to form a radical counterpart to the 1917 Workers' Committee. This Workers' National Council was to be based on local workers' councils already formed in some places in the country. The council movement was obviously inspired by its Russian counterpart and it may have been hoped that the name Workers' National Council would strike terror into the hearts of the bourgeoisie, but at this time it was almost entirely an organization on paper and it never exercised any leadership within the Swedish working class. The 1917 Workers' Committee—on which the Social Democratic Youth League, the Social Democratic Leftist party, and the syndicalists had unsuccessfully sought representation—had already established itself as the focal point for the labor movement.

The situation stabilized slowly during July. The revolutionary groups had lost the initiative and the food situation improved temporarily as the new potato harvest became available. The revolutionary feelings, to quote an old labor union member, lay "in the worker's stomach." In April 1917, the impact of the Russian Revolution together with the very serious food situation had created a feverish expectation among the workers that "something should happen." It is possible that a social revolution was closer at this time than at any other in Swedish history. The otherwise solid reformism in Sweden was shaken for several weeks under the influence of everything that happened in Russia. But it became clear that those who controlled the organizational apparatus in the Swedish labor movement, especially the union movement, also possessed the power to make binding decisions. The Social

Democratic party, on the other hand, found itself temporarily in
a crisis. Branting's undisputed authority among the older and
thereby often leading men in the party organization could always
be relied on, but Branting was severely limited in his actions as
long as the more radical element remained in the party. It was
only during the last days in May that the effects of the split on the
old party's strength could be discerned, and only at the fall elections that the effects on the voters could be observed. In Sweden,
as in Denmark, only a minority joined the new party, but it
should be remembered that the new currents won a majority both
in Norway and in Finland and the radical wings could take over
the greater part of the old party apparatus there. For the time
being, Branting had succeeded in avoiding this in Sweden. There
was undeniably some validity in the characterization that Lenin
made of Branting when he met with the young Leftist Socialists
on his trip through Sweden in April 1917: "Branting is smarter
than you. He is much smarter than you."

The riskiness of prophesying political developments is illuminated by what happened—or rather what didn't happen—in the
spring of 1918. In brief: Would the previous spring's hunger demonstrations be repeated? Famine was felt most in the late spring
(a remnant from the old peasant society), when the past year's
harvest was used up and the new year's had not yet been gathered
in. Since the food situation had by no means improved during
1917, rather the contrary, it was expected that severe hunger riots
would break out in the late spring of 1918. All sides seemed to
agree on this point. Within the military security service there
were people who expected organized violent actions, and extensive security measures were set in motion in various quarters. But
the labor movement's leftist groups did not entertain such plans;
on the other hand, there was extensive preparation for creating
positive public opinion for the left's demands. The Workers'
National Council came to life as an instrument of cooperation
among the various leftist elements, and a "minimum program"

was worked out focusing on demands for improvements in the food supply. The program exhibited striking similarities in content to the resolutions that had been accepted during the hunger demonstrations in April 1917. The intent was clearly to turn opinion in a new direction in the hopes of gaining support for the leftists from groups of unorganized workers and even those workers who were organized in the reformist movement. The threat was felt very strongly in the reformist labor movement. The Workers' National Council, which had not made much noise in 1917, now became the object of protracted deliberations within the Social Democratic party leadership, which discussed various proposals on how to meet such an opinion campaign.

The National Council laid plans to go into action in April 1918. But the workers refused to demonstrate. The minimum program that was to have been given dramatic exposure had to be absorbed into the Social Democratic Leftist party's May Day resolution. It is impossible to give a simple explanation for the apathy shown by the working class in this case, of course, but a few explanations can be offered. For one thing, the energy within the labor movement had been used up in an intense campaign of meetings on the Finland issue during February and March. For the working class, this had been a defensive battle. The object was to prevent Swedish intervention on the White side—not to support fellow workers in Finland. In the spring of 1918, the stimuli that had been present after the Russian Revolution the year before did not exist either. On the contrary, the Finnish Revolution was ending and the workers and their organizations had suffered total defeat there. Little wonder that the Swedish worker temporized in the face of incitements that, he suspected, could lead to open social conflict even in Sweden. Also, in the spring of 1917, the power of state and the bureaucracy could be identified with the governing Conservative party and thereby all the workers had what might be called a common "enemy." One year later, the Social Democrats sat in the government together with the Liberals. A demonstration, even if it was directed against "authorities" in general, could be interpreted as a disloyal action against those who clearly supported the reformist labor movement. The Social Democratic counterpropaganda, if nothing else, would see to that. Therefore, after the vehement conflict on the Finland question a great calm again descended on Swedish domestic politics. It lasted during the spring, the summer, and into the fall; then it was over.

During the first days of November 1918, the Social Democratic Riksdag caucus had been called to several meetings before the opening of the extraordinary Riksdag. It was primarily the food situation that was the object of the group's deliberations. A number of members demanded that the Liberal agriculture minister, Alfred Petersson af Påboda, resign. This would lead to a government crisis, of course, but that would be better than ignoring the workers' discontent with the government's food policy, which could jeopardize the Social Democratic voting base. Branting, however, warned his party associates against concerning themselves only with food policy. Dissolution of the government would lead to the formation of a new government by the Conservatives or by a coalition of Conservatives and Liberals, with greatly increased social and political conflicts as a result. The Social Democrats could not take over the responsibility of government in the existing situation, since this would require cooperation with the Social Democratic Leftist party; yet they should not abandon their government position to the Conservatives and Liberals, for in the politically important phase that could be expected in connection with the end of the war, the Social Democrats ought to be in power.

At this time the Central Powers stood on the verge of a complete military and political breakdown; on November 9 the German emperor abdicated; his Austrian colleague followed suit; and it seemed as if all of the old social system stood on the brink of collapse. The general unease also spread immediately to Sweden.

Swedish politicians had to seize their opportunity quickly. Zeth Höglund was fastest with his pen. He wrote a manifesto which was accepted on November 10 by the Social Democratic Leftist party's working committee, called together in great haste, and by the Social Democratic Youth League's executive committee. Only eight people attended the meeting, but Höglund declared that the majority of those not present had privately agreed with the issuance of a manifesto in the spirit of the one accepted. The governing body of the Soldiers' and Workers' League had also said that it was ready to sign. The manifesto presented these demands: formation of a socialist government supported by workers', soldiers', and farmers' councils; a republican form of government; abolition of the First Chamber; a constituent national assembly elected by all men and women over twenty years of age; an end to military exercises; wage increases; an eight-hour day; worker control of industry; and nationalization of all large landholdings. The points on the creation of councils, worker control of industry, and nationalization of land were clearly written under Russian influence; the last two points were included in Lenin's April theses in 1917. It was significant, however, that the manifesto did not contain any appeal for an immediate general strike or other unifying action. The workers should keep themselves ready "to win the victory with the weapons of a general strike, if necessary." Höglund was faced with two alternatives: either he could set in motion an action on his own, at great risk and in open conflict with the central leadership of the reformist labor movement, or he could try to cooperate with the Social Democrats in an effort to break up the government coalition. He seemed to choose the latter alternative, a decision perhaps influenced by the situation within his own party. Against a little radical, Bolshevik group, to which Höglund himself belonged, stood a group of Leftist Socialists who consistently clung to the parliamentary system. When the manifesto came before the party's representative assembly on November 14, several members of the

Riksdag caucus opposed its contents, and Fabian Månsson entered a reservation against its ratification. The Riksdag caucus did not sign the manifesto; Höglund had not mentioned at the meeting on November 10 any attempts to make private contacts with its members.

Certain soundings were now made, partly with other left organizations, partly with the trade unions. The Leftist party hoped to include especially the food workers in any general strike action and probably also hoped that the increasingly heated mood would spark such an action. The party press took a very hard line against the Social Democrats in the beginning; *Norrskensflamman* especially used very militant language. "On the Battle" was the headline of an editorial on November 16, but at this point the Social Democrats and the Confederation of Trade Unions had already mounted a counterattack.

When the news of the German Revolution reached Sweden, the Social Democratic party government was occupied with a great food demonstration that was launched on the same day, November 10, in Stockholm, but the party's secretariat immediately sent out an appeal to the party districts and the larger workers' locals to start at once action aimed at influencing the government. On the following days Prime Minister Nils Edén received telegrams from the Social Democratic party districts in Dalarna, Värmland, Halland, and Skåne and from a number of workers' locals demanding that the government consider the constitution question at the extraordinary Riksdag. Branting had urged this in vain at deliberations among the party leaders on October 29, but now the question had to be taken up. Since the spring Riksdag that year, the "constitutional question" had come to mean a demand for change of the suffrage provisions on elections to the Riksdag, county councils, and city councils, but it could also include proposals on the position of the First Chamber and a republican form of government. Precisely what was meant by the term in early November is not entirely clear from the records, but the general issue would soon become of overwhelming concern within the party. The first problem was a tactical one. How radical must a program of action be to provide an effective alternative to the Leftist Socialists' manifesto? How radical a program could the Liberal members of the government be pressed to accept? During the following days, the Social Democrats' program was given final shape in frequent deliberations, mostly informal, within the party and the union leadership. Contact was also continued with the Liberal members of the government. On November 13, at a meeting of the Riksdag caucus's secret council and the Social Democratic cabinet ministers, the party functionaries wanted to proceed with a radical program. Both Per Albin Hansson and Gustav Möller demanded that the introduction of a republic be included in the program, and they were supported by a few members of the Riksdag, but Branting and Rydén, along with other members of the government, pointed to the necessity of assuming continued unity within the government. After a four-hour debate, demands for universal suffrage, a parliamentary form of government, immediate new township elections, an end of conscript exercises, liquidation of the national defense establishment, and a normal eight-hour day were agreed on. At continued negotiations with the Liberal government members on the same day, a government program favoring suffrage and a parliamentary form of government was accepted. The Social Democrats had to agree to omission of the demands for disarmament and a standard eight-hour day.

This program, which the government immediately put to a vote of confidence, was presented by Branting at a large meeting that had been arranged on November 14 by the Stockholm workers' local. The leaders of these workers, led by Per Albin Hansson among others, had drafted a proposal for a resolution in which the demand for a republican form of government was included. To be sure, all agreed that it was practically impossible to establish such a government. Yet it was considered tactically expedient to include the more extensive demand in the resolution proposal. But Branting, who came directly from the central negotiations, forced the leaders of the Stockholm workers to change their resolution proposal from a demand to a request that the question of a republic be referred to a future plebiscite. Without direct abandonment of the demand, it could thus be removed from the political business of the day. Branting then presented this program to the Stockholm workers in a speech which stressed the great benefits that could ensue from adoption of the program but which also warned of a fate like that of the Finnish labor movement if the workers allowed themselves to be carried away and to make demands not yet within the power of the society to realize. The "Marseillaise" and the "International" were sung, whereupon the group's chairman read the resolution proposal, which was accepted unanimously. "Discussion was regarded as superfluous." By this couplike procedure, Branting succeeded in the difficult task of temporarily reconciling the need for political cooperation within the government and the mood among the party's members.

The representative assembly of the Confederation of Trade Unions met that same night, November 14, to discuss the political situation and—at the urging of the government—the Social Democratic Leftist party's plans to issue a call for a general strike. With one exception, G. Lagergren of the Bakery Workers, the union leaders agreed that such a call could not be heeded. The secretary of the Metal Workers' Union, Social Democrat Johan Olof Johansson, thought that the government's proposal should be complemented by a separate union program, however, and that the unions should be prepared to use strong measures in support of both. On the following day, negotiations between the representative assembly and the Social Democratic party government went on, and the union leaders promised that, if the Conservatives did not accept the government's proposition without change, the unions would be prepared to go out in a general strike on their own initiative. In return, they insisted that the government try to implement the eight-hour day as soon as possible.

With its manifesto on a social democratic republic, the Social Democratic Leftist party had undeniably rocked the government coalition. It also succeeded in making a number of raids on the reformist organizations, where many workers responded positively to the Leftists' proposals. But the Social Democratic leaders were on guard and also could exploit the general fear of bolshevism that existed in Sweden as in all of Europe at this time. The Leftist party therefore abstained from issuing any strike call on its own but continued its attempts to break up the government coalition by directing on November 15 an open appeal to the Social Democratic party leadership for cooperation. Branting considered the invitation to be only a tactical maneuver to win sympathy in the country. The party government's executive committee therefore replied that such cooperation could only come to pass if the Leftists expressly repudiated bolshevism. Out in the countryside, and even among the central leadership, for example Per Albin Hansson, there were strong sympathies for closer cooperation. The split in the Social Democratic party had affected deeply both the party apparatus and its voting base, and the Social Democrats were very willing to contemplate cooperation with the wing within the Leftist party represented by Ivar Vennerström, who had several times expressed himself in favor of a parliamentary system and against any form of violence or dictatorship. There was a possibility of reuniting these Leftists to the old party and isolating the group around Höglund. On the local level, the left had some success in its bid for unity, and in some places resolutions were produced that were signed jointly by the chairmen of the workers' groups in both the old and the new parties. Local deputies, especially those of unions, often considered the party split unnecessary "bickering" and in a serious situation like the present one felt that the workers should stand united. The Social Democratic party government, however, kept watch over the formation of local public opinion through the workers' groups, which generally obediently delivered an unceasing flow of resolutions to the government and the party in support of the official party line. On the central level, the only result of the efforts toward unity was inclusion of Ivar Vennerström on the special Riksdag committee to consider the government proposition. Höglund got in touch with the Young Socialists and the syndicalists in order to bring about a union on the extreme left but this organization, or "action committee," did not have any political importance.

For the Social Democrats and the Liberals, the suffrage issue had long been relatively clear. The Liberal majority, which actually wanted only equal suffrage in township elections, had had to come closer to the Social Democratic demand for equal and universal suffrage in township elections. A radical wing within the Liberal party had already spoken in favor of universal suffrage and even of a republic. Edén had opposed this position, however, in deference to the farmers among the party's voters.

If a change in suffrage was to be executed legally, there had to be acceptance by the Conservative majority in the First Chamber of the government's proposal. If the Conservatives rejected the proposal, the government threatened to resign, with immeasurable consequences under the existing conditions. What might induce the Conservatives to accept a change was the knowledge that in the uncertain situation that prevailed the Conservatives could not form a government without a civil war resulting. According to semiofficial statements, the Conservatives' attitude toward suffrage reform during the years 1917–1918 had remained unswervingly negative. But behind the scenes, there were strong antagonisms within the party. Among the intellectuals in the party as well as in the Youth League, there was a desire that the right should work out a counterproposal based on class elections to the First Chamber; Karl Hildebrand was among the most zealous champions of this line.

In the fall of 1918, a campaign for "building a bridge" in the

constitution question was begun in certain conservative newspapers. The purpose was to undermine the government coalition
through a separate agreement between the right and the Liberals.
Carl Swartz initiated contacts between the Conservative leaders
and the government but they did not lead to any positive proposals, and neither did direct negotiations among Edén, Trygger,
and Lindman that took place on November 11 and 14. At the
same time, internal deliberations went on in the Riksdag's Conservative parties, which numbered two: the National party in the
First Chamber with Trygger as leader, and the Ruralists' and
Burghers' party in the Second Chamber with Lindman in the
lead. As early as November 6 individual members had shown that
they were inclined to abandon the forty-degree scale in the township elections. The conservative newspapers also seemed disposed
to support negotiations, but the two party leaders were opposed.
The leaders of the right demanded that the constitution question
not be decided under the current uncertain conditions if the
parties could not agree voluntarily. Several days later greater com-
pliance was shown in an appeal from the General Electoral
League, the Conservative party's national organization, which
stated that the right should accept equal suffrage in township
elections and women's suffrage in order to calm the situation in
the nation. This was also the thrust of a motion that the right
presented at the end of the month. However, the right and the
farmers' parties refused to discard the tax qualification, which
was strongly opposed by the Social Democrats. The tax qualification was the provision that only those who had paid all taxes to
the state and the township had the right to vote; this provision
hit the Social Democrats' voting base very hard. In the 1917
elections in certain voting districts, 30 percent of the total
electorate had not been able to meet it.

The dispute now came to a head; all the parties had taken a
position and opinions clashed strongly in the special committee
that was appointed to prepare a recommendation on the consti-

tution question. Some of the Conservatives on the committee seemed inclined to go for a settlement, but both rightist leaders were still doubtful. "If there are people who want to drive through their demands by revolution, there are people who will prevent the revolution," Trygger declared at a meeting on December 3 in an argument with Mauritz Hellberg and Gustav Möller. Negotiations were continued within a smaller delegation of ten persons, where it was clear that the tax qualification was still the issue on which agreement could not be reached. The unusual step was then taken of forming a new, still smaller delegation with Branting, the Liberal Herman Kvarnzelius, and the Conservatives Swartz and Adolf Dahl. After the Conservative leaders had thus been sidestepped, this group reached a final compromise on December 6. The government representatives had to retreat from their "minimum program" to be sure, but on the whole the compromise still meant a victory for the left. The tax qualification disappeared completely in the general elections and for the township elections paid taxes in only one of the three previous years was required. Equal and universal suffrage for the township elections was also won, as well as completely equal voting status for women.

Did the First Chamber's Conservatives go along with the extensive compromise because they felt a direct threat? Officially, the right definitely denied this, but Trygger had revealed great uncertainty about the near future in personal notations at the end of October. "Under all circumstances one must keep up one's courage and strengthen the timid." That the threat of revolution was an important, perhaps decisive factor for Swartz is apparent in the *pro et contra* notations he made before he took a final position. The royal house was also animatedly engaged in inducing the right to make concessions on the suffrage question—the king urged compromise in the spring of 1917, out of fear of a Branting government, and, in the fall of 1918, out of fear of the implementation of a republic. In a confidential conversation with Hjalmar

Hammarskjöld, Gustav V remarked that his crown had never been as insecure as on the evening of November 14. He was also greatly disturbed at the thought of Queen Viktoria's possible fate in Karlsruhe, where she was staying with her mother. Prince Karl was convinced that a suffrage reform would give Sweden "truly Norwegian conditions," as he put it. The prince meant that in the face of a threat of approaching civil war, the reform should be accepted.

The Leftist Socialist wing had been isolated as a result of the government's quick action, and it did not dare proclaim a strike or arrange demonstrations. The policy followed by the Leftist Socialists and that of the Social Democrats shared fundamental points. The work of transforming society should be carried on within the limits of parliamentarianism, but the solution of certain crucial problems for the workers, which was stubbornly resisted in the Riksdag, should be executed with the help of extra-parliamentary measures. The Social Democratic party's young ideologue Ernst Wigforss touched on this when he wrote a letter to Östen Undén concerning the demand for a republic: "As long as it is a matter of creating the actual foundations for a continuous democratic development in legal forms, I am not afraid of revolution."

After the Leftist Socialists had refrained from taking any initiative in implementing a strike, there remained the threat of a general strike by the Confederation of Trade Unions if the right did not accept the government's proposition. This threat was strongly emphasized by Per Albin Hansson in a speech in Linköping at the end of November. When the negotiations continued within the special Riksdag committee, Herman Lindqvist, head of the Confederation of Trade Unions, let it be understood that he was having a great deal of difficulty in preventing a general strike. This threat hung over the country during the succeeding days and the Riksdag purchased candles so that it would not have to conduct its negotiations in darkness should the strike eventuate.

How did the Confederation of Trade Unions react to the prospect of having to make good on its threat of a general strike? The answer is clear from the debates at an extraordinary meeting of the Confederation of Trade Unions' representative assembly and the Social Democratic party leadership on December 6–9. It was pointed out that economic conditions were much less favorable for a general strike than they had been in 1909. None of the speakers thought that the workers in the countryside were inclined to go on strike in the middle of Christmas month; a couple of union leaders with leftist sympathies spoke in favor of a strike, but they were conscious that the burghers and farmers would very quickly win a crushing victory. It was the food situation and not political issues that bothered the workers most. "Ideas are good, but bread is better," as a union leader argued. The general strike that Lindqvist said he was having such a hard time holding back was pretty much a phantom; as a deputy put it, "if the right knew of the debate that has been conducted here today, we would surely get a nice compromise proposal." The negotiations were interrupted by a telephone call from Prime Minister Edén who wondered uneasily what was happening. He explained that if the government proposal was defeated, the government would resign.

The mood at the deliberations between the union and political leaders on the following day was one of irritation. The Social Democratic leaders felt that the union leaders ought to stand behind their promises. The union men responded that it was the government that had arranged the whole thing and that now it was up to the government to force a resolution. Attempts were made on both sides to disclaim responsibility, but the rightists and the Social Democrats on the committee finally agreed on a compromise. Then they had to weather the storm of public opinion that they themselves had been involved in stirring up. The situation was undeniably most painful for the Conservative party. At the General Election League's executive committee meeting on December 16, Lindman declared that the concessions that had had to be made meant that the Conservatives' position must be reoriented completely to accommodate the accepted democratic idea. If the party did not want to endorse the leaders' actions, they were prepared to resign. The Social Democratic leaders were also exposed to severe criticism, primarily from the Social Democratic Leftist party, which started a protest campaign against the compromise. But worse was the very strong reaction within their own party. In order to press the right to concessions, the Social Democrats had carried on an intense campaign of meetings since the end of November, and all the resolutions that resulted had stressed that the government proposition was an absolute minimum demand, on which there could be no concessions. The campaign may have been of some use in countering leftist criticism at the time, but it undeniably backfired later when the Social Democrats found that Branting had made considerable concessions instead of hewing to the "absolute minimum." Criticism even appeared in resolutions that were accepted at meetings where the leading Social Democrats participated in an attempt to appease the rank and file. Perhaps the leaders welcomed such resolutions as an outlet for discontent that might otherwise turn into hidden opposition within the party. As to the union leaders, to what extent did they reflect the desires of the country's workers? On one point clear agreement emerges: for the individual worker, food and wage issues played a larger role than purely political ones. The individual worker's revolutionary disposition was governed more by his empty stomach than by his heart and mind. On the other hand, there was a greater tendency toward drastic and extraparliamentary solutions of problems among those on the local level. The union leaders in considering such solutions were faced with the possibility of being primarily responsible for a civil war which they—in light of the Finnish experience—did not believe would bring victory to the workers. At the local level the threat of catastrophe did not always seem as great and the responsibility was not as heavy. But it must be admitted that it is almost impossible to try to determine the actual opinion among Swedish workers at this time.

In any case, in the tense situation in the late fall of 1918 the leading Social Democratic politicians had a strictly limited freedom of action in responding to what they understood to be the mood of the workers in the countryside. Hansson, Möller, and Rydén, all from Skåne, feared a shift to the left within the party in Skåne. There the Leftist Socialists had not succeeded in creating an independent party apparatus and hence the radical workers, still members of the old party, had a direct influence on it. Their discontent, if not sufficiently appeased, might even lead to a new blowup within the party, with large groups moving to the left. The volatile situation among the youth was also a matter of grave concern to the party leaders. Unemployment and military service made them especially vulnerable to the appeals of the radical labor movement's propagandists. This was a serious problem for the future of the Social Democratic party. Its leaders, then, were engaged in a delicate balancing act, with concerns of party or special interests on the one hand, the realities of national politics on the other.

Introduction to Chapter 10

Parliamentary democracy triumphed in Sweden by 1920. With the help of the pressures created by World War I, the left parties had finally achieved their political goals. Having achieved this milestone, the left coalition collapsed in March 1920 because of general disagreement over social issues and specific disagreement on a township tax reform. As the largest party in the Riksdag, the Social Democrats built the first socialist government in Swedish history. It lasted only six months. In September 1920, the Social Democrats suffered the first serious election setback in their history and resigned. A nonparty, conservative-oriented ministry replaced them. In the next twelve years, Sweden would have nine separate governments with the longest tenure in office two years. The period was marked by factionalism. C. G. Ekman, who led the Prohibitionist Liberal party, was able in the later part of the period to be a significant force because of his skill in playing the "balancer" of political scales even though the actual number of his party's seats in the Riksdag decreased. Such a result had hardly been the expectation of the men who had fought so long and hard to achieve parliamentary democracy. What had gone wrong?

Of course, nothing had gone wrong in the sense that the system did not function correctly. What had happened was that the parliament mirrored the splintered social and political interests of Swedish society. The Liberals were extremely naive in their hope for continued cooperation among the left parties; indeed the Liberals themselves could not even stay together and split into two parties between 1924 and 1934. The Socialists who accepted the Marxist view that the industrialization process would inevitably produce an absolute majority of "workers" were equally naive and found their expectations unfulfilled. What existed instead, not only in Sweden but also in almost all Western industrialized countries, was a number of different interest groups whose size and strength tended to counterbalance one another. No one group could dominate the others and alliances of convenience developed whereby cooperation was achieved on a given issue; once that issue had been settled the alliance would disappear. Thus a small, middle party like Ekman's could affect parliamentary politics in a way far out of proportion to its popular support in the country as a whole. In these circumstances no broadly conceived political program could be initiated. Pressing needs such as major social reform were not dealt with effectively because of the inability of the Riksdag to find a program acceptable to a stable majority. Many in other countries of Europe where this state of affairs existed spoke of "the failure of parliamentary democracy" and were attracted to parties which advocated non-parliamentary means of achieving power and fulfilling their political programs. The inability of the Western democracies to respond quickly to the depression increased popular support for authoritarian solutions to social, political, and economic problems. In Sweden the experience of twelve years of minority governments led not to a widespread movement for an authoritarian state but rather to an attempt to find a parliamentary and democratic solution.

By the fall election of the Second Chamber in 1932, the need for a new form of politics was self-evident. Social progress in the twenties had been painfully slow. The depression had created mass unemployment. And the collapse of the economic empire of Ivar Kreuger, who had monopolized the manufacture in Sweden of safety matches, had exposed serious cracks in the nation's economic and political façades. The exposé which followed Kreuger's suicide in March 1932 implicated Prime Minister Ekman in dirty political deals and seemed to underscore the weaknesses of Sweden's political system. The election led to a striking victory by the Social Democrats but they assumed office in 1932 as still another minority government. The problems of the day demanded strong medicine if they were to be cured. A minority government would have great difficulty in getting a broadly designed program through the Riksdag. Swedish leaders therefore turned again to a coalition government.

The following essay by Docent Sven Anders Söderpalm is a study of the building of the coalition of 1933 between the Social Democrats and the Agrarian party. The importance of the "crisis agreement" that led to coalition can hardly be overstated. The Social Democrats have remained in power continuously since 1932 except for a three-month period in 1936. Yet rarely have they had an absolute majority in the Riksdag. They have had to rely upon support from other parties, primarily from the Agrarian party (renamed the Center party), with which they shared power more or less continuously from 1933 to 1957, and secondarily from the Communist party which during the succeeding decade held enough seats to make a socialist majority in votes of confidence. Cooperation between the Social Democrats and Agrarians over such a long period of time led eventually to each adopting much of the other's program in certain critical areas. (The former have supported high price supports for agricultural products while the latter have taken over much of the Social Democrats' social reform program.) Today the reconstructed Center party with considerable nonagrarian support is the major political threat to the future leadership of the Social Democrats. The program and tactics of the Center party today are a direct legacy of the 1933 coalition agreement. Unfortunately the changing political attitudes of rural agrarian elements in recent Swedish history have not as yet received the attention they deserve. Docent Söderpalm's essay indicates how fruitful research on them will be.

10

The Crisis Agreement
and the Social Democratic
Road to Power

by Sven Anders Söderpalm

The cooperation between the Social Democrats and the Agrarian party is a well-known phenomenon in modern Swedish politics. It was inaugurated with the 1933 "crisis agreement" on an agricultural and unemployment program and proceeded in several stages. Minority parliamentarianism thereby was transformed into majority parliamentarianism. The Social Democrats could continue to hold power and to establish a new employment policy. But the subject involves more than purely economic and parliamentary aspects. The crisis agreement should be seen in the larger context of interest politics. How could a party dominated by industrial workers in a country that was still strongly agrarian win the necessary voters among the poor rural population? This question became especially topical after the reform of 1909 enfranchised petty freeholders and rural workers. It was still a significant issue in the decisive Second Chamber election in 1936, when the Social Democrats took up the old and very elastic slogan "Workers and Farmers"; under the circumstances, "Farmers" could mean anyone from agricultural entrepreneurs to those who were completely or partly working for wages on farms.

How deep was the class cooperation? What consequences did it have, in the long run, for the Social Democrats' relationship to industry, for example? In one sense Sweden's modern history can be described as a drama depicting the triangle of workers, farmers, and big businessmen.

In 1911 the Social Democrats in practice abandoned Marxist agricultural views and accepted a genuine petty freeholder program. But the new policy, which aimed at creating "a true people's party" of workers and farmers and was supported by groups in part identical to the later Leftist Socialists, was not pursued with any great vigor. Hjalmar Branting, who took rapid industrial development for granted, continued to promote almost exclusively the interests of industrial workers, and the party gradually aroused resentment among all categories of agrarians. Farm owners were strongly antisocialist and sided with other employers in party politics. Both the Conservatives and the Liberals were basically farmer parties, although the latter were oriented more than the former to petty freeholders. The Conservative party, which was protectionistic and pro-defense and held back on the issues of suffrage and worker protection, was largely built on the solidarity between larger scale agrarians and industrialists. This was especially clear during the battle over defense and the castle courtyard crisis, when the farmers helped bring Hammarskjöld's ministry (1914–1917) of civil servants and big businessmen to power. During the Hammarskjöld and Swartz (1917) ministries, a community of interest between workers and the entrepreneurs in big industry was demonstrated for the first time. Both Social Democrats and influential businessmen opposed the farmers' demands for higher food prices, and both also opposed Hammarskjöld's trade policy, which they saw as a hindrance to agreement with England on the importing of raw materials from the West, vital for industry and the national economy. The cooperation that resulted was personified primarily by Branting and the heads of Stockholm's Enskilda Bank, Knut and Marcus Wallenberg, who were active as foreign minister and trade negotiator respectively. It became an important element behind the Social Democrats' rapid rise to power. The Conservative party and the Conservative government were weakened by internal conflicts. The prime minister and foreign minister came into conflict, and Hammarskjöld was overthrown. The 1917 election resulted in the formation of a Liberal–Social Democratic coalition government under Edén and Branting (1917–1920), which, with a representative of Enskilda Bank as foreign minister, concluded a trade and tonnage agreement with the Western Powers the following year and at the end of the war sponsored legislation establishing equal suffrage in township elections, women's suffrage, and the eight-hour day. Even the big banks and industry supported the demand for suffrage and exerted pressure on the Conservative party to do likewise; they wanted to avoid interruptions in production and saw democracy as a natural consequence of the victory of the Western Powers in the war.

But the established parties were on the verge of losing control over developments. In a time characterized by hunger-prompted demonstrations and by rumors of revolution, conflicts between the industrial and agricultural sectors became acute. The Leftist Socialists seceded from the Social Democratic party, demanding a policy favoring proletarian labor and petty farmers; the farmers in the Liberal Riksdag caucus required intensive persuasion before they would accept the suffrage and working hours reforms; and the right, which had been the big loser in the election, threatened for a while to split into urban and rural factions. During the battle over defense and parliamentarianism that brought Hammarskjöld to power, the right had defeated the Liberals in the struggle for votes from southern Swedish farmers, but the political attention focused on them made these voters more conscious of their class and interests. In 1914–1915, two special farmer parties had been formed, the Agrarian party and the Farmers' National Association; after a modest start they suddenly rode high on the discontent with the government's food policy and in 1917 captured ten Riksdag seats.

For a long time, the new movement belonged on the far right, a situation that the authorized party historians have not considered it opportune to mention. The Agrarian party was more smallholder-oriented than the National Association and in the beginning opposed all cooperation with the right in elections, but the party's often-mentioned anticapitalism was of an extremely conservative type and went hand in hand with strong enmity to socialism: it regarded big capital and supranational socialism as children of the same spirit. Both farmer groups described the old parties as mouthpieces for banking, trust, and speculative interests, which allowed a good business cycle to profit only trade and industry while the agricultural population was exploited; big industry in an unholy alliance with the socialists pushed through price ceilings, export prohibitions, and numerous other regulations. Both similarly opposed demands for democratization and were strongly pro-German, at least as far as their press was concerned; the Western Powers were regarded as representatives of a bellicose capitalism, whose victory would mean a breakthrough for "the ideological party system" and "plutodemocracy." The farmer parties received a small but much-noted element of support from academic intelligentsia, and the young Conservative ideologue Rudolf Kjellén interpreted the movement as "a new step in the direction of renewing the representation of interests, which sooner or later will come over our corrupt parliament."

Of the more famous Social Democrats, Arthur Engberg, editor of *Arbetet* and later minister of ecclesiastical affairs, was the only one who welcomed the farmer movement and felt that it would open the way to cooperation between the workers and farmers. But he was not as perceptive in his assessment of the situation as has sometimes been asserted. As a staunch free-trader, Engberg thought along rather traditional lines. He underestimated the conservative element in the farmers' anticapitalism and believed that they would depart from the protectionist camp as they liberated themselves from the right; his ideal was an agrarian left of the old type. The thought of cooperation at the price of a new Social Democratic agricultural policy never occurred to him, and he played no role in the creation of the crisis agreement.

The battle of interests during the war years locked the parties into attitudes and positions that remained characteristic of them for more than a decade. Consideration for farmer opinion thus continued to play a central role both for the right and for the Liberals; this was especially clear in the social field, where the farmers' employer-oriented attitude was often more strongly negative than that of industry. The working hours reform turned out to be a clear burden for the Liberals, who, after the downfall of the Edén ministry, never again undertook any regular cooperation on the left with the Social Democrats. For the latter, the farmers and especially the Agrarian party stood out as the core of reactionism.

Despite a number of temporary successes, the twenties did not become the decade of Social Democracy as many had expected. The newly won political rights were exploited badly, participation in elections was low, and parliamentarianism functioned only through short-lived caretaker and minority governments. As in the rest of the Western world, liberalism in Sweden experienced a last period of glory as the arbiter of social programs; in the Riksdag, to which power was now shifted, Liberals and freethinkers held the balance.

The Social Democrats formed the government three times—Branting, 1920, Branting, 1921–1923, Branting (Sandler), 1924–1926—but largely had to content themselves with administering bourgeois policy and working along Liberal lines. During the postwar years, this party more than any other protected the value of money and free trade; it promoted a strict deflationary and thrift-oriented fiscal policy, which elicited a number of protests from agriculture and industry; but it went to battle in earnest only on certain issues concerning unemployment policy: a softer line on help to workers affected by industrial conflicts, higher relief-work wages, more state-township jobs, and the introduction of unemployment insurance for industrial workers. Both in 1923 and in 1926 the Social Democratic governments fell on unemployment policy issues. Their policy on unemployment strengthened the Social Democrats' grip on trade unionists but at the same time made the party seem even more a bastion for industrial workers and contributed to the loss of the marginal voters in the rural population, which was decisive for the period's political development. Unlike industry, agriculture suffered throughout the twenties, especially at the end of the decade when the crisis became international owing to depressed business cycles. Agriculture's already large lag in income and profitability was greatly increased, which naturally affected the rural workers.

The Agrarian party, which in 1921 incorporated the Farmers' National Association, had very good relations with the right during the whole decade. Cooperation during elections was cordial and relations were especially close in the Riksdag, where members visited each other's caucus meetings and the party leaders, Arvid Lindman and Olof Olsson af Kullenbergstorp, a former member of the National Association, were on good terms. The liberal newspaper *Dagens Nyheter* characterized the Agrarian party on one occasion as "the farm hands' quarters of the right." All the bourgeois parties could unite on the unemployment question. Both agriculture and industry were interested in a mobile labor market and therefore tried to limit relief work to a minimum; they clung to the principle that relief-work wages should remain below those of the open market. The farmers, who were often most negative about "the principles of trade unions," thus demanded that work wages in any area not rise above the agricultural workers' wages.

The Swedish agricultural workers' movement was weak and divided for a long time, following the international pattern. In

1909 it had been adversely affected by the defeat of the general strike; after a considerable recovery during the good agricultural cycles in the years around the end of World War I, the number of members again decreased sharply. In the middle of the twenties, not even 5 percent of a total of 250,000 agricultural workers were organized, and only in the large estate areas in Skåne, Östergötland, and the Mälar provinces was there any great support for the movement. The decline in part resulted from the advantage the agricultural crisis gave to employers, but it was also connected to the lack of interest which for a long time had distinguished the labor movement's attitude toward the rural proletarians' efforts. The decline had dire political consequences.

In the Second Chamber elections in 1928, the Social Democrats suffered their greatest defeat up to that time. All the parties increased their vote totals, but the right gained most strongly. The Social Democrats lost fifteen seats, Ekman's Prohibitionist minority government (1926–1928) was replaced by a Conservative one, and Lindman became prime minister (1928–1930).

The propaganda campaign preceding the election had turned into a battle between the bourgeois parties and the socialists. The right's exploitation of the electorate's unease over bolshevism and socialization, which had grown since the Social Democrats had presented such proposals as that advocating a radical inheritance tax and had entered into technical election cooperation with the Communists, has been pointed to as one reason for the outcome of the election. But the agricultural crisis played an equally important role. The lower agrarian classes united with agricultural employers to defend their threatened sector of the economy and, in the agitation at the grass-roots level, they were strongly susceptible to arguments like "industrial workers are better off than farm workers," "their wages force up prices and place burdens on agriculture," and "the Social Democrats aren't interested in farm workers." In most of the election districts, the majority of farm workers voted for the bourgeois parties.

Clearly aware of this, the Social Democrats now began a more intensive political self-analysis. Shortly after the election, Gunnar Myrdal, a young Social Democratic economist of growing importance, and Rickard Lindström, the chairman of the Social Democratic Youth League, undertook similar analyses, in which they showed how conflicts of economic groups and interests crossed party lines; they strongly criticized the trade union movement for having ignored the farm workers and through monopoly hindered them from trying to move into industry during the agricultural recession. According to Myrdal, "if the Social Democrats want to collect and hold the farm workers in the party, they must soften the entire trade union policy, which will happen most easily by extending the organization to include all workers, even farm workers." Lindström also cited the division of interests within the bourgeois parties and the labor class regarding demands for a Social Democratic policy aimed at leveling the distinctions between social classes; the goal should be a "people's party" where socialism built on common sense and conviction. These were views which Per Albin Hansson openly concurred in, and which during the following years clearly influenced Social Democratic ideology and tactics. Generally conciliatory notes were struck, a number of union methods were criticized by Social Democratic leaders, the party's agricultural and rural social programs were extended, and union and political activities among farm workers were initiated.

At the same time, the party made a pioneering political contribution by outlining a program for combating permanent unemployment in line with Keynes's still little-known theories. At the 1930 Riksdag, the Social Democrats proposed that the entire relief-work system should be abolished and replaced with productive state work at wages set by contract agreements. Ernst Wigforss, later finance minister, who was not a national economist but was well acquainted with Marx's theory of underconsumption and therefore very early became aware of the arguments of liberal English economists, was a leader in the program. It is more difficult to determine if the Social Democrats at the same time were influenced by the Swedish Communists and by the older Fabianist view of unemployment.

But the new unemployment policy played a role only in the longer range. It took time to influence opinion, and industrial employment was still comparatively high. The township election in 1930 was a victory for the Social Democrats, but it had been preceded by what was in part a rather traditional battle over duties, which solidified the conflicts between farmers and industrial workers. Nothing yet pointed to a decisive shift among the mass of rural voters; the Agrarian party gained strongly and Liberals and Prohibitionists were the only clear losers.

In 1929 the agricultural crisis had become acute because of increasing international competition, but when the right and the Agrarian party demanded increased duties on sugar and cereal, the Social Democrats united with the Prohibitionists and defeated the proposals. The idea of cooperation among the groups on the left was again considered, but the Social Democrats took no initiative of their own. In 1929 only half of the party could be persuaded to vote for the alternative proposed by the Prohibitionists which provided for subventions to the beet growers, and, when the decisive vote was taken in the spring of the following year, the Social Democrats did not join the Prohibitionists in promoting the proposal that eventually won, a proposal forcing the mills to blend Swedish rye and wheat with imported grain, the so-called mixing and blending obligation. The result was a government crisis, in the resolution of which the Social Democrats, to the disappointment of Per Albin Hansson, were completely left out. Lindman resigned but was followed by Ekman and a new Prohibitionist minority government (1920–1932).

During the next two years, the Social Democrats drove their criticism of minority parliamentarianism to the absolute limit, but they were attacking a system that was basically conservative, not the Prohibitionists as such. The idea of cooperation on the left was still strong and was abandoned only after the world depression had shaken the old order to its roots and created a receptive climate for the party's new economic policy. The agricultural crisis was further deepened, and at the end of 1930 the depression reached industry. Domestic market production and the high-quality engineering industry got along remarkably well for a long time, but the export of wood, pulp, iron, and iron ore was strongly affected, harming the national economy as a whole. In the fall of 1931, Sweden left the gold standard without being able to break the generally declining economic trend, and at the end of the year approximately a quarter of the union workers were unemployed.

At the 1932 Riksdag the Social Democrats presented in a series of motions a general program to meet the crisis; it was based on the stimulation of employment and buying power through state work and placing of orders on the open market. Special relief-work wages would disappear, subventions would be doubled, and money would be obtained through loans. It was also proposed that agricultural supports be strengthened. The party was not ready for protectionism, but a great effort was made to illustrate the connection between the agricultural crisis and unemployment within industry, to show that workers and farmers were dependent on each other's buying power. Thus support loans were proposed for small-scale farmers. Ernst Wigforss was now, as before, the prime mover. He had long searched for ways to liberate the Social Democrats from their dependence on the Prohibitionists and perhaps was the first to realize that the new economic policy, if consistently followed, would mean the death blow to cooperation on the left and perhaps end in a rapprochement with the Agrarian party; he demonstrated his deep interest in the relationship between workers and farmers in several contributions to the party journal *Tiden*.

The Second Chamber elections in 1932 resulted in large losses for the right and the Prohibitionists and the formation of a Social Democratic minority government; the inner circle of the government was composed of Per Albin Hansson, Wigforss, Gustav Möller as minister of social affairs, and Per Edvin Sköld as minister of agriculture. During the campaign, the Social Democrats had again promoted consumer and free-trade views, and, after the election, the possibilities for cooperation on the left with the Prohibitionists were once more considered, but Wigforss especially was skeptical. The new government did not want to be bound by Liberal principles and concentrated on a program which gave priority to the new economic and unemployment policy and accepted the existing grain regulations and a newly introduced system of milk fees that would increase the price of butter. Sköld's first important action as agriculture minister was to establish regulations on the latter.

Compromise was necessary on the agricultural question. After the grain market was successfully stabilized in 1931, prices had begun to decrease sharply on butter, pork, and beef; the price index for animal products ended up more than 25 percent below the pre-crisis level. While cereal grains had required only the regulation of imports, animal products were a major export article. The decline in their price was caused especially by the worsened market conditions in England and Germany. The producers then took an interest in the Swedish domestic market that found expression in a dynamic development of the economic association movement within agriculture. In order to eliminate middlemen, free purveyors, and create an effective distribution system, farmers, aided by the state, soon attained monopolistic power over the entire marketing process. Local associations were combined into provincial and national societies that not only worked in the field of commerce but also were authorized to collect obligatory fees and apportion all state agricultural support. In the spring of 1932, the Swedish Dairies Association was formed, in part to administer the milk fees, and somewhat later, organizations like the Swedish Farmers Meat Marketing Association, the Swedish Egg Marketing Association, and even the Association of Swedish Forest Owners appeared. After having been primarily interested in production techniques during the twenties, farmers soon emerged as an interest group whose economic solidarity and consciousness could only be compared with that of the labor movement.

The economic association movement was strong enough by 1932 to dictate continuation of the Prohibitionist government's agricultural policy, despite the outcome of the election. But the movement could at the same time be exploited by and for the benefit of the new government. Farmers were receptive to arguments about purchasing power, and the acceptance of agricultural regulation opened new possibilities for the Social Democrats in the still undecided battle for rural voters. The Social Democrats could no longer be characterized as directly hostile to agriculture. The party had just elected its first farm workers to the Riksdag and strengthened the representation of small farmers; only the 1928 loss of votes and seats had been compensated for, however.

At the same time, the bourgeois front was beginning to crack. The right and the Prohibitionist party, which both experienced internal tensions between agriculturalists and industrialists and between consumers and producers, were irritated by the success of the Agrarian party. Their leaders accused the party of campaigning on the basis of class and making promises that could not be fulfilled, and after the election they opposed a Kullenbergstorp proposal for the formation of a bourgeois coalition government with the special task of looking after the interests of agriculture; Lindman felt that such a government would lack homogeneity and become very weak. Agrarian party members took due note of the bourgeois parties' attitudes and the majority, especially the many new members in the Riksdag, felt free to go their own ways in the future. Per Albin Hansson and Sköld later always denied that there were any plans at the time for a rapprochement of Social Democrats and the Agrarian party, but with hindsight it is not difficult to see portents of the approaching agreement.

At the 1933 Riksdag, which met in the worst period of the depression, it looked as if the government would fall on its proposal for reserve jobs at wages, financed by loans, corresponding to those of the open market. But it was made clear in repeated private contacts with the Agrarian party that if the unemployment proposal were accepted, the Social Democrats were willing to go along with general agricultural supports including the especially detestable excise tax on margarine. Thereby the bourgeois front finally dissolved. At the end of May the two parties concluded their crisis agreement, or "cow-trade" as opponents condescendingly called it.* After the government guaranteed animal products prices of at least 75 percent of the pre-crisis level, the unemployment policy was passed with certain minor modifications. The appropriation for public works on the open market was decreased from 115 to 110 million kronor, and wages for workers on them, even if the usual unskilled workers' wages now became the norm, would be calculated "with regard to the wage situation within agriculture and forestry as well." The unemployment commission was retained, and the proposal for state unemployment insurance was omitted from the agreement and later voted down.

The agreement, which came about only after Axel Persson Bramstorp, of a Skåne agricultural cooperative, and Professor K. G. Westman had assumed leadership within the Agrarian party through a coup, led to violent debate. In Conservative quarters, where the possible long-range parliamentary consequences were fully clear, it was, however, presented as a meaningless political deceit; rightist leaders scoffed and insisted agricultural supports would have been passed with only bourgeois votes. But the members of the Agrarian party, who distrusted the Liberals

---

* "Cow-trade" in Swedish was meant as a pun on the word "coalition."

and did not discount the possibility of cooperation on the left to the detriment of agriculture, saw several obvious benefits in the agreement. The party not only had broadened the base for the new agricultural policy but in the continuing battle for farmer voters had an important psychological advantage over the parties of the right after years in their shadow. It was also known that there were farmers even within the right who held expansionist economic views and were more willing than the party leadership to reach compromises with the Social Democrats. Bramstorp was a firm supporter of the new theories of purchasing power; he had shown this in statements in the association press a year before.

Scholars have justifiably seen a connection between Hitler's takeover of power and the desire for compromise and unity manifested in the crisis agreement. But it was primarily the right that directly felt the Nazist tendencies. The Agrarian party had slowly liberated itself from most of its old antidemocratic attitudes, and reports that the party's south Swedish voters had been moving toward Nazism before the agreement are based on rumors in the contemporary conservative press.

From an international perspective, the crisis agreement is an episode in the general development toward national economic planning, autarchy, and popular-front thinking that followed in the wake of the world depression. But, at the same time, there is reason to speak of a specifically Swedish and Scandinavian crisis policy. The cooperation between workers and farmers in Sweden had counterparts in Denmark and Norway and the similar development in the three countries was in part the result of widespread internordic ties within these groups. The Nordic Social Democrats had formed a special cooperative committee in 1932, and among the farmers it was characteristically the new interest organizations that primarily felt the need for contact and cooperation. Their development was strikingly parallel in the Scandinavian countries and they quickly coordinated a number of their economic activities and established principles for the relationship of the association movement to the state.

The Nordic Social Democratic cooperative committee discussed worker-farmer cooperation at a meeting in Helsinki in December 1935. The subject had been made especially timely by the "crisis agreement" reached by the Norwegian labor and farmer parties in the spring of the same year, but the Swedish and Danish as well as the Norwegian prime ministers described their experiences of cooperation.

Per Albin Hansson recalled that the two groups had regarded each other earlier with distrust. The industrial workers had demanded lower prices on food and through the trade unions had challenged the farmers indirectly by raising wages in the countryside. Even in 1932 "almost no one" had counted on the possibility of cooperation with the Agrarian party, which had been regarded as a conservative party, but slowly the workers came to understand that the farmers had become so poor that they could not buy any industrial products. After prices in Sweden were no longer determined by the world market, the farmers had become strongly dependent on the workers' purchasing power, especially for meat and milk products, and thereby the way to an agreement was prepared. The experiences of cooperation were good, according to the prime minister, and therefore he looked to the future with great optimism. The old distrust had been replaced by a new feeling of solidarity both in the Riksdag and out in the rural areas, and Bramstorp was alleged to be following the same line as the government: "The present farmer leader wants to put aside the big farmers and continue the cooperation with the Social Democrats. A number of older conservative farmers are dissatisfied, but the younger ones look at the matter more idealistically and want the two main laboring elements in the population to form the basis for the future democratic policy. I believe in the possibility of extensive future cooperation. The National Swedish Farmers'

Union is cooperating with the trade unions against company domination. In the defense question, the farmers want larger appropriations than we do but declare that they are willing to negotiate."

Johan Olof Johansson from the Confederation of Trade Unions described a rather spectacular example of local cooperation between workers and farmers: a blockade of the Körsnäs Company's forest work at Stora Kopparberg which had been organized by the National Swedish Farmers' Union, RLF (formed in 1929 to look after agriculture's social and economic interests), and carried on through the winter of 1935. The small farmers in the area demanded the right of collective bargaining; they were supported by the Forest and Flotation Workers' Union and a campaign in the cooperating parties' press. The employees won. (Locally the conflict may have played a critical role for the Social Democrats in their battle against the Communists, who were strong in the forest provinces involved. The Communists were violently opposed to the crisis agreement, which they characterized as a fraud against the consumers and small-scale farmers.) Johansson also reported that cooperation had occurred even within home districts and study circles, and all the Swedish participants also emphasized that their purpose was not to turn the "real" farmers into socialists. This was neither possible nor desirable. The party included only "3000 true farmers, but all of 10,000 petty freeholders, who also work for wages, and 10,000 farm workers." But differences in principle had not prevented workers and farmers from understanding each others' interests and guarding democracy and, if the Social Democrats wanted to secure their position among the rural little people, it was important that they not appear directly hostile to agriculture. According to Gustav Möller, who could speak from a background of many years' experience as party secretary and election strategist the main thing was to free the farmers from their animosity toward the labor movement. On this point the Swedes had clearly been more successful than their Nordic party comrades. Local and union cooperation was a specifically Swedish phenomenon.

The Danish crisis agreement, the Kanslergade agreement between the Stauning government of Social Democrats and Radicals (Radikal Venstre) and the liberal farmer party Venstre, had been reached only months before the Swedish agreement, and on one decisive point it had the same background: because of the curtailed animal products trade in England and Germany, even the strongly export-oriented Danish agriculture had become more dependent on the domestic market and workers' support for "an artificial price increase." Although the Danish workers' and farmers' organizations had the same general view of economic policy, they had not been able to strengthen their relationship. Thorvald Stauning commented at the Helsinki meeting that he hoped for closer cooperation, but the farmers were still strongly critical of the trade unions' wage policy, and furthermore rapprochement was made more difficult "by class and interest conflicts within the farmer population itself." Here he obviously alluded to discord between Venstre and the Farmers' Association, which had resulted in the formation of a new Agrarian party and a farmers' march and production strikes earlier in 1935. A new election in October had secured Stauning's position, but his relations with the opposition were very tense.

Cooperation did not occur in Norway, either locally or within the government, because of the country's extreme smallholder structure. The Agrarian party was almost a party of big farmers, while the Labor party, unlike its counterparts in the other Scandinavian countries, had a very strong smallholder wing and for a long time followed a policy related to that of the Swedish Leftist Socialists; the Labor party formally joined the Nordic cooperative committee only in 1936. Prime Minister Johan Nygaardsvold confessed that there were forces within the Labor party that opposed the "policy of profitability" implied in the crisis agreement and would rather cooperate with the working farmers' special interest organization, the Norwegian Farmers' and Smallholders' League, than with the Farmers' League, which stood closer to the Agrarian party.

The Finns, finally, because of the fascist-tinged Lappo movement had special reasons to want to safeguard democracy and parliamentarianism. The conflicts from the civil war were still deeply felt, and the Social Democrats were weaker than in the rest of Scandinavia. Finland was industrially underdeveloped and the smallholders in its Agrarian Association were accustomed to holding the political balance. It made them less willing to cooperate, while the workers, with their low wages, had a hard time understanding the point of cooperation. The Finnish Social Democrats were staunch free-traders and did not want to increase the already large support of agriculture by export premiums and other subventions. The latter viewpoint was especially emphasized at the Helsinki meeting by the party leader, Väinö Tanner, who surely also was speaking in his capacity as head of the Finnish consumer cooperative; it is characteristic that the Swedish consumer cooperative was the Social Democratic pressure group that had the hardest time reconciling itself to the crisis agreement and the monopolistic tendencies of the economic association movement. The first Finnish Agrarian–Social Democratic government came in 1937.

In Sweden conflicts over defense and pensions led to a government crisis in the spring of 1936 and the formation of a minority government by the Agrarian party under Bramstorp. But this government served only as a caretaker until the election. Despite the efforts of the right, no bourgeois coalition government came into being, and after the election Per Albin Hansson returned at the head of a "red-green" (Social Democratic–Agrarian) coalition; Bramstorp and three other members of the Agrarian party joined in the government.

The Social Democrats had won a convincing election victory,

and in Hansson's comments on the outcome, he said with pardonable exaggeration that the party had "conquered Sweden's countryside." The great goal had been reached. The party lost votes in Stockholm and Göteborg, but otherwise its progress was even and strong both in the North and in the South and in all types of forest and agrarian areas; in several of the forest provinces, the party quadrupled its already large proportion of the vote, and in a south Swedish agricultural province like Kalmar, where it had been exceptionally weak, it had as much as octupled its proportion since 1928. The right suffered greatly, and the bourgeois Second Chamber majority was lost, even though both the Agrarian party and the Liberal party held their positions.

The Social Democrats and the Agrarian party continued governing jointly in the national coalition government of 1939–1945 and in the new two-party coalition of 1951–1957. (See Table 1

Table 1. Riksdag Seats and Agrarian Element of the Parties in the Second Chamber (the Figures in Parentheses Indicate the Number of Farm Workers)

Party	1918	1928	1938	1948	1958
Conservatives	56 (35)	65 (36)	44 (22)	39 (16)	45 (18)
Agrarians (including Farmers' National Association)	14 (14)	23 (23)	36 (35)	35 (35)	32 (29)
Liberals	61 (42)	32 (21)	27 (12)	26 (11)	38 (5)
Socialists (including Leftist Socialists in 1918)	96 (11)	105 (14)	115 (24)	115 (21)	111 (14)

Source: B. Ulfvinge, *Jordbrukarinslaget i riksdagen.*

for some statistics on representation in the Riksdag.) They carried out the agricultural policy that had been established in the crisis agreement; within this part of the economy, "normal times" never returned. But agricultural supports were not dear to Social Democratic hearts. When the party created a new agricultural program at the end of the thirties, the assistance measures were presented as a costly and, from the point of view of equality, very dubious form of social policy, which could be accepted only if there were continued rural depopulation and streamlining in agricultural procedures. Among leading Social Democrats, Per Edvin Sköld was one of the few who in the future was concerned with the special interests of the small farmers.

After the Social Democrats had secured their power, they wanted to carry out new social reforms and increase and safeguard employment in preparation for any future crisis; they were completely dependent in both cases on the development of industrial production. They were fully aware of the necessity of increasing the effectiveness of the national economy, and they approached big industry with proposals for joint economic policy deliberations. The negotiations that resulted were broken off by World War II, but the government carried out several measures to stimulate production and capital formation, and it sought to relieve the uneasiness of business over national economic planning and wartime socialism by giving businessmen the majority of key posts in the quickly swelling war administration; influential entrepreneurs were even involved with plans for a regular government coalition between the Social Democrats and big industry represented by a number of nonpolitical specialists to replace the red-green coalition of the thirties.

Furthermore, the Swedish Employers' Confederation and the Confederation of Trade Unions had reached accord on the rules for industrial conflict in the Saltsjöbaden agreement that made the Swedish labor market one of the world's calmest. By it wage determinations were centralized, and policies were emphasized that would secure employment and high wages through a rapid development toward concentration and rational large-scale production. Or, as a radical young historian, H. Arvidsson, recently put it, "the ostensibly paradoxical result . . . was that the Social Democrats and the Confederation of Trade Unions came to support the largest and most sound companies, in other words, big business."

Against this background, the continued cooperation between Social Democrats and members of the Agrarian party gradually became only a parliamentary marriage of convenience; this became abundantly clear during the coalition in the fifties. Subsequently there were large election rebuffs for the two parties. The radical slogans about workers and farmers disappeared before the war and will hardly be revived. The smallholders and other more proletarian rural groups that once gave them meaning are well on the way to being completely eliminated. The highly systematized Swedish agriculture soon will not employ more than a twentieth of the working population. The most important worker-farmer cooperation occurs today *within* the Agrarian party, which continues to live as the Center party (1957) and recently has won wide support of its demands for a new environmental policy opposed to the tendencies toward centralization; the party has made great inroads in the cities and now includes more workers than farmers.

The slogan about workers and farmers tells us less about modern Swedish politics and social development than concepts like the spirit of Saltsjöbaden and Harpsund.* The relationship between the Social Democrats and business is sometimes tense but as spokesmen for the industrial workers, the Social Democrats have had an economistic view of fundamental structural and production questions. Forty years of the exercise of power have only strengthened the characteristic in the party's policy that appeared during World War I.

---

* Harpsund is the official residence of the prime minister. It was used by Tage Erlander, 1946–1968, as the meeting place of influential businessmen, labor leaders, and politicians in frank discussions of Swedish economic policy. "The spirit of Harpsund" is an expression implying a desire to compromise and to build a broad consensus.

Introduction to Chapter 11

No socialist party other than the Communist party of the Soviet Union has governed in its country longer or more continuously than the Social Democratic party of Sweden. The Social Democrats have held or shared power in various forms during most of the years since 1917: first in a coalition government with the Liberals, 1917–1920, later as a minority government, 1920, 1921–1923, 1924–1925, and since 1932 (with the exception of the summer of 1936) continuously either alone, 1932–1933 and after 1957, in coalition with the Agrarian party, 1933–1936, 1936–1939, 1951–1957, or in a wartime coalition with all the non-Communist parties. The ability of the Social Democrats to maintain this commanding position in Swedish political life over the past five decades is a unique record for a socialist party in a democratic country. Why and how have the Swedish Social Democrats succeeded in achieving political dominance over an extended period of time when other Western European socialist parties have failed? The question cannot be answered definitively in this volume although a number of essays, including the following one by Docent Leif Lewin, suggest at least partial answers.

Our knowledge of the early history of the Social Democratic party in Sweden is still rudimentary. There exists no thorough analysis of the social foundations for the labor movement nor is there a large-scale study of the political development of labor groups. Virtually no studies exist on the party's organization and its decision-making process. And no recent work has been published on the two men who have had the greatest impact on the growth and direction of the party: Hjalmar Branting and Per Albin Hansson. What exist are simplistic, often dogmatic, general treatments of the entire labor movement, a few suggestive general surveys, and some excellent monographic studies on very narrowly defined topics. The most influential work to date has been a two-volume study of Herbert Tingsten, *Den Social Demokratiska Ideutvecklingen* (1939).

Tingsten's work is a fascinating study in many ways but is unfortunately too much a personal testament. Tingsten has been one of the major intellectual figures of Sweden for the past forty years and his own ideological disenchantment with socialism in the 1930s found expression in his analysis of the Swedish experience. Docent Lewin's essay raises some serious questions about Tingsten's interpretation. Until we have a wider range of historical literature on the labor movement in Sweden, our conclusions about its nature and success will have to be highly speculative. Nonetheless a few observations might be made.

Classical forms of socialist ideology, particularly Marxism, have had less influence on the political activities of the Swedish party than they have had on most other European socialist parties. Although the Social Democratic party platforms used Marxist terminology freely at least until the late 1920s, many of the ideological planks in the party program that were direct translations from other socialist programs, particularly the German Social Democratic party programs, had little relevance to Swedish conditions. From the very beginning of the party's history, its leaders tended to take a practical rather than a theoretical approach. The party's founding fathers exhibited a strong desire to keep all the elements of the labor movement together, i.e., the party and the labor unions, and to set as the top priority of the party the establishment of parliamentary democracy. These concerns led naturally to the so-called reformist approach to the achievement of a social democratic state and to cooperation between labor groups and other organizations in Swedish society. This latter fact differentiates Sweden particularly from Germany, where the German socialists were forced to exist as "enemies of the Reich." The Swedish Social Democratic party has never been as isolated from the nonindustrial labor classes as have other European socialist parties. Of course this fact is partly explained by social and economic forces quite uncontrolled by the political parties. The first generation of party and union leaders also learned that large-scale, direct confrontation with antilabor institutions and organizations would more likely than not produce negative rather than positive results and hence these leaders tended to seek forms for compromise. That Swedish institutions and organizations eventually proved responsive to the ideas of the labor movement also must be considered of prime importance. One should not, however, get the impression that modern Sweden is more or less a product of the Social Democratic party. The party's contribution has been extensive but was seldom made in a political vacuum. The Social Democrats have followed an imaginative ideological and political path for almost five decades which has permitted them to speak for a far larger percentage of the Swedish people and to have more support from nonsocialist parties than a socialist party normally does. Docent Lewin's essay concentrates on the development of one of the most critical aspects of the Social Democrats' program: the use of economic planning.

11

The Debate on Economic
Planning in Sweden

by Leif Lewin

At the end of World War I a government consisting of Liberals and Social Democrats introduced universal suffrage to Sweden. An issue that had dominated political discussion for over two decades had finally been solved. Only after its resolution could the Social Democrats seriously turn their attention toward major social reform. However, the Liberals, allies on the suffrage reform, rejected the radicalism of the Social Democrats. They were driven to cooperate with the Conservatives. Out of this there arose a new grouping in Swedish politics: instead of a division between the left and the right, there was a division between, on the one hand, the Social Democrats and, on the other, all the nonsocialists—the Conservatives, the Liberals, and the Agrarian party—stemming from differing attitudes toward socialism or, as the Social Democrats often said, economic democracy.

The essence of the ideology held by the nonsocialist parties was an adherence to the free-market doctrine of liberalism, an absence of state intervention. The freedom of the individual and the freedom of industry to begin new enterprises, to exploit the country's natural resources, and to offer employment and opportunities of

wage earning were, to the nonsocialist, values that would be sti-
fled by such state intervention as the Social Democrats favored.
Their rejection of the state was not, however, as thoroughgoing
as that of the Manchester Liberals. For social and political reasons a certain amount of state intervention was necessary. But
the power of the state should not be allowed to expand to the
extent that it damaged the "productive powers" within society.
The nonsocialist parties believed that there existed a harmony in
the economic system whereby every man in his attempt to advance
his own interest also contributed to the national welfare in the
best possible way. According to this liberal doctrine of harmony
the driving force in this system lay in private ownership, the prospect of profits, and wage differentiation. But it was these forces
of the market that the Social Democrats now wished to bring
under control. When the nonsocialist parties opposed plans that
would lead to a significant increase of state power in economic
life, they were fighting both for freedom and for the national
welfare as they conceived it.

Their fight was successful during the 1920s. The liberal system
was preserved intact. After the depression, the economy displayed
extraordinary powers of recovery. Extensive rationalization was
carried out and the national income of Sweden as well as its
export industry grew more rapidly than in most other countries.
Toward the end of the decade there was talk about "Sweden's
second Great Power Era."

The Social Democrats on the other hand had neither the parliamentary strength nor the ideological qualifications to carry out
a socialist reform of society. Their ideology was conditioned by
a materialistic conception of history. According to Marx's works
the conditions within a society were not characterized by harmony
but by an irreconcilable conflict of interests between capital and
labor. Exploitation was spreading rapidly in society; wealth was
being gathered into a few hands, and the working class was being
turned into a proletariat. But the capitalists would not succeed

in finding outlets for their products, which they were manufacturing at an increasing tempo. The exploited working class could not afford to buy them. Constant marketing crises would therefore afflict the capitalistic system. Eventually, Marx prophesied, the proletariat would rise against the capitalists during a final violent crisis. The means of production would be taken over by society and the classless society of socialism would be established.

This philosophy of history did not provide much guidance in everyday political life. The Social Democrats wished to work for an increased "economic democracy"—that is to say, a fairer sharing of the national product and economic control of the means of production. But did the Marxist system permit reforms of this type? The essential condition for the great socialist program was the existence of an exploited working class. If the living conditions of workers were gradually improved, this would represent a departure from the anticipated development. How would it be possible to combine social-political reforms carried out on a short-term basis with loyalty to the larger perspective of Marxism? This was the dominant question in the ideological discussions among the Social Democrats during the 1920s. But they did not come up with an answer. They did not formulate any definite course of action, and the radical plans made in the first years of the decade seemed increasingly utopian. The deterministic view of Marxism crippled the day-to-day political life of the Social Democrats.

There was, however, one exceptional Social Democrat who with greater success than others meditated on the ideological situation of his party. This was Ernst Wigforss. He devoted himself especially to the study of unemployment, one of the greatest political problems of the 1920s. Economists and politicians had tried in vain to find a solution. The nonsocialist parties applied their doctrine of harmony to the problem of unemployment. They traced its cause to the high wages demanded and obtained by the trade unions. The policy of high wages had made it, they said, too expensive for firms to employ all those available for work. Unemployment was the market's own corrective against an abuse of economic laws. Only through the lowering of wages could a balance be restored and unemployment brought to an end. On compassionate grounds the Social Democrats tried to resist this line of reasoning, but by and large they did not succeed in refuting the liberal wage theory. Wigforss, however, had not found any empirical relationship between low wages and high employment. On the contrary, he claimed that by means of high wages the purchasing power within society could be increased, so that manufacturers would have more outlets for their products and unemployment would be eliminated. Toward the end of the 1920s, Wigforss had arrived at a theory of underconsumption, which in its essential points anticipates the full-employment program that Keynes, an economist whose works Wigforss had studied at an early date, subsequently set out.

It was Marx's crisis theory that set Wigforss on the path that finally led him to the idea of the expanding economy. There are great similarities between the economic doctrines of Marx and of Keynes. Perhaps no one has described them with greater precision than Joan Robinson, a liberal British economist. In a period, she has written, when academic economists were concentrating exclusively on micro-economic problems, withdrawing their attention from the real problems within the economy as a whole and conducting abstract arguments that could not be verified empirically, Keynes revived Marx's more realistic macro-economic approach. Like Marx, Keynes was especially interested in crises within the capitalist system and its inability to realize full employment. But while this situation persuaded Marx that the capitalist system must go under, Keynes, using his expansion theory, devised a method for solving the unemployment problem in capitalism.

For the Social Democrats solving the unemployment problem presupposed considerable state intervention. When the private sector of the economy could not afford to support the unemployed, the state should do it. Public works should be started to combat unemployment. In this connection the Social Democrats had found a way of increasing the power of the state in economic life other than through socialization of businesses, a better way, Wigforss pointed out. If one business after another was nationalized, this would guarantee state control but the same state-controlled businesses would be caught in "the chaos of the free market"; in the event of a crisis, production would still have to be reduced and workers laid off. But by means of a new unemployment policy—complemented by increased state influence over credit facilities and by the rationalization of the economy—it would be possible to transform capitalism gradually and increase the rate of employment as well as its efficiency. This was called the policy of planned economy.

This ideology can be subsumed under the phrase "socialist concept of freedom." This is something quite different from freedom in the liberal sense, freedom from the state. When the Social Democrats talked of freedom, they were referring to freedom from the domination of capital, from poverty, and from the effects of inevitable underproduction. To overcome society's ills they put their trust in the state; their idea of freedom included a freedom *for* the state. There already existed many different forms of state activity that increased the individual's sense of freedom: in the social field, in education, and so on. Through the expanding unemployment program such an opportunity was now to be available in the economic field. On the most practical level the concept of the planned economy would find expression in particular parliamentary decisions, by means of which economic, commercial, and full-employment policies would be carried out.

Wigforss quickly won over the leading figures within the Social Democratic party to his program. In 1930 the party proposed a parliamentary motion demanding a reform of unemployment policy on the lines of the new theories, but the motion was rejected. Shortly afterwards the first symptoms of the Great Depression appeared in Sweden, and the election campaign of

1932 occurred in the shadow of an unemployment crisis. This crisis was interpreted by the nonsocialist parties as a painful but natural reaction of the economy; during the purifying and restorative periods of crisis, the disturbed harmony would be reestablished and wages and prices returned to their natural levels. State intervention in the course of the crisis would only exacerbate the interplay of economic forces. The Social Democrats won the election and formed a minority government. However, in the interests of forming a majority government, the Social Democrats built a coalition with the Agrarians. At the base of the coalition were two concessions: the Social Democrats accepted the Agrarians' farm policy, while the Agrarians agreed to support the unemployment policy of the Social Democrats. As a result of the coalition the government increased its opportunities to carve out in parliament new economic policies. The foundations had also been laid for the Social Democrats' long tenure of office in Sweden. During the thirties the Social Democrats carried out their policy of expanding the economy, a policy that most Western democracies did not initiate until the end of World War II. "As late as 1939 Sweden was still the only country that had made any serious attempt to put a compensatory public works policy into practice," says British economist Mark Blaug. The Swedish Social Democrats were the first socialist party in the world to be able to increase gradually the power of the state in economic life without revolution or large-scale nationalization. The rest of the world began to talk of "Sweden, the middle way."

It should be noted that the foregoing analysis differs from Herbert Tingsten's classic interpretation of the development of Social Democratic ideology. Tingsten did not understand—partly because of a self-confessed lack of interest in economic theory—the change in Social Democratic ideology at the end of the twenties. Even during the debate in the Great Depression, he believed the issue to be a conflict between Marxist determinism and the demands of daily politics, which meant in practice from his point of view a nonsocialist, general welfare policy. Tingsten failed to comprehend the ambitious new economic policy of the thirties; he wrote that the Social Democrats' full-employment policy was "at no point over the border of general social welfare."

The second phase in the planned economy policy concerned increased public control over credit facilities and the rationalization of economic life. A large number of public committees were established, but little progress was made, one of the reasons being incessant criticism from the opposition. With great energy the Conservatives and most of the Liberals criticized both the unemployment policy and the general economic measures of the Social Democrats. Against what they saw as a "socialist coercive economy" they asserted the principle of freedom and the doctrine of harmony. The prime minister, Per Albin Hansson, was not combative but tried to reach understandings and decided to move forward cautiously. The outbreak of World War II also caused the postponement of further plans.

With the war the interparty struggles vanished and a coalition government was formed out of the Social Democrats, the Conservatives, the Liberals, and the Agrarian party; maintaining a policy of neutrality and solving the consequent domestic problems were its principal commitments.

At the end of the war the Social Democrats decided to resume their economic plans on a more ambitious scale. Led by Wigforss, they worked out a special program that had some similarity to a program introduced in Great Britain about the same time, the Beveridge plan. Full employment was stressed as an important goal, especially since a severe postwar depression was expected; in order to cope with this the "honored traditions" of the thirties had to be further developed. But full employment was not enough; it was also necessary that the means of production should be put to use as efficiently as possible, that the structure of the economy be made as rational as possible. If the private sector of the economy accomplished the task assigned to it—of giving the public as much of the good things of life as was technically feasible with full and efficient employment—it would be possible to leave the organization of the economic system much the same as before the war. But if the economy did not meet the needs of the labor movement the state would then intervene in order to make production efficient and speed up the rationalization of its structure.

The Communists, who in the 1944 election had increased their parliamentary representation in the lower house from three to fifteen seats, backed up the postwar policies of the labor movement. But they believed that full employment and efficient productivity could not be attained without state ownership of industry and therefore demanded—in opposition to the Social Democrats—unconditional nationalization of the vital sectors of the Swedish economy.

Among the Conservatives and Liberals a change of view took place at the end of the war, associated with the fact that a new generation was taking over the leadership in both parties. Both parties now accepted the main lines of the Social Democratic unemployment policy from the 1930s. The doctrine of harmony of the interwar years was modified to the extent that state responsibility was accepted for the development of the economic situation. This ideology was given the name of social liberalism by Bertil Ohlin, a Keynesian economist who was the new leader of the Liberal party. On the other hand the opposition to the other economic plans of the Social Democrats was as intense as before. When the Social Democrats tried to carry out their postwar program through parliamentary motions and official committees, the three nonsocialist parties left the coalition government. The policies of the Social Democrats were subjected to extreme criticism through the medium of campaigns in the public press and in certain propaganda organs financed by private industry. The early postwar years, called by the optimistic Social Democrats "harvesttime," were the classic period of the debate on the planned economy in Sweden. Neither before nor since have ideological antagonisms been expressed with such force.

The ideologist of the nonsocialists was the economist F. A. Hayek, whose book *The Road to Serfdom* had had an enthusiastic reception and received worldwide attention. Hayek tried to show that a planned economy was inconsistent with political democracy. If the state is to decide on the direction economic production should take, it must then as a logical consequence exercise control over private consumption and the individual's choice of work and wages. Furthermore the prerogatives of a parliament would have to be set aside. Such a complicated matter as an overall plan for economic production is something that only experts can work out. When a central plan is submitted to a parliament it is bound to be marked by compromises and concessions to various interests. No single part, therefore, can be separated from the whole. A parliament must either pass or reject the plan in its entirety. Finally individual freedom would also disappear. When the time comes for the plan to be carried out, no criticism could be tolerated. It could thus endanger the very future of politics. The individual would be liable to punishment for insufficient loyalty to the plan and free society would disappear.

The nonsocialists attempted to use this approach in discussions with the Social Democrats. However, the nonsocialists did not correctly interpret the intentions of the Social Democrats. The former contended that after a temporary period of moderation during the 1930s, the Social Democrats were now prepared to join with the Communists in a far-reaching socialization of Swedish economic life. This was not true. More importantly the nonsocialists did not understand the Social Democratic idea of planning. The Social Democrats were not trying to draw up any "central plan" for the economy. Only if private enterprise failed in some sectors would the state intervene to maintain employment and rationalize the structure of the different sectors of the economy. When the Social Democrats had given government support to various industries in difficulties during the 1930s, no attempt had ever been made to draw up a central plan for the economy. Nor did this happen when a stricter control on monopoly was instituted, or when selective state ownership was carried out, or when at the end of the war many committees were set up to investigate the structural problems of the economy. It follows from this that political democracy was not endangered in the way described by Hayek. His analysis lacks application to the political conditions of Sweden.

But a critical analysis of the relationship of a planned economy to political democracy can still be justified. Now as earlier the central concept in the ideological debate was the controversial concept of freedom. The nonsocialists accused the Social Democrats of using the word "freedom" in too wide a sense; they were said often to use this word when in fact they meant security or equality. The Social Democrats, on the other hand, said that the liberal demand for freedom from state power was far too limited; if a rather considerable amount of state intervention was not to take place, many would be left in insecurity and poverty. For the nonsocialists the Social Democratic program of economic development and equality contained a conflict of goals. A certain wage differentiation was a condition for a rise in prosperity. Absolute equality presupposed such protection from the state that freedom would disappear for all. Freedom would therefore have to be purchased at the price of a certain inequality, but it was such a valuable treasure that it was worth the price.

The Social Democrats refused to accept the idea that there was a conflict in their goals as the nonsocialists claimed. Economic equality and state intervention could very successfully combine freedom and political democracy, they believed. The distinctive mark of democracy was that people could cast out their governors through free voting. So long as this right existed, so did political democracy—this was true even if the government was conducting a radical economic policy. Against this the nonsocialists argued that political encroachment could also take place in the name of the majority. The only safe guarantee of freedom, therefore, was to keep state power *limited*.

To take sides in favor of either of these opposed ideologies is no function of the scholar. It is a question of value—the amount of faith one has in the alertness of the electors and in the control of politicians over the administration. How great is the ability of the state to increase the individual's feeling of freedom? How great is the risk that the power of the state will instead be used to stifle personal freedom? Here lies the heart of the ideological discussion concerning a planned economy.

The nonsocialist argument on freedom won a victory during the election of 1948 when the Social Democrats lost some seats. At the same time the government was faced by an inflation crisis which to a certain extent was caused by its financial policy of stimulating purchasing power. Accordingly new economic problems awaited solution, and the major plans for the economy had to be laid aside before any great results had been achieved. During the immediate postwar period, when a boom was in progress, the economy seemed to manage quite well without the state. But what happened then to the planned economy? At the end of the war the Social Democrats had anticipated an increase of state power in the life of the economy. Could this state intervention be attained now in any other way? For the second time the Social Democrats had experienced failure in their major economic program.

After what the nonsocialists called "the nationalization program" had been laid aside, they regarded it as their primary task to oppose those controls that survived from the war years. During the 1950s these controls were gradually removed; only in the housing sector did they remain. At the same time there occurred a relaxation of the strained relations between the Social Democratic government and industry. Regular meetings were begun at the prime minister's residence at Harpsund between representatives of these groups.

The fifties were characterized by election successes for the non-socialist parties. They themselves saw an inevitable connection between these successes and the increasing national prosperity. In the middle of the 1950s Poor Sweden had become Welfare Sweden; the country's standard of living was, with Switzerland's, the highest in Europe. At the same time as poverty was being eliminated, so too—according to the interpretation of the nonsocialists—were the future prospects of socialism. A liberal epoch would be inaugurated in Swedish politics. The power of the state in economic life would be diminished. The accumulation of private capital would be encouraged and each citizen would be turned into a small capitalist. Small enterprises and shareholding would be given priority. The Conservative party—like its counterpart in Great Britain—called this political utopia a "property-owning democracy." This term was not used by the Liberals or by the Agrarian party, but their economic ideas coincided in the main with those of the Conservative party.

Despair prevailed in the Social Democratic party. But in 1956 Prime Minister Tage Erlander attempted to assign new goals for his party in new Welfare Sweden. It was true, he admitted, that dissatisfaction with poverty had been one of the principal forces behind socialism, and of that dissatisfaction little now remained. But another dissatisfaction had arisen instead. Erlander called it "the dissatisfaction of great expectations." Full employment had caused people to look to the future with even greater expectations. They made greater demands on life. New requirements arose in education, housing, health, roads. These demands could only be met by collective efforts. It was in these matters that Erlander saw new goals for socialism. In the welfare society the economic role of the state should not be lessened—as the nonsocialists said—but on the contrary increased in order to meet the new requirements of the people. These ideas preceded what the famous American economist John Kenneth Galbraith would write in his *Affluent Society*. During the sixties Social Democratic speakers often referred to Galbraith.

A critical problem in postwar economic policies was the inflation that came in the wake of full employment. Nonsocialist politicians and economists wished to solve the inflation problem primarily by attacking its cause: by lowering the level of employment. But such a proposal was contrary to the ideology of the Social Democrats. Gösta Rehn, one of the trade unionist economists, suggested another alternative. He advised the government to diminish excess demand by means of a strict financial policy with high company taxes; excess purchasing power should be "sterilized." Rehn was aware that the businesses that were the least sound would as a consequence run into difficulties and "pockets of unemployment" would tend to develop. To counter this, Rehn proposed a thorough overhaul of labor market policies. Its aim would be to increase the mobility of manpower, so that an individual would have the opportunity of moving from a "pocket of unemployment" to another sector or branch of industry that could give him higher wages and greater security. Through instruction courses a worker could be given greater freedom of choice concerning employment and way of life. For Rehn this active labor market policy represented a step toward the realization of socialism's concept of freedom. From the nonsocialist side, however, the proposal was sharply criticized. With the downturn of the trade cycle at the end of the 1950s Rehn's ideas concerning the labor market began to be put into practice. The active labor market policy aroused great international interest and even had imitators. For the second time in one generation Sweden had become a pioneer in employment policy. The government, however, was not able to carry out a financial policy strict enough to halt the rise in prices.

A policy that would affect the structure of the economy had long been sought by the Social Democrats. Toward the end of the 1950s the old ambition of obtaining greater public control of credit facilities was also realized. The basic national pension was supplemented with a service pension which was related to the individual's income from work during the active part of his life. A large state fund was set up, which contained within a few years billions of crowns. Toward the end of the decade new instruments had been placed at the disposal of those shaping economic policy and it was being asked how the Social Democrats should employ them for a continued socialist reform of the Swedish economy.

The advent of the service pension resulted in election victories for the Social Democrats, and they were able to remain in power. In 1961 the trade unions issued a pamphlet entitled *Coordinated Economic Planning* in which the ideas on economic policy of the Social Democrats were set forth. In it Tage Erlander's thoughts on the dissatisfaction of great expectations were further developed, as well as Gösta Rehn's program for a labor market policy. The pamphlet claimed that the liberal economy had never functioned in the way that liberal doctrine presupposed. The perfectly functioning free competition of which the Liberals spoke had been contradicted by an economic reality of inertia and bottlenecks, incompletely utilized production facilities, and monopolistic and protectionist regulations. These deficiencies caused slower economic development than was necessary. The economic theory of socialism had originated in a desire to replace, later to improve, this inefficient system of competition. With great consistency the authors asserted that it now ought to be the task of Social Democratic economic policy to bring into being the economic system that the doctrine of harmony implied. But this meant a significant modification of the liberal ideology: the state must take a leading role in economic policy since the market had shown itself incapable of attaining its own ideals. No controlled economy, however, was being sought. The market forces should themselves point out the direction in which economic development should go. The task of the state would be to remove obstacles and factors causing sluggishness in the market forces, ease the mobility and adaptation of production, and deliberately encourage the most expansive tendencies. The economy's capital support ought to be arranged in such a way as to increase structure rationalization. Through continued expansion of the labor market policy the mobility of manpower would be increased and along with it the opportunity of the individual to move from a low-wage concern to more effective businesses with larger wage-paying potential. The program of the planned economy policy of the sixties, explained Gösta Rehn, would thus set out to "realize what the free market according to its claims ought to but could not realize."

In certain parts this program has been realized; this especially applies to labor market policy. But the increasingly rapid rationalization of Swedish economic life has in recent years caused the closing down of more and more firms with consequent unemployment and a brief recession during 1967–1968. The issues of economic policy have as a result acquired renewed topicality. In 1966 the Social Democratic party suffered one of the greatest defeats in its history, and a period of self-examination commenced. At the beginning of 1967 the government announced that it intended to set up a large economic fund so as to facilitate the supply of capital for the rationalization of the economy.

In the following year, which was an election year, the Social Democrats made huge sums available to help the unemployed. The campaign was hot—the nonsocialist parties believed that, for the first time in many years, they had a good chance to win the election and form a government. But the results were quite the contrary, the largest victory ever for the Social Democrats. This was a result primarily of the mobilization of ordinarily nonvoting industrial workers. The 1968 election was the culmination of the ideological struggles between the Social Democrats and the nonsocialists in Sweden on the question of economic planning. The intensity of debate on this issue during the campaign parallels the campaigns of 1932 and 1948.

Even during the debates of the sixties the nonsocialist parties had repeated their classical ideological positions. The demands of the state for power over the economy were then as before rejected by the nonsocialists at least so far as the issue of freedom was concerned; the ability of the state to bring about an increase in welfare was distrusted because of a fear of bureaucratic inefficiency. Assistance to the unemployed within the framework of the active labor market policy was accepted. But when the right to assistance was broadened in 1966 to include everyone who wanted to move from low to high incomes, notes of warning were sounded by the nonsocialists. The socialists' craving for experiment and state management of the economy would be calamitous to the future development of Welfare Sweden. Why, the nonsocialists wondered, should the state experiment with all kinds of interference to bring about an economic development that would in any case take place automatically?

During the sixties the Social Democrats were also subjected to criticism from the left—criticism much stronger than it had been for many years. The new left displayed a greater faith in basic Marxist views than the modern Social Democrats. The left claimed that it was not possible to arrange the forces of the market in such a way that the values of the labor movement could be realized. Not even through the Social Democrats' active economic policies was it possible to create harmony out of the conflict between labor and capital. Why did the Social Democrats, for example, think that they served the interests of society in general by backing the most progressive industries? By virtue of the refined sales techniques of highly developed capitalism these industries could thrive on the socially meaningless manufacture of luxury or semiluxury goods. This identification of the good of the individual with the good of society seemed in the eyes of the new left just as unrealistic as that maintained by economic liberalism in the interwar period. Society could only be improved if capitalism were eliminated, that is to say if the vital sectors of the economy were nationalized and a thorough democratization of industry undertaken.

In recent years many political observers have spoken of the "end of ideologies" in the rich lands of Europe, America, and Australia. This view has been put forward by such men as Raymond Aaron, T. H. Marshall, S. M. Lipset, and Daniel Bell, and in Sweden primarily by Herbert Tingsten. The following distinctions and definitions might help to throw a clearer light on the discussion, which has often been diffuse.

It is first of all necessary to identify the participants. At what levels in the forming of public opinion has ideological prediction been decaying? Care should be exercised in comparing the different levels; the fact that the average member of parliament in our day reasons with less eloquence than Karl Marx cannot be brought forward as proof of the death of ideologies. It is necessary to distinguish between different intellectual levels in the process of forming public opinion—such as the creator of ideas, opinion makers, and the general public—and not compare a high level at a certain time with a lower at a subsequent time in order to obtain support for a theory. (The terminology suggested here also points to a limitation in political scientists' criticism of ideas. Only the thoughts of the creators of ideas and opinion leaders and the relationship between these levels are analyzed by political scientists in this field of study. If the political views of the public are to be known it is necessary to use other, political-sociological methods.)

In the second place the notion that politics was a "pure struggle of ideas" in earlier historical periods is probably wrong. Politics has always been a composite of tactics and technique and ideology; these are not characteristic features just of our own time.

Furthermore one ought to distinguish between the decay of ideologies and social equalization. To mix these two ideas is a frequent mistake. Proof of the end of ideologies is seen in the rise of the affluent society and the political and economic integration of the working class into society. But the conflict of ideas on a certain issue—for example, the role of the state in economic life—*can* be just as great even if the national income rises. Whether a certain development of ideas took place can only be decided through a study of source material, not through economic-historical sketches.

Finally, only a certain type of political conflict is of interest here. In other words we must establish a definition of the term "ideology." To conform with Herbert Tingsten's usage it seems wise to reserve the term for "a collection of political concepts that is meant to present a systematic whole and give a general and definite directive for action." If a person defends monarchy on the ground that this form of government gives a greater guarantee of competence in the head of state than a republic or criticizes a political proposal as expensive and inefficient, he is not regarded as being an adherent of a political ideology. "If he explains, however, that the principle of personality belongs to the natural presuppositions for all social life and that this principle is inconsistent with the holding of office by inheritance, or he condemns social politics as a crime against the principle of free competition which is bound up with the human being, then ideological points of departure are said to be decisive."

When in the Swedish debate an attempt is made to take a position on whether ideologies have declined, a number of strange features appear. Those who oppose the theory often allege that the majority of politicians say that they themselves are impelled by ideological motives. But the participants' own description of the idea structure in society does not possess any scientific value as evidence. Others say that in such difficult questions as these the question is whether the truth can ever be reached. Those who agree with the theory and those who oppose it are both in their own way right to approximately the same degree. Perhaps the best thing to do would be to try to arrive at a compromise between those holding opposed views. But such an intellectual recognition of defeat is as unacceptable as to agree with the claim of the majority of politicians, who, according to what they themselves say, are propelled by ideological convictions. When one attempts to solve theoretical questions it is as unjustified to try and arrive at compromises as it is to apply majority rule.

The picture that Tingsten's supporters paint of Swedish politics is approximately as follows. Since the Social Democrats gave up their belief in nationalization and the nonsocialists became social liberals, ideological conflicts have diminished and disappeared. The extensive discussion on freedom focuses upon an illusory problem. Do not all the parties commit themselves to the ideal of freedom? Do not all the parties wish to increase the individual's sense of freedom? Political debate has been reduced to marginal disagreements on the percentage growth that should be permitted the public sector.

According to Tingsten's view it is characteristic of ideological statements to arise not out of immediate evaluations but from systematically formulated principles. In both of his examples, on the head of state and social politics, those views were called ideological that were maintained against the background of a certain conviction of principle. The actual viewpoint, in other words, was not critical. The main thing was the *motivations* cited for a given position. In the same way one should say that what gave the struggle during the nineteenth century between the Conservatives and the Liberals its ideological characteristics was not the different technical-economic solutions; rather it was the conceptions and ideas that were brought forward as arguments for the proposal—those concerning the true nature of the state and the obligations arising from patriotism or the international validity of free competition and the law about comparative costs. What gave the right-to-vote controversy its ideological character was not the technical solutions to the problems of parliamentary representation; it was the motives that were put forward—the people's in-

competence and the connection between economic accountability
and political rights or the equal value of all human beings and the
desirability that through everyone's participation in the running
of the state the civic spirit of the individual would be developed.

It is in the same way that the debate on the planned economy
was analyzed. What gave the struggle over the unemployment
policies its ideological characteristics in the thirties was not the
energetically discussed question of how high a wage should be
paid for public works; it was the conflicting opinions on whether
the higher wages would spoil the self-regulating mechanism of the
liberal economy or, on the contrary, lead to an increase of production and employment. It was not the actual economic and commercial issue concerning the state's opportunities to help toward
the rationalization of certain branches of industry that created
the ideological struggles of the forties; they stemmed partly
from the Social Democratic hope of "a better world after the war,"
free of the recurrent crises of capitalism, partly from the fear of
the Conservatives and Liberals that the growth of the state would
lead to the fall of democracy and civic freedom. The ideological
character of the property-owning democracy was not its concrete
proposals for the extension of shareholding to all social groups,
but its belief that only such capital ownership could lead to that
personal freedom and independence that the Conservatives
wished to realize. The resistance to the "active economic policies"
of the Social Democrats in the sixties did not receive its ideological stamp from criticism of individual points, but from the conviction of the nonsocialists that these policies would lead to total
planning of economic and political life by the state.

But this is only the first of two steps toward proof of the vitality
of ideologies. All this argument about freedom could be what
Tingsten calls a "Sunday sermon," empty chatter without any
practical significance for politics. The investigation in this essay
can be seen, however, as an empirical examination of the hypothesis, leading us to the conclusion that the problem of "freedom" is

real and so Tingsten's view of the end of ideologies must be rejected. Since World War I the ideas concerning freedom have been the driving forces for political work in the economic and industrial transformation of society. The frequency with which this discussion on freedom arises when the particulars of every-day politics touch on the role played by the state in economic life, and the tendency of the political parties to allow their different ideas of freedom to be decisive in their practical political work, provide evidence that the ideologies still possess vitality.

Introduction to Chapter 12

"Politics are adjourned" is the cry that is normally heard when war begins. Twentieth-century warfare has demanded the complete participation of the entire population of an engaged nation in order to meet the challenges of a wartime effort. Partisan politics during periods of war are viewed particularly by those in positions of power as unnecessary and severe handicaps. The famous *Burgfrieden* of World War I where dissident political parties in almost all of the belligerent nations buried their own grievances and joined a common front to eradicate the enemy is a well-known example of such experiences. But what happens to those countries that are lucky enough or smart enough to avoid war? Usually the pressure is as great within the nonbelligerent nations to support a common effort to stay out of the war as it is in the warring nations to support a war policy; perhaps it is even greater.

In Sweden's case the common policy during both of the world wars was neutrality. In both 1914 and 1940 almost all elements in Swedish society supported a neutrality policy. In 1914 the government of Hjalmar Hammarskjöld, which had originally been something of an imperial ministry, became a national government with enormously increased domestic support for its wartime program, while in 1940 the coalition government of the Agrarians and Social Democrats was extended to include all non-Communist parties in a grand coalition. There was clearly a tendency to try to ignore prewar domestic struggles in the face of an external threat but did that threat in fact eliminate internal politics? The following essay by Karl Molin examines this problem in the context of World War II. Some comments can be made here about the experiences of World War I.

There can be little doubt that after August 1914, Hjalmar Hammarskjöld's policy of active neutrality became a unifying force in Swedish political life. At least during the first two years of the war he drew support from all of the major political groups. Only the small and ineffective pro-German activists worked against the prime minister's policies. The great domestic struggles of the immediate prewar period were set aside in the hope that war could be kept from the shores of Sweden. But the issues that had caused the prewar upheavals did not disappear and as the war extended into its third year the domestic consensus began to collapse. By the fall of 1916, partisan domestic politics were in full swing again and in 1917 Sweden witnessed two governmental changes and the establishment of parliamentary democracy. Even in the last year of the war, domestic politics had a clear partisan ring. What is of interest to note about this is that the very apparent disagreements between Swedish political groups about Sweden's domestic and international course may have been an important factor in Sweden's success as a nonbelligerent. The belligerent Great Powers, fearful that a group in Sweden opposed to their interests would achieve power, tried to support the forces in Sweden that would keep a balanced neutrality policy. In short, the lack of nonpartisanship in Sweden during 1917–1918 did not injure or weaken Sweden's ability to remain neutral. Obviously it would be dangerous to suggest from this one example that disharmony may be as desirous as harmony for the maintenance of neutrality, but at least it can be demonstrated that rarely can real domestic disagreements be shunted aside for any extended period by external pressures.

12

Parliamentary Politics during World War II

by Karl Molin

"Sweden is the point of departure for all of our efforts," the Social Democratic defense minister, Per Edvin Sköld, declared at the end of a long speech in the Riksdag in June 1942. He continued: "Without an independent Sweden, our efforts are ended. If we wish to improve social conditions, if we wish to work for peace on earth, if we wish to create a society that is better in this or that respect, then first and foremost we must have a free place to work, where we can make full use of our powers. This place is Sweden, and in order to preserve it there is in fact no limit to the sacrifices we ought to take upon us."

Nationalism was not among the fundamental elements in the Social Democratic party program. But Sköld's thoughts and hopes in the face of a recognizable threat to the integrity of his own country did not differ from what other responsible politicians thought and hoped. Sweden did not participate militarily in World War II but the threat of invasion was constantly present, at least until the time of the Allied invasion of Normandy, and national declarations about preserving Sweden's integrity were legion. They did not always have the rhetorical unpretentiousness of the example given above, but the simple basic idea was the same: the country would be defended at all costs.

The majority of the Swedish people were participants in this nationalistic movement in one way or another. The men capable of bearing arms had to do emergency military service for various lengths of time; small savers bought government bonds in order to support defense. The celebration of May Day was transformed into demonstrations of national unity, with participation by the four large parties. National holidays were celebrated with new enthusiasm and increased interest. People were reminded of and confessed their national allegiance constantly and everywhere. Gustav Adolf pastries were eaten in all homes and the Swedish flag day lasted all year around.

On the level of party politics, this effort toward national unity resulted in the formation of a coalition government. On December 1, 1939, the day after the outbreak of the Finnish-Russian War, a discussion that had been suspended in the middle of October was resumed; this concerned enlarging the government coalition between the Social Democrats and the Agrarian party to include the Liberal and Conservative parties. The earlier discussion had been initiated by the Agrarian party; the other parties had not shown any enthusiasm then, but by December a reconstruction of the government was generally approved. The Conservatives thought of temporarily abandoning parliamentarianism in favor of a "national government," in which representatives of parties would be blended with representatives from institutions not tied to parties. It was, however, the Agrarians' view that finally triumphed. After twelve days of intensive negotiations, the two-party government was succeeded by a four-party government, in which the Social Democrats had five seats and the bourgeois parties two seats each. On December 13, the new government's program was read in the Riksdag by the Social Democratic prime minister, Per Albin Hansson, in the Second Chamber, and by Gösta Bagge, the new ecclesiastical minister and leader of the Conservative party, in the First.

In the government declaration, it was announced that the coalition of political parties was "a manifestation of national unity on the essential tasks for Swedish policy internally and externally." That such unity could not be achieved without mutual sacrifice was underlined: "a prerequisite for the work of the coalition government is that internal political differences of opinion be put aside." The Riksdag was also informed of the political questions primarily of concern: "The situation at this time invited joint effort to solve the great tasks of which continued strengthening of the defense and the security of the food supply are dominant." The leaders of the Riksdag groups saluted the declaration with short answering speeches. The chairman of the Social Democratic group in the Second Chamber spoke of the new government's stamp of "rugged manliness and strength" and assumed that it would win full response in all parts of the country. On his group's behalf, he announced his complete support, and all his colleagues within the Liberal party, Agrarian party, and Conservative party did the same. The party groups swore their fidelity to the ideal of national unity.

The concept of national unity can be described as the mainstream in Swedish politics during the crisis period. But there was an undercurrent running in an opposite direction. The war between the Great Powers meant for Sweden not only a threat to Sweden's security, which created unity, but also a stimulation of economic conflicts of interest, which acted as a splintering force.

Through the blockade of foreign trade that culminated in the establishment of the Skagerack blockade in connection with the German invasion of Denmark and Norway in April 1940, Swedish imports were reduced by approximately one-half and exports by about one-third in comparison with the average volume of 1936–1938. This meant, among other things, that the importation of food drastically decreased and that the Swedish economy was almost exclusively reduced to domestic production. The likelihood of achieving a satisfactory domestic volume was worsened at the same time by the lack of imports of artificial fertilizer and fodder and by the cold winters and dry summers that made both 1940 and 1941 years of severe famine. For consumers, this development meant a considerable curtailment of food supply; for farmers, on the other hand, one dares to suspect, it meant a not unwelcome opportunity to close through price increases the gap between the agrarians' standard of living and that of industrial workers which had developed in the thirties.

The trade blockade also meant a shortage of raw materials within industry. In several areas substitute production appeared but at the price of increased costs and reduced profits. Difficulties grew because of a shortage of labor caused by the military mobilization. The result was a tangible reduction in the volume of production: in 1944, the production index for industry was on the average about 12 percent below the 1939 level. At the same time as the volume decreased, a reorganization of its direction to the advantage of the military sector took place. Up to a fifth of industry's personnel were occupied with defense orders during the war years. The production concentrated on "normal," civilian needs thus decreased far more than the total production.

The shortage of goods led to price increases which in turn forced wage increases. In the spring of 1942 the government concluded that further price and wage increases must be regarded as inflationary. After long negotiations with business and labor organizations, the government announced on the last day of October 1942 that, from the following day, a general wage-price freeze would be in force. The real wages of industrial workers were thereby locked at a level that lay approximately 15 percent under that of the last prewar year.

Rearmament for defense affected not only industrial development but also, and not least, state finances. From 1938–1939 to

1944–1945, defense costs increased from 248 million to 2 billion crowns. Even if loan financing in large measure was resorted to and payment left to the future, immediate tax increases were inescapable. By the end of 1943 the total tax burden had increased approximately 35 percent. The Swedish levels of taxation, which during the prewar years had been low in comparison with other countries, came up to the standard that had been prevalent in countries with the heaviest taxes.

The problems of industry and of state finances like those of agricultural policy could not be solved without the risk of severe conflicts between various interests in society. Through the wartime crisis a number of social and economic problems strained the coalition. Who would bear which burdens of the crisis? Who would pay most of the raised taxes? Who would suffer the greatest decrease in real wages? Who would receive extra benefits in the distribution of food? Earlier a person who had only a little piece of the economic pie could comfort himself that this piece would tend to grow; now even minute improvements were unlikely. In fact, if he was just to maintain his standard of living, those who had bigger pieces would have to resign themselves to still bigger reductions: ever larger pieces for defense had to be sliced out somehow. These problems, probably unavoidable for a stagnating or regressive economy, swelled the undercurrent in Swedish politics of the war period.

The general tendencies that characterized Swedish politics during World War II can be summed up in the following way: on the one hand, the foreign political threat worked to the advantage of political unity and encouraged compromise solutions; on the other, a number of problems related to the economic situation led the parties, tied as they were to different interests and ideologies, in opposite directions. Obviously these two tendencies asserted themselves in varying strength in different situations. It may be said that there were two different groups of political issues: national issues, which include the questions connected with foreign and defense policy; and issues of allocation policy, among them the questions touching the economic interests of various social groups. During the following analysis of parliamentary life during the war period these two sets of issues will be contrasted.

When members of the Riksdag acted on questions which involved defense or foreign policy, they can be characterized as being aware of walking on thin ice, where any wrong step could be disastrous. This feeling was expressed by one Conservative this way: "Time today has big eyes and listens with attentive ears; what is said in this room is noted very carefully outside of its walls, and this may give rise to reflections or measures that cannot be useful for our country." Many of his colleagues in the Riksdag expressed the same or similar thoughts on various occasions. The purpose was to impress on fellow members of the Riksdag how important it was that they watch their words. The Riksdag should behave in such a way that the surrounding world would realize that Sweden's people were determined, united, and strong.

The Riksdag should thus stand together. But what should it stand together on? In the matter of foreign policy, the new foreign minister, Christian Günther, commented in his first Riksdag speech in January 1940: "I expect increased difficulties during the time to come and for the foreign policy leadership it is naturally necessary that it can count on the Riksdag's support and understanding." His answer was simple: the Riksdag should stand together behind the government's policy. It also became a ritual that the various party leaders at the beginning of every general or foreign policy debate professed their loyalty to the government and its foreign policy.

Farther down in the party hierarchies, however, there were those who could not restrain their feeling that this unity was nothing but a fiction. "The Riksdag in fact does not know what will happen and has no possibility of judging whatsoever," declared one of the doubters. The statement was made on February 21, 1940, during the war in Finland. With hindsight, it is rather easy to state that the comment was justified and also that it was valid even during later phases of the war. It is clear that the government was parsimonious in the flow of information considered a necessity. The government could not risk the nation's welfare through excessive communicativeness, nor could it expose other nations to difficulties by disclosing what they had reported in confidence. An information gap between the government and the Riksdag was thus presented as something perhaps regrettable but unavoidable. For the Riksdag, this meant that its passive role was even more emphasized. The Riksdag's support of and confidence in the government's directed policy were not the result of an independent judgment, which would have required equal information, but an a priori recognition of the rightness of the government's actions.

This lack of information contributed to the general tone that distinguished the foreign policy debate of the war years and also to the fact that the number of debaters was very limited. It is sometimes possible to distinguish certain nuances of difference between the parties, at least for those who want to consider emotional values. As early as the government negotiations in December 1939, the Conservative party, for instance, indicated that its position could not be presumed under all circumstances to agree with that of the other parties. Gösta Bagge attached a reservation to the unofficial government program wherein he dissociated himself from a categorical rejection of military intervention in Finland. He maintained that Sweden's attitude toward Finland, considering the uncertain future, should not be set in advance but decided by Sweden's vital interests and the course of events.

In the Riksdag debates where the Finland question was central, neither Conservatives nor any others presented explicit demands for intervention in the war. But when the Conservatives spoke of the government's decision not to intervene, they were more anxious than others to stress that other possibilities of material help, for example the outfitting of a voluntary corps, were available. They also wanted to emphasize that the decision was only dictated by concern for protecting Sweden and not by any indifference to the fate of their neighbor. The difference in attitudes from those of the other parties had its most sensational expression during the "February crisis." The trigger was a newspaper report on February 16, 1940, that a Finnish request for military intervention had been rejected by the Swedish government. On the same day, the prime minister reported rather abruptly in a communiqué that an inquiry had been presented by the foreign minister of Finland and that as an answer the previous negative stand was referred to. The statement was characterized in the press comments as cool and aroused great excitement. On February 19, Gustav V intervened with a public statement wherein the king repeated the same conclusion as the prime minister but in different words. "With sorrow in my heart" he had found himself compelled to adhere to the negative position which he earlier "unfortunately" had to take. He also stated that Sweden in other ways was trying to support "our neighbor Finland's heroic battle against the superior power." This difference between the pure rejection and the sympathetic expression of regret characterizes the difference between the Conservative party's and the Riksdag majority's performance in the Riksdag debates on Finland. When J. B. Johansson, the leader of the Conservative party's First Chamber group, delivered his obligatory loyalty declaration on February 21, he formulated it as support not of "the government's policy," but of "His Majesty the King's proclamation."

The other party groups primarily and without observable difference in nuance followed the governmental line but occasionally Social Democrats and Liberals chose to speak in the same phrases as the Conservatives. The Agrarian party normally delivered a loyalty declaration through its leader but otherwise did not participate in the debates.

Sweden's geographical position meant that the country, despite its proclamation of neutrality, was drawn into the combatants' strategic calculations. This expressed itself concretely in combatant demands for passages in transit through Swedish territory. A petition from England and France for permission to transport troops to Finland through Sweden was rejected in the beginning of March 1940. More demands would follow but from another quarter. On July 5, the Swedish government announced that it had entered into an agreement with Germany for the passage in transit of war matériel and personnel through Sweden to occupied Norway. This "permittent traffic" continued until July 29, 1943. The second and most sensational of the transit permissions was given in connection with Germany's attack on the Soviet Union at midsummer of 1941: the German Engelbrecht division was transported from Norway to Finland on Swedish railways.

To judge the Riksdag's attitude toward these developments, it is again necessary to take into account the information provided it. What was reported to the Riksdag's representatives on the foreign affairs committee regarding the agreement in July 1940 is uncertain, but the Riksdag as a whole was informed first on August 16, 1940, when the foreign minister in his account exaggerated the freedom of action left to the Swedish government by the agreement and thus to a certain extent deceived the popularly elected representatives. When the demands for transit were made in the summer of 1941, the Riksdag groups of the four governmental parties were heard before a definite answer was given. Information was given by government representatives, there was a long debate, and votes even occurred. This procedure was characterized later by a member of the Riksdag as "highly exemplary" behavior on the part of the government. What he did not know then, but what we know now, is that a preliminary affirmative answer had been given to the Germans before a summons to recall the recessed members of the Riksdag had even been sent. While the members of the Riksdag sat on the express train to Stockholm, technical negotiations between the Swedes and the Germans had already been started. In comparison with earlier foreign policy crises, the events at midsummer 1941 meant that the Riksdag had become a piece on the chessboard but, as had previously been the case, it could not affect the game's outcome. The real difference seems to have been that the government considered a formal hearing of the Riksdag to be a prerequisite this time so that its members would feel themselves bound by the decision and obligated to defend it publicly.

It was the prime minister and the foreign minister who had let the German negotiators understand that the Swedish answer would be positive. Clearly, they both wanted the Riksdag groups to exercise little real influence on the decision-making process; they only wanted to be able to assert that the positive decision had been made with unified parliamentary approval. In the bourgeois groups all went well. The members of the Agrarian party without exception agreed with the government policy, as did the Conservative party with one exception, and in the Liberal party group approximately two-thirds were in favor of granting permission. There was more difficulty with the Social Democratic group. In the government four Social Democrats, Wigforss, Möller, Sköld, and Axel Gjöres, had taken a firm position in favor of a negative answer. It became apparent that large parts of the Riksdag group also were opposed to the government recommendation. Only a few made statements in favor of giving permission. The debate in the Social Democratic meeting was dominated by a demand for new negotiations with the bourgeois parties in which the Social Democrats would ask that they join in a refusal. Only after an answer on that appeal should the group make a definite decision. An overwhelming majority voted to accept this plan. Only two voted against. On Hansson's instigation a further vote took place, however, wherein it was decided by a slight majority and with many abstaining that if the bourgeois parties said no, the Social Democrats should cooperate "in the interest of unity" on a compliant answer to the German demand. It was the result of this latter vote that Hansson reported to the bourgeois parties when the government continued its deliberations. This meant that, in the presence of five fellow party members who had participated in the group meeting, he disavowed the group's decision. The bourgeois parties were thus informed that the Social Democrats were prepared to follow their line and no new negotiations were suggested. The other Social Democratic ministers were obviously disturbed, as was noted by the diary keepers present. But the result was clear: the technical preparatory work concerning the railways did not need to be broken off.

As to the Riksdag's position on the "permittent traffic," we must again refer to the Riksdag protocols. In the debates where the question was under discussion, the group leaders declared their support for the government's "foreign-policy outlines." Only the Communists as a party were openly critical; logically and emphatically they accused the government of breaches of neutrality. Insinuations in the same vein were heard occasionally from members of the Liberal party and from a handful of Social Democrats. In November 1942, the insinuations for the first time became explicit demands for termination of the transit agreement. The Conservatives allied themselves in full force with the government line, and, as far as the members of the Agrarian party were concerned, foreign-policy questions were obviously matters that they found no reason to express themselves on.

The chairman of the committee on foreign affairs, Östen Undén, a former Social Democratic foreign minister, belonged among those who were earliest in demanding an end to the "permittent traffic." In March 1943, he gathered the committee and tried to bring the members to favor termination. But the prime minister stepped in and at a later meeting collected declarations of confidence in the government's policy. Undén, who continued his demands, received support in the committee only from Rickard Sandler, former Social Democratic prime minister. These two were authoritative critics, to be sure, but even in a forum which was withdrawn from the public eye, the government's authority was overwhelmingly powerful. This attempt to get a minority of the members in the Riksdag who had seats on the foreign-affairs committee to abandon their passive role failed. As far as we know, this was the only serious attempt in this direction.

The hints of party lines that were found in consideration of the Finland question, 1939–1940, were lacking in the discussions on transit. It was not unusual for the various speakers to say that they represented a broad opinion in the country but, with the exception of the Communists, they never said that they represented a party. This did not mean that critics and those faithful to the government were evenly divided among the parties. The Conservatives' earlier mistrust of the government line had now been exchanged for full support. The Social Democrats and Liberals who had engaged themselves in the Finland question in a conservative way now figured as promoters of a quick termination of the transit agreement.

It became apparent during the foreign-policy debates of the war years that the government never succeeded in convincing all the members of the Riksdag that its policy was the only one possible for Sweden. Even aside from the Communists, there was a continuous stream of those who in more or less veiled language suggested critical views or recommended alternative lines of action. But the ideal of national unity worked to the government's benefit and prevented the appearance of party-oriented opposition as well as the formation of opposition groups free from party politics. This was of inestimable help in secret diplomacy, since the government had a free hand to withhold from the Riksdag facts which could have influenced the formation of opinion—dangerously, from the point of view of the government.

The importance of unity for defense policies had been agreed to during the negotiations over a coalition government in December 1939. The fact that the parties agreed that defense should be strengthened to the extent technically and economically possible meant a radical break with earlier tradition. Both the 1925 decision on trimming the defense apparatus and the 1936 decision on reconstruction were the result of a long search for compromise between strongly divergent ideas.

Agreement by the parties on a positive defense program did not mean that continued calls for unity came to be regarded as unnecessary. On the contrary, such appeals were especially in evidence when defense questions were debated. This could be a result of the great importance ascribed to these questions, but also of a feeling that the newly won unity rested on fragile supports. The question of what the future direction of armament should be lay behind the immediate measures to strengthen preparedness. To be sure, everyone wanted to have the strongest possible defense as long as the war lasted, but, at the same time, completely irreconcilable ideas about the future of defense were expressed in the debates.

In these debates, one view common since the twenties regarded defense as an elastic issue and proposed a barometer theory of expenditures. That is, international politics were thought to follow a cyclical development: times of crisis and times of relaxation succeeding each other at something like regular intervals. Therefore military strength should be increased and decreased in tune with changes in the international climate. With a certain amount of oversimplification it can be said that this conception was primarily embraced by Social Democrats and to a somewhat lesser extent by Liberals. The theory probably lost many proponents when the blitzkrieg became a fact of life at the end of the thirties. However, new proponents came to replace apostates. Those who were not totally opposed to defense spending, those who had not actually been pacifists but who had—even in the spring of 1939— talked about the country's exceptionally favorable strategic position and the peaceful disposition of its inhabitants as the best guarantees for peace, became the new proselytes of the elasticity theory. When millions and billions of kronor began to be eaten up by the insatiable war apparatus, and when the Riksdag in 1941 decided on an extended period of conscription, they did not offer opposition but they did, at every opportunity, give voice to this comforting thought: what is now being built is only a temporary thing; one day all this money—and all this time in young men's lives—will be used for something else, something better. They also believed that the Riksdag should retain freedom of action and not commit funds for future defense expenditures. In the debate in 1942 over a new five-year plan in which limits on defense spending were many times higher than had been the case previously, a group of ten Liberals and Social Democrats moved to cancel long-range plans for building three cruisers. They declared that they were prepared to support measures effective immediately but wanted to bind the government's hands as little as possible for the future. The single member of the Liberal party who urged rejection of the whole five-year plan reasoned even more openly along the lines of the elasticity theory.

These views did not play a decisive role in the 1942 debate. But two years later, when peace was approaching, the opposition to long-range expansion of Sweden's defense forces had grown. Especially the Social Democratic group in the Second Chamber was then regarded as holding what a Conservative called "anti-defense attitudes." In the spring of 1944 the Social Democrats succeeded in persuading the supporters of the government line to compromise on a proposal for civil defense to the extent that a time limit was included. When the government requested funds for the establishment of a defense research institute the following year, criticism was renewed. A group of Social Democratic women in particular was active in urging rejection of the proposal. This time the attacks were not successful.

As on foreign policy, the unity in the Riksdag on defense policy was superficial to a certain extent; however, it was not the members' lack of knowledge that gave an impression of unity but rather their immediate perspective. The members were united on

rearmament to meet the nation's needs in the period of international war but not on any long-term defense policy. At the same
time those who criticized rearmament beyond immediate needs
had greater freedom of movement than the critics of foreign
policy. If they gave their support to the measures for immediate
needs, they could then criticize long-range plans fairly freely.
However, these critics in the Social Democratic and Liberal parties lacked support from their party leaders. Especially among the
Social Democrats there were many who allied themselves with the
Conservatives against what they regarded as destructive tendencies in their fellow party members. Also, these proponents of the
elasticity theory would not prevail at the end of the war, when the
majority of the young generation within the parties, who had previously been lukewarm toward defense expenditures, had come
to accept a strong defense as an inescapable necessity.

A pruning of the political freedom normally guaranteed by a
democratic form of government was also accepted during the war
years. The right to distribute printed materials was limited by an
ordinance approved in the spring of 1940 by the Riksdag giving
the government the power to forbid transporting through public
or private channels such publications as were considered to
endanger the country's internal and external security. Later in
1940 and in 1941 the Riksdag accepted a change in the constitution which empowered the government to exercise censorship and
to prohibit importation of printed materials when the country
found itself at war or in danger of war, as well as to prohibit pub-
lishing activities during wartime. Furthermore, the rights of
assembly and association were curtailed by a law, approved in
May 1940, which allowed the government during war or danger
of war and after consultation with the Riksdag to disband "antisocial organizations." Of these provisions for government intervention, only that prohibiting the transporting of "inflammatory"
materials came to be used; Communist newspapers and the
aggressively pro-Western publication *Trots allt!* were especially

affected. The Swedish press was subjected not only to newly legislated reprisals but also to old, revived ones; a law, long considered obsolete, on confiscation of individual issues of newspapers,
without trial, was used periodically, particularly against the
strongly anti-Nazi press.

The attitude of the Riksdag groups toward these curtailments
of political freedom, like the attitudes on foreign policy and
defense, was distinguished by a verbal unity on important points.
All were agreed, or at least said that they were, that political freedom could not be maintained at the cost of national security. The
right of a democratic state to defend itself against destructive
forces was stated many times as an obvious premise for every
debate on the subject; no assertions that democratic values should
be given priority above national values appeared. Nevertheless
within a theoretical framework of unity conflicts on this issue
were far sharper and more unconcealed than was the case with
foreign-policy and defense questions. The Communists, who were
also the primary target of the restrictive measures, were constant
critics. But also within the parties that formed the government,
a sometimes many-voiced and often authoritative band of critics
appeared.

That complete political freedom was disruptive and potentially
dangerous in the situation in which the nation found itself was
asserted by the government and those who defended its policies.
By simply reversing this argument, opponents could defend their
views without denying the priority of national security. The risks
for the Swedish nation, they claimed, were greater with curtailed
freedom than with full freedom, because confidence in the government and the people's will to resist would be lost if debate were
smothered.

The greatest proportion of opponents in relation to the size of
the group was found within the Liberal party, where they
amounted at times to a clear majority. The largest group in num-

bers came from the Social Democrats. The right had a few who were constant opponents and on one occasion a member of the Agrarian party delivered a critical statement against government policy on political freedom. The opponents were thus spread over the party spectrum, and none could say that they advocated a party position even if the members of the Liberal party asserted that opposition *ought* to be a Liberal line. Although the critics were not from the same party, they had a common characteristic: they were usually well educated; more than half of them had taken academic degrees. Also, they had often appeared as critics of the government's concessions to Germany. For them curtailment of freedom of the press was understood as a link in the government's concession policy and thus their support of the press (few were themselves newspapermen) was in part a means of opposing a humiliating foreign policy. The opposition group grew with the years and succeeded in 1944 in rescinding the constitutional changes made four years earlier. The last defender of limiting freedom of the press was the foreign minister. Much in his behavior indicated that even he understood the action of the Riksdag in abolishing constitutional restrictions to be a demonstration against the foreign policy he had been a leader in carrying out.

In the matter of prohibitions against party activities during the war period, the opinion pattern was primarily the same. But an important difference must be noted here. The Conservatives were united and, as a party, favored passage of a law prohibiting the introduction of new parties and also its enforcement, which was more controversial. During lengthy debates in the government, the two Conservative ministers pushed their demand that the new law should be used against the Communists. In that case, the Social Democrats insisted, it should be used against the Nazis too. The Conservatives could not accept such an application and no decision on enforcement was ever made. Opposition against both the law's introduction and its enforcement was raised primarily within the Liberal and Social Democratic parties, but neither formulated a party line on the issue.

On all these national issues, then, the major parties tended to exhibit certain central views: that the government's neutrality policy was the only one possible, that no use of appropriations could be more urgent than defense, and that the protection of the nation was more important than the protection of democracy. For the great majority of the members of the Riksdag, support of these views meant support of the government's concrete proposals. But some even within the parties forming the government wanted to air divergent views. For them the problem was in finding forms for criticism that did not disturb the national unity, that did not make hidden eyes widen or ears prick up. The foreign-policy opponents chose to present their views in heavily veiled words or, even better, to speak, as it were, in camera. The critics of defense policy emphasized insistently that they did not aim at stopping defense construction for immediate purposes and that their attitude was not, as the defense minister usually intimated, pacifistic, but realistic in light of Sweden's long-range needs and goals. The opponents of curtailment of freedom of the press, on their part, stressed that they were not attacking the national ideology that underlay the government's policy but rather the belief that curtailments on democratic processes would benefit this ideology. A number of techniques were thus developed for the purpose of influencing the government's policies without disturbing the national unity. Political single-mindedness as a result never became a reality.

When questions of allocation policy came under debate in the Riksdag, the demand for unity was far more muted than in the debates that directly or indirectly concerned foreign policy. No one could miss the fact that issues of allocation divided the Riksdag on party lines. The tone in the debates on them is reproduced rather well in a diary notation which Gösta Bagge made on May

11, 1943. After a meeting of the drafting committee that day, he had a conversation with the finance minister, Ernst Wigforss, concerning the allocation of price rebates on food fats and milk; it was not especially genial: "Wigforss showed an outburst of emotion when I talked with him about the matter and said in the most demagogic way that the proposal would take from the poor and give to the rich. I maintained that so far as food fats were concerned it could only mean that those people for whom a dime made a difference would buy margarine instead of butter and that one should not take the matter so demagogically. He spoke, however, of deep differences in the view of life."

At issue essentially in the debates was how the necessary lowering of the standard of living in the war years should be distributed among the various social groups. This was a matter affecting the nation's everyday life and one would have expected the several parties either to agree on a common program of principle or to formulate separate programs. But only occasional efforts in this direction were made. Apparently the unity that was necessary for a common declaration of principle did not exist but at the same time there were mutual apprehensions about showing a split publicly. On a great number of concrete questions, however, this split was evident. The conflicts in most cases came down to what was meant by justice. Wigforss, who to a certain extent was an exception in favoring public debate, stated in a brochure published in 1942 that burdens should be distributed according to the ability to support them; that is, it was only just that a person who was better situated should have his standard of living reduced more than one who was worse off from the beginning. When Conservatives spoke of justice they meant, on the contrary, that the same burden should be borne by all. If the burden then became too great for anyone, he should be helped with special measures.

The conflict was illustrated concretely when the government had to take a stand on cost-of-living compensation for civil servants: Wigforss wanted the payment of compensation only to the lowest-paid groups, while Bagge maintained that all wage-earning categories should be treated in the same way. The issue of civil servants' wages was settled by a compromise, but only after a number of Social Democrats and even Agrarians protested against it, asserting that a strict principle of burden-according-to-ability would better have been followed. A similar problem came up in connection with tax policy, but then it was the Conservatives who found reason for discontent with a compromise. In 1940 deductions allowed on general income and capital taxes were increased by 50 percent. This resulted in more progressive taxes, and in effect sharply increased the amounts paid by those with greater ability to bear tax burdens. The bourgeois parties made no apparent protests. It would have been difficult for the Conservatives, who traditionally advocated defense increases, to fight a tax which would make possible the rearmament for which they had pleaded for so long. But two years later, at the spring Riksdag of 1942, when the government proposed an additional surtax of 25 percent, the protests came. In committee and chamber Conservatives unanimously demanded strengthened guarantees that no one should have to pay a tax that was so high that it exceeded income and caused capital reductions. But the opposition from an equally unanimous Social Democratic group, which also had support from a majority of Liberals and Agrarians, overwhelmed them.

The question of how much sacrifice it was reasonable to ask of those with fortunes became an even more controversial matter in connection with the 1942 election campaign. A debate then began on demanding from the rich a "one-time sacrifice." Conservatives promptly declared that such a tax could only be regarded as confiscation of capital and that its effects would be devastating on private savings, the prerequisite for maintaining social and cultural standards and for supporting defense. They warned that the small savers of the country would be ruined. In the face of this, the Social Democrats adopted a careful watch and wait position and said no more than that they thought the possibility should be kept open. Obviously they were worried that the Conservatives' propaganda on this issue would be a threat to their own party's election campaign.

The following year Communist motions demanding quick action reopened the question. The motions were abruptly rejected by the government. But when the question came up yet again in 1944, the Social Democratic committee majority, obviously with the approaching Second Chamber elections in mind, asserted that any tax eventually passed would not affect small savers. The main Social Democratic view was still that the possibility of the one-time tax should be kept open and that it should be investigated. The bourgeois parties, on the other hand, who now presented a united front, wanted no further discussion. They said that just having the question debated did harm. In a vote on initiating an investigation, the grouping of Social Democrats (plus Communists) versus the bourgeois parties was completely broken.

What contributions higher income earners and capital owners should make toward state expenses thus showed itself to be a politically divisive issue. Similar party differences arose concerning how much the lowest income earners or those most oppressed should pay in taxes. In connection with the increase in income and capital taxes on higher incomes, the Conservatives had demanded in vain that the amount assessed those who had earlier not been subject to any tax be ten kronor instead of five as proposed. The dispute was renewed when a general sales tax and social rebate system were discussed.

Forced by necessity, the finance minister in June 1940 introduced a form of taxation that his party's program had opposed. A 5 percent general sales tax was approved. In principle the tax was to be levied on all consumer goods, which meant that those who used a bigger part of their incomes on consumption would have to pay a relatively heavier tax than others. The tax would thus affect the poor hardest. In mitigation, provisions were introduced to exempt certain important consumer goods. Social price rebates had the same purpose, that is easing the tax burden for those worst off. In public discussions it was maintained that the proposed measures were not far-reaching enough and demands were presented, in the name of poor and large families, that exceptions from the tax be extended and the rebates raised. Those who spoke for the merchants opposed such proposals. Exceptions and rebates increased the paper work of retail business and should therefore be as few as possible. In this apparently trivial but politically important conflict, the Conservative and Liberal parties took the side of the merchants. In a government debate on price rebates, Gösta Bagge rendered a further objection against exemptions: it would be, he said, "unhealthy" if too large a part of the population received support from the public.

The Social Democrats in the government seem to have been responsive to this bourgeois view: both the exceptions and the rebates proposed became fewer. The opposition to this stance that appeared in the Riksdag's chambers did not follow party lines but was concentrated in the Social Democratic group, spear-headed by consumer-oriented women representatives. In June 1942, they succeeded in mobilizing a majority of the Social Democrats in the Second Chamber against the government proposal in a debate on the rebate system, but the minority of the Social Democrats with bourgeois support was able to vote through the government proposal. Nevertheless the pro-consumer group was large enough so that its views in later discussions had to be considered.

The most difficult dispute by far in the economic debate of the war years concerned the effect of the budget deficit on the value of money. Somewhat pre-Keynesian thinking was applied by the Conservatives, who took the view that the national deficit was the actual driving force behind price increases. The Social Democrats, i.e., the finance minister and his undersecretary, Dag Hammarskjöld, took the deficit less seriously and instead pointed to primary price rises as the most effective force prompting general price increases. The Conservatives' view, which for long periods was shared by more "modern" economists like Bertil Ohlin, led to demands for the greatest possible budget limitations on expenditures. Appropriations for defense had to be exempted. Their main attention therefore came to be directed at the general subventions distributed by the finance minister since the fall of 1939 in order to counteract the effect on consumers of increased prices for flour, milk, bread, and other staples. Hundreds of millions of kronor were appropriated over the years for this purpose. This expenditure should be stopped, the majority of the bourgeois members of the Riksdag believed.

The subventions had implications for allocation policy. Their cost would lead to increased taxes either immediately or at the time of repaying the national debt. It is not unreasonable to see the political split on subventions as a consequence of the context of allocation policy. The increased tax burden stemming from subventions could be anticipated to affect primarily the social groups whose political interests were administered by the bourgeois parties, especially the Conservatives. Nothing was more natural than that they saw it as a central political task to hold state expenditures and thereby the tax burden down.

Gösta Bagge was in the lead of the bourgeois opposition on the subvention question. In June 1942 when the Riksdag discussed the latest subvention proposition, the ecclesiastical minister delivered a sweeping criticism of the finance minister's proposal. Bagge pointed out that the state's expenditures for subventions then amounted to 400 million kronor; the subsequent budget deficit seriously threatened the value of money. He also declared himself to be an opponent in principle to the idea of giving support to all regardless of their income and capital situation. In the only vote that took place on the question, the Social Democrats and the bourgeois parties followed party lines almost without deviations.

The conflicts in party politics that have hitherto been touched upon can all be said to have reflected conflicts in interests between income groups. There were also conflicts between the interests of producers and those of consumers. Outside the Riksdag these conflicts produced headlines chronicling the activities of trade unions and economic organizations: intricate negotiations, threats of strikes, strikes. When the perspective is limited to the Riksdag, the account appears comparatively undramatic, in large part because the Riksdag occupied a subordinate role in the central event, that is, the negotiations on agricultural prices.

Representatives of the agriculturalists negotiated on prices with representatives for the state, and it was on this level that the actual decisions were made. The Riksdag had to give formal approval after the fact, which it never refused. In the parliamentary debates, to be sure, the farmers' strike actions were brought up and spokesmen for the labor movement did not fail to recommend their own organizations' cooperativeness and social consciousness as models. But only on one occasion was the Riksdag made the arena of controversy in this sphere. The price of sugar beets was at issue. Prolonged negotiations between the producer organization and the state had reached a stalemate and in March 1941 the government considered that a compromise was impossible. A forced cultivation law was therefore recommended. In the Riksdag the Agrarian party group presented a motion demanding rejection of the proposed law and in the debate that followed all participating members of the Agrarian party but one recommended rejection. The exception was the party leader, who believed that the economic associations ought to show greater social solidarity and not simply think of their own economic advantage. He, alone of the party members, urged approval of the law. In the final vote, all those present from the other parties voted for the law.

On the allocation policy questions, whether they concerned income groups or producers versus consumers, the pattern for the parties' actions in the Riksdag was thus very different from that where national policies were under consideration. There was, to be sure, a general agreement that all party disputes should be put aside but no one asserted that the world outside Sweden was paying much attention to Riksdag debates on wages, taxes, subventions, and agricultural prices and hence controversies on these issues could not affect national security. On these issues there could be some freedom of movement for the parties. In the controversies that thus arose, it was without exception one or more of the bourgeois parties that played the role of opponent, and it was the Social Democrats, usually the finance minister, who were criticized. The Conservatives can be characterized as the most pugnacious of the three bourgeois parties. The Agrarians were active on a number of issues that had obvious special interest for them, while the Liberal party only rarely joined in attacks.

At the same time as there were expressions of partisan interests, other features in the parties' behavior showed the influence of the prevailing doctrine of unity. The clearest sign is the lack of purely party motions; that is, motions presented with the support of a party's central committee in the Riksdag and bearing the group leaders' names first. The only exceptions were the Conservative motion to prohibit formation of new parties and the Agrarian party's motion against the compulsory cultivation law. On the other hand, it was not unusual for sharp criticism of a party nature to be presented in motions signed by one or more members of the Riksdag who did not have seats on the central committee. Often too an individual speaker's remarks would have a critical and party-tinged stamp but did not urge rejection of the proposal being debated. In both these ways a party group could demonstrate its disagreement but avoid bringing a difference of viewpoint to a climax.

Since the possibilities for pursuing party politics were sharply limited during the war years in Sweden, the methods of attracting voters necessarily had to be modified. "Naturally cooperation is tactically inopportune for the parties," it was pointed out in a guide for the Liberal party's campaign speakers in the 1942 election. But it was stressed there that "the general opinion" surely would "appreciate and value the parties which at this time follow the laws of the political party truce." This judgment was reflected in the conduct of all the parties, most obviously in the 1940 election campaign, which more than the others was stamped with the spirit of national coalition. The best thing the parties could do then was to join in the chorus and try to stand out there as a pillar. The Conservative party, for example, tried to present itself as the most reliable of the five pro-defense parties by reviewing its historical stance on defense. It hoped by this tactic to cast some doubt on the Social Democrats. In view of the outcome of the election—the Social Democrats won their biggest victory ever—the tactic was not successful.

The election campaigns of 1942 and 1944 were livelier; the threats to foreign policy were then not as obvious and conflicts over allocation policy had stirred people up. Now Riksdag activities became usable in campaign propaganda. The Conservative party referred to its opposition to the subvention policy and to capital taxation, the Liberal party to its criticism of the curtailment of freedom of the press, and the Agrarian party to its greatly diversified commitment to the rural population. The parties also made clear to potential voters what individual members of the Riksdag, without support of the party leadership or a group majority, had achieved in the form of motions and of contributions to debate. Those who had been critical, even in secret, thus had an opportunity to build up a profile that could attract voters. Those who could not do this were the Social Democrats. The Riksdag's majority had in the main defended government economic policy and the criticism Social Democrats had offered was all too similar to that presented by the Communists to be in any way usable in election tactics. As a result the Social Democrats had to play a defensive role; defending themselves against attacks from Communists as well as from the bourgeois parties was their lot.

Despite the fact that the bourgeois parties kept their opposition within the boundaries that had been drawn around national unity, they made it clear that responsibility on allocation policy rested with the Social Democrats. They allowed the government no opportunity to show that responsibility was shared by all, as on the national questions, for there was always someone who in debate or by motion had stated objections and it was enough for the bourgeois parties to be able to show that their members had spoken their minds. In the 1942 and 1944 election campaigns the special parliamentary situation improved the starting position of the bourgeois parties; the Social Democrats were bound to government compromises that permitted both Communist and bourgeois attacks. This tactical dilemma was probably one of the reasons why the Social Democrats more than the other parties urged a quick dissolution of the coalition government in the summer of 1945.

Introduction to Chapter 13

Sweden: The Middle Way, Sweden: The Model for Democracy, and *Sweden: Prototype of Modern Society* are the titles of books written abroad in the past forty years about Sweden. In much of the Western world Sweden has become a symbol of the progressive welfare state, a model to be examined and in some cases copied. The international interest in Sweden began in the 1930s and was particularly influenced by Marquis Child's book *Sweden: The Middle Way.* His emphasis, in fact exaggerated, was on the role of the cooperative movement in Swedish economic life and on the "middle way" Sweden had found between unfettered capitalism and socialism. After World War II attention again focused on Sweden as the country embarked upon a series of major social reforms including a radical transformation of the school system, a compulsory medical care program, and a vast new old-age pension scheme (the so-called supplementary pension, ATP). In studying Sweden, many have assumed that Sweden has always been a leader in social reform and that welfare programs have deep historical roots in Swedish history. These assumptions are not entirely correct.

That Sweden has had a long history of governmental support of welfare programs is undeniable. Since medieval times Swedish kings and various governmental units have provided certain basic albeit crude forms of social help. Hospitals, for example, have traditionally been a province for governmental activity. However, in this respect Sweden is hardly unique. Europe has had a tradition of rulers providing the ruled with basic social services. Indeed it was within this traditional framework that the first modern social welfare reforms in Europe were initiated (the Bismarckian reforms in Germany in the 1880s). But the great break in the traditional relationship between ruler and ruled also came in the nineteenth century with the advent of liberalism. Liberalism eschewed governmental interference in the private lives of citizens and many liberal politicians advocated separation of the state from institutional solutions to social problems. In respect to governmental acceptance of responsibility for existing social conditions, the late nineteenth and early twentieth centuries were not periods of widespread innovation. Only under the cumulative pressures created by industrialism, competitive nationalism, World War I, the depression, and so on did European governments begin to take affirmative steps to deal with social problems. Although there were important milestones reached even before 1914—including Sweden's old-age pension program of 1913, largely the creation of the Liberal government, which while financially inadequate accepted the principle that social welfare should be treated as a right of all citizens and should not be based upon need or other limiting criteria—the great spate of welfare legislation did not occur until the 1930s and afterwards. The modern European welfare state is of recent origin, by and large a product of the post-World War II period. If one uses Sweden as an example, social reform until the mid-thirties was remarkably sparse and entirely inadequate. In comparative European terms Sweden was relatively backward in the amount and quality of its social legislation until the late thirties. Even now one should be careful in generalizing about how advanced Sweden really is. Many other West European countries have welfare programs that are the equal (certainly in cost if not quality) of the Swedish programs. There are many areas where the Swedes feel they themselves could make vast improvements. Eastern European countries of course provide even wider benefits than Sweden but at a severe political cost. The growth of the Swedish welfare state should be viewed as an example of a general European development. The following essay by Kurt Samuelsson, which traces the philosophical supports of Swedish welfare legislation over the past one hundred years, could also be, to a large degree, an essay on general West European development.

13

The Philosophy of Swedish Welfare Policies

by Kurt Samuelsson

Generally, and without excessive abstraction, the following values or "ideas" can be seen as the philosophical foundations for the historical development of Swedish welfare policies: (1) humanitarianism or mercy; (2) resocialization or rehabilitation; (3) integration; (4) solidarity; (5) equality and justice; (6) social security. In part, these values have overlapped, so that the same program has often been derived from several of them—or been regarded as fulfilling several of them, at least for propaganda purposes. To a certain extent they also are means for realizing each other; for example, all of the others lead to the goal of integration. On the other hand, a single idea has sometimes been interpreted in far different ways during various periods or at the same time by various supporters. In other words, rather unwieldy phenomena are involved which may be made more wieldy here through "analytical language." If the ideas are given sharper, and sometimes alternative, meanings we should be able to distinguish them from each other more easily. The fact that certain of these ideas have crowded out or gained ascendancy over certain others— whether known or noticed or not—must also be considered. One of our tasks here is to try to determine these shifts.

The idea of humanitarianism or mercy coincides with what has been called the relief of distress. Intervention occurs when people otherwise would succumb or suffer great need. It can be said to be based on two traditions—the idea of Christian love and, to put it rather crudely, the idea of public cleanliness (that is, it is not sanitary to have people lying in the streets, possibly dying there). Both concepts placed limits, more or less strictly drawn at various times, on the degree of humaneness to be exercised, on the amount of relief to be provided. For both held that it was a person's own fault if he was poor and needy; this was seen as a punishment by God or at least as the sign of a bad life. God did not create people without providing them with the ability to support themselves. The more profane of the concepts regarded need in very general terms as proof of laziness, good-for-nothingness, conscious "asociality."

This view was clearly expressed in the Swedish debate on poor relief in 1869, for example. The temporary parliamentary committee formed to consider a new poor relief law declared that the mildness and generosity of the 1847 and 1853 poor relief laws were the cause of the prevalence in the country of poverty (which had been especially widespread since the beginning of a famine in 1867). Poor relief should not be obligatory but should be based on "voluntariness, sympathy, and Christian help," for all help was a "work of love." A *right* to receive help took away a person's incentive to think for himself, to secure his position "through work, thriftiness, and privation," and led "easily to laziness, and an idle life." Therefore, obligatory help for the needy from the townships should be limited to orphaned children and the insane. In 1871 the township's obligation was extended to people incapable of supporting themselves because of age, physical or mental illness, disability, or deformity. But it was emphasized that this obligation was a responsibility of the township to the state, not to the needy individual. The right to appeal a relief decision of the local authorities, introduced in 1847, was rescinded.

An inverted reasoning often accompanied this evaluation of the indigent. The presence of those who needed help was not the reason for social support; rather it was argued that the poor were needed to provide an opportunity for works of Christian love. There was something good in people devoting themselves to charity; therefore, the needs of the poor should not be alleviated by official measures that would endanger the private activity of love. What made this view possible was the general lack of familiarity with the causes and extent of poverty and distress. The situation between 1867 and 1871 is a case in point. The effects of the famine in Sweden had not been understood, and therefore in 1869 the increased poverty, the extent of which was not fully seen, and the increased mendicancy could be blamed on an all too generous and morals-destroying poor relief. In 1871, when the economy had improved strongly and poverty decreased, complaints about a declining work ethic lessened, but few connected the "change in morals" and the greater ease with which individuals could maintain a work ethic when more jobs were available. Only gradually was there recognition of the relationship between job opportunity and poverty and a concomitant appreciation of distress relief as basically humiliating and therefore unhumanitarian.

A transformation—in effect only procedural, not ideological—took place into the idea of resocialization and rehabilitation. When the dependence of poverty and other difficulties on economic and social conditions began to become clear, distress relief shifted from help to self-help. At the same time, the need for contributions by society was emphasized. This concept of help to self-help retained—and still retains—the idea that the individual is to some degree responsible and shares in the blame. Help to self-help thereby was strongly linked to education, in part coercive education. This view was given expression by Ebba Pauli of the Central Association for Social Work in 1906, characterizing poor relief as "a factor of importance in the history of a people's moral development." It was primarily people who should be adapted, educated, not the society that should be changed. Hjalmar Branting characterized this attitude as the millionaires' recipe for the art of getting rich through industry and thrift.

The idea of resocialization or rehabilitation could lead to various practical results, from poor relief granted only upon proof of need to certain more "insurancelike" arrangements. It could emphasize the right to assistance in contrast to the old idea of mercy. But still the goal was self-help, the responsibility essentially the individual's.

A somewhat different approach emerged in discussion in the Riksdag in 1912 on general pension insurance. The 1907 old-age insurance committee's report had stressed the material insufficiency of the already existing forms of assistance and underlined their humiliating character. The committee declared increased security not only was urgently needed but was an earned right: "It does not satisfy the present consciousness of justice that, for example, a man who has worked throughout a long life to support himself and his family and thereby at the same time contributed in his degree to society's progress shall perhaps see no other way out than to turn to poor relief or to accept the dole from his relatives when his working strength ebbs. Rather, even the most modest career must be regarded as giving the right to support, which may not be extended in humiliating forms."

It is especially interesting that the committee's statement of principle was not limited to support of citizens in old age, the specific subject matter assigned to it. The committee took the position that all branches of social insurance (covering "illness, accident, old age, involuntary unemployment, or other unprovoked causes") should have the character of general national insurance. In some of these areas, it would be a long time before this principle was accepted—and it has yet to be practiced in toto. Interior Minister Per Axel Schotte (Liberal) emphasized that old-age insurance was only a first step. Accident and health insurance too were a claim on justice in opposition to the humiliating dole of poor relief.

In the debates in parliamentary committees and in the Riksdag, sharp conflicts emerged between the supporters of poor relief and of social insurance. The former clung to their belief in the importance of educating the individual. The supporters of social insurance offered a kind of ideological compromise, by incorporating the old idea that each person should save for his own old age into the argument for social insurance. Social insurance would be the means of forcing citizens to save for their future needs. The dispute between the proponents of the new official ideology—which was realized in a general national insurance system—and those urging retention of poor relief did not mean that the latter were satisfied with the way poor relief was administered. On the contrary, they wanted to improve this form of assistance and make it less humiliating. They believed that general social insurance would in practice perpetuate the wretchedness of poor relief in its prevailing form. They also believed that permanent support by social insurance—especially represented by proposed pension supplements—would morally ruin people. This was not a new idea. In 1895, a parliamentary committee had repudiated a proposal for a workers' pension on the grounds that it would end the workers' reliance on their own powers and undermine their confidence. In this debate on welfare policy the differences between "macro-thinking" and "micro-thinking," between general benefits based on objective criteria and measures for individually need-proven assistance, emerge for the first time in Sweden.

Neither side won a clear-cut victory. But the scope of social insurance gradually expanded while that of poor relief contracted. The concept of rehabilitation was still cherished by many, but the practice of relief continued to suffer from the problems cited by the 1907 old-age insurance committee: its "bitter bread of mercy, its lack of freedom, and the social lowering that

occurs with its support" were serious disadvantages. In effect rehabilitation measures could become a help to self-destruction rather
than a help to self-help. The risks of a rehabilitation program
became especially acute when coercion was an element. Political
pressures could not easily be defended by poor-relief proponents.

The idea of the integration of all parts of society increasingly
took the upper hand. In part, to be sure, "integration" can be
said to be simply a term encompassing the ideals of solidarity,
equality, and social security; the "partial goals" deriving from the
latter values can be said to coincide in the "goal of integration."

The conditions in Sweden for success of the idea of integration
were good. The milieu in which Swedish welfare and social policy
had developed can be characterized generally as highly integration-oriented and even integrated. Although the labor movement,
formed during the period of industrial expansion, had felt that
it was in a position "outside of society," it had chosen to work by
democratic and parliamentary means to become a part of that
society. Perhaps this was possible because industrialization in
Sweden was free from the worst of the social misfortunes that
characterized it in other nations, above all concentration of population and activity in gigantic cities. In its efforts at integration
the labor movement rather early met a positive response from
economically propertied and politically and socially leading
groups: there was a striving by employers to organize themselves
and thereby accept the free play of negotiations; there was a
desire on the part of the industrial lords to establish legal norms
through certain state controls of working conditions. Indeed
socio-political state intervention was accepted by a remarkably
widespread portion of the political groups in Sweden.

There was not, however, any large-scale consensus on either the
specific goals or the philosophical underpinnings of state intervention. The idea of integration was expressed during the first
periods of social policy debate—until shortly after the turn of the
century—in a kind of "platform" or bourgeois socialism. The aim

was to mitigate the worst abuses and ease the worst discontent by establishing a certain basic security for workers. There was fear that in the obviously oppressed segments of society "antisocial" attitudes smoldered which new, "dangerous" socialistic teachings would fan. E. Westin put this view clearly in 1882. The poor workers' problems, he said, should be thought of in purely humanitarian terms and, by wisely and expediently regulating the relations between employer and worker, between capital and labor, a healthy development should be promoted which might forestall "the socialistic tendencies which in other countries instill justified apprehensions and compel strict legislative measures." S. A. Hedin in 1884 quoted approvingly a German statement according to which "the safest guarantee for a reformist, not revolutionary, progress would be won provided that the great majority of the laboring population could be united in the preservation of the existing state organization." The same perspective is to be seen in Pontus Fahlbeck's *Estates and Classes* in 1892, in Gustav Cassel's *Lectures on Social Policy* in 1902, and, although less explicitly, in the 1907 old-age insurance committee's argument.

The criticism directed by the Social Democrats against these concepts of integration emanated from their desire for more radical reforms or a more general transformation of society. Platform socialism—or "state socialism," as it was also called—was, said the Social Democrats, only intended to preserve the prevailing social system through marginal improvements that calmed discontent. In support of its view the party quoted the arguments of Liberal reformers, who, in responding to Conservative accusations that freedom had been curtailed and state socialism established, emphasized that the controls already generally accepted had not endangered the liberal society and that the new measures proposed were not more dangerous than those already in effect, such as the 1881 child labor law; on the contrary, the new measures could prevent the raising and realization of far more dangerous demands. A program that could be presented in such a soothing way for Conservatives could only be regarded as a tranquilizer by the more radical.

As the Social Democrats were transformed into more radical reformists, the party came to accept a more advanced and sophisticated idea of integration. The Social Democrats believed that the measures taken in the name of marginal, platform socialism would not subdue discontent. Instead the causes of every justified social discontent had to be eliminated, if only step by step. Integration would be won through "social transformation"; in the long run, integration would be fully realized in a society different from the one in which the work was begun. The prospects of eventual great changes and improvements made the support of gradual reforms easier.

The idea of integration thus encompassed what may be termed defensive and offensive positions. Those supporting integration on the defensive side regarded a specific reform as a bulwark against too-great changes, while those on the offensive side saw the same reform as a link in a considerably more extensive reform policy.

A coalescence in goals of those holding either integration position existed largely during the thirties. It is especially clear in connection with the population issue. Radical demands for social policy reforms, which in themselves were dismissed by many Conservatives, won a certain support because they favored a growing population, "the preservation of Swedishness," and similar, traditionally Conservative, postulates. At the same time, "platform socialist" conceptions reinforced radical demands. A new "social liberalism" had arisen that regarded social improvements as a significant element in national preparedness against risks of ideological contagion from the south, from Nazi Germany.

How the new philosophical consensus emerged as a combination or compromise of rather widely divergent values was illuminated in statements by Gustav Möller in the guidelines set down for the 1935 population commission. Möller noted that "no people with an unweakened vitality and will to live in the face of the verifiable tendency of development [Nazism] could fail to bring about a change." More and earlier marriages should be promoted, as well as a rise in the birthrate. A wisely organized information campaign should awaken in Swedes a sense of responsibility for the future of the nation. The words were not very different from those of the Conservatives in debate on the same subject in the 1935 Riksdag although the nuances are important. Under consideration was a family-supportive tax. The Conservatives declared that the population question was "literally the question of the life of the Swedish people"—adding, however, that "the Conservative party's fundamental national and social view obliges us to cooperate in such a policy without thereby abandoning the principle that personal self-responsibility constitutes our greatest social resource." In a statement at the Social Democratic party congress in 1936 responding to a motion from a workers' group for a "policy that aims directly at an increase in fertility," Möller declared frankly: "I may say that I do not for a moment hesitate to frighten any number of Conservatives and Agrarians and Liberals with the threat that our people will otherwise die out if I can induce them with this threat to vote for social proposals which I am presenting. This is my simple view on the population question, and it suffices for me."

For the Social Democrats—or in any case for Gustav Möller—the population issue thus was important primarily because it could be used in forcing through social policy reforms, even if we allow for some tactical exaggeration in the statement quoted. Möller reflected the offensive position. Those who were concerned with the population issue in and of itself, and for its sake *accepted* social reforms that they otherwise opposed, took a defensive position.

Integration as the main value in social policy received a boost from a change in the prevailing economic thinking. According to older static economic theory, social policy measures always constituted a sacrifice for society, society being identified largely with the leading and better situated social groups. The latter's interests were understood as identical with the society's. In purely economic terms—which naturally were not "purely" economic but ideologically influenced—social policy measures meant the transfer of social resources from economically good to economically bad use. Means that in the hands of the better situated were used for saving and the building of the nation's economic life were transferred to the poor who used them entirely for consumption and who also, as a result of being given assistance, in many cases remained sick and unemployed or generally useless to a greater extent than would otherwise have been the case. National economic policies of the time in Sweden were developed in line with this theory. State expenses were debilitating and should be held low and in balance; this had especially important implications when "times were bad," that is to say when business declines resulted in unusually widespread unemployment and mass poverty and needed political intervention was vetoed by the policy of state frugality.

The work of the Stockholm School and Keynes brought about a change in the views of economists. The static theory was replaced by a dynamic one, in which social and welfare policy was understood to be economically justified and wise. A conflict of interests could no longer be sustained by "cold economic facts." Integration as simultaneously a joining with the society and a change of the society could lead to economic growth.

Integration in the existing society could occur even as the integration process meant a change of the society. At a given time this can be called integration in expectation of a better society in the future. At the same time, the philosophy of integration compelled a certain carefulness in implementing goals. Otherwise the disintegration of previously established groups could result. Offensive integration could not be pursued so vigorously that the defensive integrationists could not follow along tolerably comfortably. The former needed to find the "right" combination of carefulness and change in any given situation. Would integration (in the sense that the majority were satisfied and those remaining unsatisfied were too few and weak to force further measures) achieved at "too early" a stage stop the intended process? Would a period of offensive policies evoke a return to the defensive line on a higher level? This philosophical and political dilemma had to take account of two "support values"—the idea of solidarity and the idea of equality.

The idea of solidarity meant in its most general and vague—and thereby presumably most politically usable and used—form a common responsibility for all citizens of a society. It had strong connections with the idea of brotherhood: that all felt obligations to each other like those the members of a family were supposed to feel. Per Albin Hansson expressed the idea in the concept of the nation as the "people's home." The connection to Christian parables was also clear in the demands to "help your neighbor," "care for your brother." An apparent relation here to the idea of mercy and humanitarianism can be misleading. The society's responsibility to the individual was emphasized in a completely different way in the idea of solidarity. The responsibilty in solidarity was both responsibility for and responsibility to. It was society's fault that inequities and problems prevailed and its duty to remedy these conditions.

Solidarity primarily concerned the weak, poor, oppressed: it was the worse positioned groups or their advocates who requested solidarity from the others. A rather pure vertical transfer from "the rich" to "the poor" was envisioned in the solidarity model. But in a somewhat longer perspective the goal was more than assistance in present difficulties for certain groups in the existing situation. Today's well-off could become tomorrow's poor and needy because of illness, unemployment, or other risks. The concept of national insurance grew out of the idea of solidarity, from one point of view, although it had several roots, not least the idea of security. National insurance involved protecting not only those who were burdened but also those who could possibly come to be, as everyone could in principle. Solidarity thus necessitated society's functioning as a kind of gigantic insurance company for all citizens. This naturally led to the idea of social security.

Often the idea of solidarity seems to have been used synonymously with the idea of equality. There are reasons to keep the two separated in principle, however. To be sure, solidarity measures decreased certain existing inequities. But while equality presupposes solidarity, under "natural" social conditions, solidarity does not presuppose equality, except in a very modest sense.

The value of equality is more advanced in principle than the value of solidarity. At the same time its lack of clarity is even greater. The concept was used with various meanings, ranging from the idea that people should be regarded as equals, in the sense "of equal value"—"wherever a wretch is found he is my friend, my brother"—to the idea that all should live under completely equal circumstances. In the latter, more politically active meaning, sometimes equal conditions in all respects, sometimes an equality in sum was meant. Complete equality in every particular is an impossibility since complete equality in a certain respect in a number of cases inescapably makes complete equality impossible in some other respect. Equalizing sums is theoretically possible, but difficult to describe in practice. How shall social and economic differences be evaluated in terms of each other?

The ideal of equality and the general welfare policy goals derived from this concept have never been concerned with such ideas in practice. Equality has been a grand expression for more limited ambitions, namely to decrease inequities in certain respects. These ambitions, however, have seldom defined which inequities have been relevant with regard to various other social values or purposes (economic growth, structural change, social basic security, "just" wages in relation to efforts, etc.). The labor movement's postwar program speaks of "reasonable and just distribution of the profits of common work" as an inescapable part of society's transformation: "It extends from the immediate demand for higher real wages all the way to an essential general equalization and democratization of the citizen's economic, social, and cultural conditions." Equal income for equal effort and equal pay for equal work is also mentioned. The emphasis is placed more on equalization between different groups, thus on a horizontal equalization, than on a vertical one within the groups: "Neglected groups of industrial workers, as well as rural and forest workers, fishermen, and working agrarians, must be given a position equal to that of other working groups." But whether such an equalization policy takes the form of wage policy, economic policy, social policy, education policy, "it must consider both the desirability of increased equality and a stronger feeling of solidarity among the citizens and the need to evoke the individual's best contributions even with prospects of a higher economic compensation."

It is clear that horizontal and vertical equalization could partly blend into each other. If geographic, occupational, and sexual differences decreased, total vertical income distribution would be concurrently affected in the direction of equalization. But it is important at the same time to emphasize how the philosophy of the labor movement's postwar program, which could through the political position of the Social Democratic party dictate the governmental policy, continued to maintain the traditional line from Sweden's first social policy reform. It proceeded from the raising of security for especially neglected groups in the society more than from equalization within the groups. Decreased inequity between groups was the goal in the supplementary pension program. Working groups and certain other groups without "service pension" would receive benefits similar to those of salaried employees. But equalization of the pension benefits between wage earners at different income levels within the respective groups was never discussed.

The prominent horizontalization of the value of equalization, or in any case in the goals derived from it, is interesting from another point of view: it was clearly easier to win more general support for such a horizontal "leveling" than for a more direct vertical equalization. Horizontal leveling was tied to both the integration and solidarity values and—at least marginally but this sufficed in many situations—politically important and easily comprehensible interests: "the industrial workers," "the agrarians," or, on a more cross-sectional level, "the old people," "the families with children." Political interests could be united in a new way under the banner of horizontal equalization, as the coalition era during the thirties showed. They could also be divided when horizontal equalization was not felt to benefit one of the parties as at the dissolution of the farmer-labor coalition in 1957.

Often, as in the labor movement's postwar program's words on "reasonable and just distribution," equality and justice were used as synonyms. As long as this synonymization was limited to "decreased inequality and increased justice," the terminology could hardly be said to collide with the rules of logic. But where were the boundaries for decreased inequality to be placed? In absolute form the two concepts are not synonymous; on the contrary they can be contradictory in certain combinations. Certain equalities have clearly been regarded as unjust from certain points of view. Equal income in spite of unequal effort, for example, can be regarded as a measure of equality from one point of view—"from each according to ability"—but has clearly been regarded as less than just from another. If social security measures were designed so that benefits became equal for all, independent of income, greater inequities would appear between, for example, the sick and unemployed on one side and the healthy with jobs on the other *within* the various individual income groups. Equality would "hit" only those for whom socially insured risks were manifested, but not the others.

In other words, there has been something vague and uncertain in the value of equality. Consequently no clearly formulated general goals, or even definite partial goals, for welfare policy can be said to have resulted from consideration of this value. This does not mean, however, that it has been meaningless. On the contrary, it has had two important effects: (1) to give welfare policy measures an ideological gilding (sometimes after the fact, as a rationalization), which in turn has benefited and legitimized the goal of integration, and (2) to work as a general driving force for reforms. The public has taken the value of equality seriously.

I have already pointed out that the horizontalization of the idea of equality in society had a connection with certain shifts in the value of social security and the goals that were entailed by this. The creation of a kind of minimal security was a goal in the first political advances on social insurance during the 1880s. The concept behind this idea was that an earlier security had been lost in the new industrial society, so that a substitute was needed. The debate of the time centered on the industrial workers' especially difficult and insecure position. In S. A. Hedin's famous motion in the Riksdag—regarded as the portal to modern Swedish social policy—the issue exclusively concerned "worker insurance." In Gustav Cassel's *Lectures on Social Policy*, the goal was "to provide the working class with better living conditions." For the state it therefore was a matter of providing the workers with insurance for old age and for survivors and with legislation on accident insurance and industrial safety, and furthermore of pursuing a purposeful policy in order to forestall unemployment and solve the housing problem, "which, however, intrudes more deeply than any other on the working family's whole economy."

The issue of security for other groups was regarded from other perspectives. It was imagined that the agrarian population had its security relatively well arranged. The small groups of civil servants had their special "position of confidence," which gave a high degree of guarantees lacked by the working class. Their needs were generally not seen as urgent in the same way as those of the workers, whether for laws on working hours, industrial safety, accident insurance, or provision for old age.

This view of industrial workers as primarily "the needy" was far from tenable on closer examination, however. Within the agrarian population there were still large groups of wage earners or smallholders with low incomes. They possessed little of the social security that for a long time they had been imagined to have. When, for example, the 1907 old-age insurance committee described the changes needed in social policy because of economic development, what we could call the socio-political private sector of the older economy was emphasized. As long as an overwhelming part of the population largely lived directly on the yield of the earth, the committee declared, there was a certain degree of protection against such misfortunes as unemployment, illness, accident, invalidism, and inability to work because of old age. Among those owning their own farms, the family ordinarily took care of their sick and old people and "the master could provide for the farm's people all the better because the assistance could ordinarily be extended in natural benefits, and besides the nature of the work often made it possible for the older and weaker to make themselves useful in some employment." There was a good deal to be said for this description. But in major respects it was a romantic gilding of the old agricultural society. Of approximately 2.8 million people who made their living from agriculture and allied occupations in 1870, slightly more than half (52 percent) were farm owners, a large part of these being smallholders with minimal farms which gave extremely low returns. Sixteen percent of the agricultural population were crofters, 18 percent were cotters and lodgers, and close to 14 percent were servants. Around the turn of the century further proletarianization of the agricultural population was halted by emigration to the United States and migration to industrial employment. Income had also improved. At the same time, many small agriculturalists had disappeared and certain consolidations had taken place. The result was that the farm owner population had declined to approximately a third of the total agricultural population when the old-age insurance committee wrote its description.

The old-age insurance committee was right that "the new forms of management and the mobility they elicit in the working population" worked for a dissolution of the former personal ties between employers and employees. Only the earlier tenacity of the ties was exaggerated. When it was further emphasized that the dissolution of the older times' more stable conditions in the "course of development" affected "even agriculture's great working field," the fact that this "dissolution" was of a far earlier date was disregarded. What actually happened around the turn of the century was that through the discovery of the new problem—the position of the industrial workers—an old problem also emerged: the social situation of the unpropertied agricultural population and owners of very small holdings.

The first discovery led to the demand for workers' insurance, the latter to the insight that such insurance did not suffice, that social policy must be extended to give security to everyone. The initial stage was the demand for general social reform as a basic right which was voiced from 1907 on. Security was to be provided under conditions which people, broadly speaking, could not control, that is to say becoming too old to manage their own support, becoming sick, unemployed, or invalided. Implementation was slow. Not until the 1950s was there health insurance reform and later the supplementary pension reform by which income security, compensation for income loss, was guaranteed. The supplementary pension program was so constructed, it should be noted, that prevailing income differences between a certain floor (the general basic security) and a certain ceiling would be preserved. This program and its philosophical underpinnings, which I would call livelihood according to social class, reflects a change in the general concept of security. In the case of health insurance, for example, Gustav Möller at first argued that it should be a uniform basic security insurance, equal for all. Later he had to rework his proposal in accordance with a modified income loss principle. The motivation for this change was primarily technical: to avoid having in part a state basic insurance and in part a private supplemental insurance. In the supplementary pension issue, the income loss principle became a value in itself: the basic security regulated by social policy depended on the level of a person's achieved income. This new income-related value of security took an important place in the ideological arsenal of Swedish welfare policy and affected strongly the setting of goals and technical management.

It is impossible to say which ideas had the greater political driving force in the formation of social policy in Sweden. They were interwoven and often thought of synonymously. To a certain extent, one's choice may depend on which perspective one has: the political parties' or the voting citizens'. The following assumptions seem to be at least reasonable. Among the politicians—and especially among those in a position in government—the value of integration (defensive and offensive) had especially high priority. This is connected with the fact that social calm, "law and order," lies in the interest not only of a ruling party, but, also, in a parliamentary system, of all other parties supporting the system. For voters, integration can be assumed to have been more a consequent phenomenon than a goal in itself. The high level of abstraction in the concept of equality, the feature of "sacrificing" for many in solidarity, the "divergence" in the "clients" of rehabilitation and resocialization—all these factors made such ideas less obvious or less urgent than security. From the time of the first social policy reforms, the need for security was felt very strongly, first in relation to extended poverty, later in relation to risks of losing positions of prosperity or at least a "tolerable" standard of living.

The idea of security was less controversial than the concepts of equality, solidarity, and rehabilitation, against which charges of "leveling," "collectivism," "support of the asocial," and similar designations have figured in debates during the course of the years. To be sure, security measures could be painted as dangerous to the will to work and threatening habits of thrift. But these problems could be handled technically by controlling the amount of benefits provided, the qualifications for them, and the time that had to elapse before they went into effect, as well as incorporating provisions encouraging or requiring individual savings. The idea of security thus became the politically most stable ideal in the philosophical development of Swedish social welfare policy, the ideal that could most easily and with the fewest risks be used by political leaders to mobilize public support.

Selected Bibliography

Selected Bibliography

The following bibliography is a selective list of works in English which the editor recommends as useful aids to the understanding of modern Sweden. The general histories often have their own bibliographies for those who want sources for specific problems. Additionally there are large numbers of excellent articles about Sweden in professional journals in the social sciences. These references were generally of too technical a nature to be included here; only those articles are cited in the following pages which have particular relevance for the topics discussed in this book. Journals in English that are specifically concerned with Sweden are *Scandinavian Political Studies, Scandinavian Economic History Review, Scandinavian Journal of Psychology, Cooperation and Conflict,* and *Economy and History.* Journals of a broader nature include *American-Scandinavian Review* and *Scandinavian Studies.*

For those who read Swedish the extensive bibliographical notes in *Från fattigdom till överflöd* (Stockholm: Wahlström & Widstrand, 1973) will be of interest; this is the Swedish-language edition of *Sweden's Development from Poverty to Affluence.* The following are general histories in Swedish: *Svensk historia,* vol. I (Stockholm, 1962) by Jerker Rosén and vol. II (Stockholm, 1961) by Sten Carlsson; *Den svenska utrikespolitikens historia,* 10 vols. (Stockholm, 1951–1961); *Sverige efter 1900* (Stockholm, 1967), by Stig Hadenius, Hans Wieslander, and Björn Molin; and *Sveriges economiska historia,* 6 vols. (Stockholm, 1935–1949), by Eli F. Heckscher.

Bibliographical Aids

Groennings, Sven. *Scandinavia in Social Science Literature.* Bloomington, Ind., 1970.
Sweden Illustrated. Stockholm, 1963.

General Histories

Andersson, Ingvar. *A History of Sweden*. London, 1956.

Hancock, M. Donald. *Sweden: The Politics of Post-Industrial Change*. New York, 1972.

Heckscher, Eli. *An Economic History of Sweden*. Cambridge, Mass., 1954.

Oakley, Stewart. *A Short History of Sweden*. New York, 1966.

Samuelsson, Kurt. *From Great Power to Welfare State*. London, 1968.

Scobbie, Irene. *Sweden*. New York, 1972.

Other Works

Allen, G. R. "A Comparison of Real Wages in Swedish Agriculture and Secondary and Tertiary Industries 1870–1949," *Scandinavian Economic History Review*, vol. III, no. 1 (1955).

Andersson, Stanley. *The Nordic Council*. Seattle and New York, 1967.

Andrén, Nils. *Modern Swedish Government*. Stockholm, 1961.

Andrén, Nils. *Power-Balance and Non-Alignment*. Stockholm, 1967.

Austin, Paul. *The Swedes*. New York, 1970.

Bagge, G., E. Lundberg, and I. Svennilsson. *Wages in Sweden, 1860–1930*. Stockholm, 1935.

Beijbom, Ulf. *Swedes in Chicago: A Demographic and Social Study of the 1846–1880 Immigration*. Uppsala, 1971.

Blake, Donald. *Swedish Trade Unions and the Social Democratic Party: The Formative Years*. Berkeley, Calif., 1961.

Board, Joseph. *The Government and Politics of Sweden*. New York, 1970.

Brown, E. H. Phelps. *A Century of Pay*. London, 1968.

Childs, Marquis. *Sweden: The Middle Way*. New Haven, Conn., 1936; rev. ed., 1961.

Childs, Marquis. *This Is Democracy: Collective Bargaining in Scandinavia*. New Haven, Conn., 1938.

Clark, Harrison. *Swedish Unemployment Policy 1914–1940*. Washington, D.C., 1941.

Cole, Margaret, *et al. Democratic Sweden*. New York, 1939.

Connery, Donald. *The Scandinavians*. New York, 1966.

Dahl, Robert. *Political Opposition in Western Democracies*. New Haven, Conn., 1966.

Dahlgren, E., E. Lindahl, and K. Kock. *National Income of Sweden 1861–1930*. Stockholm Economic Studies 5a and 5b. Stockholm, 1937.

Elder, Neil. *Government in Sweden*. Oxford, 1970.

Fleetwood, E. E. *Sweden's Capital Imports and Exports*. Geneva, 1947.

Fleisher, Fred. *The New Sweden: The Challenge of a Disciplined Democracy*. New York, 1967.

Fleisher, Wilfrid. *Sweden: The Welfare State*. New York, 1956.

Fox, Annette B. *The Power of Small States*. Chicago, 1967.

Fridlizius, Gunnar. "Sweden's Exports 1850–1960," *Economy and History*, vol. VI (1963).

Fridlizius, Gunnar. *Swedish Corn Export in the Free Trade Era*. Lund, 1957.

Gendall, Murray. *Swedish Working Wives: A Study of Determinants and Consequences*. Totowa, N.J., 1963.

Gjöres, Axel. *Cooperation in Sweden.* Manchester, 1937.

Goodwin, A., ed. *The European Nobility in the Eighteenth Century.* London, 1953.

Gustafson, Alrik. *A History of Swedish Literature.* Minneapolis, 1961.

Håstad, Elis. *The Parliament of Sweden.* London, 1957.

Hatton, R. M. *Charles XII of Sweden.* London, 1968.

Heckscher, Eli, *et al. Sweden, Norway, Denmark and Iceland in the World War.* New Haven, Conn., 1930.

Hedin, L. E. "Some Notes on the Financing of the Swedish Railroads 1860–1914," *Economy and History,* vol. X (1967).

Hendin, Herbert. *Suicide in Scandinavia: A Psychoanalytic Study of Culture and Character.* New York, 1964.

Herwitz, Nils. *Sweden: A Modern Democracy on Ancient Foundations.* Minneapolis, 1935.

Hinsaw, David. *Sweden: Champion of Peace.* New York, 1949.

Hohman, Helen. *Old Age in Sweden.* Washington, D.C., 1940.

Hovde, B. J. *The Scandinavian Countries, 1720–1865.* New York, 1948.

Husen, Foster, *et al. Differentiation and Guidance in the Comprehensive School.* Stockholm, 1959.

Huntford, Roland. *The New Totalitarians.* London, 1971.

Janson, Florence D. *The Background of Swedish Immigration 1840–1930.* Chicago, 1931.

Jenkins, David. *Sweden and the Price of Progress.* New York, 1968.

Joesten, Joachim. *Stalwart Sweden.* Garden City, N.Y., 1943.

Johansson, O. *The Gross Domestic Product of Sweden and Its Composition 1861–1955.* Stockholm Economic Studies, New Series VIII. Uppsala, 1967.

Johnston, T. L. *Collective Bargaining in Sweden.* London, 1962.

Jones, Shepard S. *The Scandinavian States and the League of Nations.* New York, 1939.

Jörberg, L. *Growth and Fluctuations of Swedish Industry, 1869–1912.* Lund, 1961.

Jörberg, L. *The Industrial Revolution in Scandinavia, 1850–1914.* Fontana Economic History of Europe, Vol. IV. London, 1970.

Källberg, Sture. *Off the Middle Way.* New York, 1972.

Kälvesten, Anna-Lisa. *The Social Structure of Sweden.* Stockholm, 1965.

Koblik, Steven. *Sweden: The Neutral Victor.* Lund, 1972.

Koblik, Steven. "Wartime Diplomacy and the Democratization of Sweden in September–October 1917," *Journal of Modern History,* vol. XLI (1969).

Lewin, Leif, Bo Jonsson, and Dag Sörbom. *The Swedish Electorate, 1887–1968.* Stockholm, 1972.

Lindberg, Folke. *Scandinavia in Great Power Politics.* Stockholm, 1958.

Lindgren, Raymond E. *Norway-Sweden: Union, Disunion and Scandinavian Integration.* Princeton, N.J., 1959.

Lindmark, Sture. *Swedish America, 1914–1932.* Studies in Ethnicity with Emphasis on Illinois and Minnesota. Uppsala, 1971.

Linnér, Birgitta. *Sex and Society in Sweden.* New York, 1967.

Lönnröth, Erik. "The Diplomacy of Östen Undén," in Gordon Craig's *The Diplomats.* Princeton, N.J., 1953.

Migration in Sweden: A Symposium. Lund Studies in Geography, series B, no. 13. Lund, 1957.

Moberg, Wilhelm. *The Emigrants.* New York, 1951.

Moberg, Wilhelm. *The Last Letter Home.* New York, 1960.

Moberg, Wilhelm. *Unto a Good Land.* New York, 1959.

Montgomery, A. *The Rise of Modern Industry in Sweden.* Stockholm, 1959.

Myrdal, Alva. *Nation and Family: The Swedish Experiment in Democratic Family and Population Policy.* New York, 1941.

Myrdal, G. *Cost of Living in Sweden 1830–1930.* Stockholm, 1933.

Myrdal, Jan. *Confessions of a Disloyal European.* New York, 1969.

Nelson, George R., ed. *Freedom and Welfare: Social Patterns in the Northern Countries of Europe.* Copenhagen, 1953.

Nicander, E., and B. Holgerson. "The Railroads and the Economic Development in Sweden during the 1870's," *Economy and History,* vol. XI (1968).

Nilsson, C. A. "Business Incorporations in Sweden 1849–1896," *Economy and History,* vol. II (1959).

Nott, Kathleen. *A Clean Well-Lighted Place.* London, 1961.

OECD. *Education Policy and Planning—Sweden.* Paris, 1967.

Olsson, Nils William. *Swedish Passenger Arrivals in New York, 1820–1850.* Chicago, 1967.

Palm, Göran. *As Others See Us.* Indianapolis, 1968.

Palmer, R. R. *The Age of the Democratic Revolution: A Political History of Europe and America, 1760–1800.* Vol. I. Princeton, N.J., 1959.

Population Movements and Industrialization: Swedish Counties 1895–1930. By the Staff of the Institute for Social Sciences. Vol. II. Stockholm Economic Studies 10:2. Stockholm, 1941.

Robbins, James J. *Government of Labor Relations in Sweden.* Chapel Hill, N.C., 1942.

Roberts, Michael. *Essays in Swedish History.* London, 1967.

Roberts, Michael. *Gustavus Adolphus: A History of Sweden, 1611–1632.* 2 vols. London, 1953, 1958.

Roberts, Michael. *Sweden as a Great Power, 1611–1697.* London, 1968.

Rosenthal, Albert. *The Social Programs of Sweden.* Minneapolis, 1967.

Rothberg, Agnes. *Sweden, the Land and the People.* London, 1936.

Rowat, Donald. *The Ombudsman.* London, 1965.

Rustow, Danquart. *Politics of Compromise.* Princeton, N.J., 1965.

Schmidt, Folke. *The Law of Labour Relations in Sweden.* Stockholm, 1962.

Schmidt, Folke. *Legal Values in Modern Sweden.* Stockholm, 1964.

Scott, Franklin. *Bernadotte and the Fall of Napoleon.* Cambridge, Mass., 1935.

Scott, Franklin. "Sweden's Constructive Opposition to Emigration," *Journal of Modern History,* vol. XXXVII (September 1965).

Scott, Franklin. *The United States and Scandinavia.* Cambridge, Mass., 1950.

Silk, Leonard. *Sweden Plans for Better Housing.* Durban, 1948.

Sjöberg, Bideon, M. Donald Hancock, and Orion White, Jr. *Politics in the Post-Welfare State: A Comparison of the United States and Sweden.* Bloomington, Ind., 1967.

Stephenson, George M. *The Religious Aspects of Swedish Immigration.* Minneapolis, 1935.

Thomas, D. S. *Social and Economic Aspects of Swedish Population Movements, 1750–1933*. Stockholm Economic Studies 10:1. New York, 1941.

Tingsten, Herbert. *The Debate on the Foreign Policy of Sweden, 1918–1939*. Stockholm, 1949.

Verney, Douglas. *Parliamentary Reform in Sweden, 1866–1921*. Oxford, 1957.

Verney, Douglas. *Public Enterprise in Sweden*. Liverpool, 1959.

Wendt, Frantz. *The Nordic Council and Cooperation on Scandinavia*. Copenhagen, 1959.

Wendt, Paul. *Housing Policy, the Search for Solutions: A Comparison of the United Kingdom, Sweden, West Germany, and the United States since World War II*. Berkeley, Calif., 1962.

Wilkinson, M. "Evidence of Long Swings in the Growth of Swedish Population and Related Variables 1860–1965," *Journal of Economic History*, vol. XXVII (March 1967).

Youngson, A. *Possibilities of Economic Progress*. Cambridge, 1959.

Index

Index

Aaron, Raymond, 298

AB Separator, 206

Åbo, Finland, 21, 27, 31

Absolutism: of Karl XII, 14; collapse, 15, 19; influence on constitution, 40, 46, 50, 57. *See also* Royal power

Act of Union, 74, 86

Adlerbeth, Gudmund Göran, 42, 43, 50, 57–58, 60

Adlercreutz, C. J., 40, 44

Adlersparre, Georg: and coup of *1809*, 40, 42; on Trolle-Wachtmeister constitutional committee, 43, 44; influence declines, 50, 51; constitutional committee recommendation, 53, 57; and Swedish-Norwegian Union, 71, 73

Adolf Fredrik of Holstein-Gottorp, 20

Age of Freedom: historical views of, 15; conditions in Sweden, 17, 38, 39–40; mentioned, 8, 14, 25, 35, 36

Age of the Democratic Revolution, The, 15, 17

Agrarian Association (Finland), 275

Agrarian party (Denmark), 274

Agrarian party (Norway), 274, 275

Agrarian party (Sweden): formation, 192, 222, 223, 260–261; coalition with Social Democrats, 256–258 *passim*, 262, 267, 270–278 *passim*, 287, 348; relations with conservatives, 261, 263, 269, 271; economic policy, 263, 266, 293, 324, 328; leadership, 270; Bramstorp government, 275; Riksdag representation, 276; worker-farmer cooperation, 278; national coalition government, 288, 303–304, 306–307, 321, 324, 328–331 *passim*; internal dissension during World War II, 312; foreign policy, 314, 315; view on population issue, 343; mentioned, 11, 279. *See also* Farmers

Agriculture: land reforms, 8, 10, 30; revolution of, 9, 10, 11, 102–106; expansion of, 92, 102, 106, 118, 121, 123, 134, 157; exports, 93, 103–104, 118, 133; crises, 105, 170–171, 263–268 *passim*; population employed in, 127, 350–351; tariffs, 128; emigration, 169–173 *passim*; and politics, 194, 260, 264, 276; and labor movement, 216, 263–264; government